Rewriting Citizenship

Rewriting Citizenship

WOMEN, RACE, AND NINETEENTH-CENTURY PRINT CULTURE

By Susan J. Stanfield

The University of Georgia Press
ATHENS

Paperback edition, 2024
© 2022 by the University of Georgia Press
Athens, Georgia 30602
www.ugapress.org
All rights reserved

Designed by Kaelin Chappell Broaddus
Set in 10.5/13.5 Garamond Premier Pro Regular
by Kaelin Chappell Broaddus

Most University of Georgia Press titles are
available from popular e-book vendors.

Printed digitally

Library of Congress Cataloging-in-Publication Data

Names: Stanfield, Susan J., 1964– author.
Title: Rewriting citizenship : women, race, and nineteenth-
century print culture / by Susan J. Stanfield.
Other titles: Women, race, and 19th century print culture
Description: Athens, Georgia : The University of Georgia Press,
[2022] | Includes bibliographical references and index.
Identifiers: LCCN 2022003492 | ISBN 9780820362618
(Hardback) | ISBN 9780820362601 (eBook)
Subjects: LCSH: Citizenship—United States—History—19th century.
| Sex discrimination against women—United States—History—19th
century. | Race discrimination—United States—History—19th century.
Classification: LCC JK1759 .S67 2022 | DDC 323.60973—dc23/eng/20220308
LC record available at https://lccn.loc.gov/2022003492

Paperback ISBN 978-0-8203-6987-7

DEDICATED TO MY MOTHER,

Betty Bell Stanfield

(1932–2020)

CONTENTS

ACKNOWLEDGMENTS

ix

INTRODUCTION
Gendering Rights and Racializing Gender
The Cultural Practice of Citizenship

1

CHAPTER 1
The Expanding Female Sphere
Creating the Citizen Woman

17

CHAPTER 2
Constructing Home and Nation
Household Advice and Civic Domesticity

43

CHAPTER 3
The Infrastructure of Race
*Citizenship, Gender, and
African American Public Culture*

68

CHAPTER 4
Creating an Empowered Private Sphere
Female Citizenship and Print Culture

101

CHAPTER 5
Rewriting Race and Respectability
African American Women and Citizenship

134

CONCLUSION
Reconstructing Womanhood
*Domesticity, Citizenship, and
Minor v. Happersett*

165

NOTES

169

INDEX

211

ACKNOWLEDGMENTS

Acknowledgements feel like an acceptance speech at the Oscars. I rattle off a list of names but provide little explanation, because I want to avoid the orchestra from playing me off, all while worrying about who I might have forgotten. A project that has taken as long as this one to complete has accumulated many debts—debts both institutional and individual. The University of Iowa, the University of Texas at El Paso, and Smith College all provided financial support for archival research or release time for research and writing. Research would be impossible without the work of archivists, and I appreciate them at every place that I visited. I was introduced to unexpected sources and provided with new contexts from people at the Historical Society of Pennsylvania, the Connecticut Historical Society, the University of Michigan's Clements Library, the Harriet Beecher Stowe Center, Special Collections and the Iowa Women's Archives at the University of Iowa, and the African Episcopal Church of St. Thomas (Philadelphia). Through his patience, kindness, and guidance, Nate Holly at UGA Press has made the process of writing a first book a positive experience.

I have been fortunate to receive support from many individuals who helped me to develop ideas, rethink my arguments, and get through the various bumps in the road. I first began thinking about women, the home, and citizenship in the very first graduate history class I enrolled in as a part-time MA student at Kansas State University. Sue Zschoche was the professor in that first class, and her encouragement is why I decided to pursue a PhD. At the University of Iowa, where I received my doctorate and taught for the first three years after graduation, there are too many people to identify by name. I learned from my classmates in graduate seminars and from the faculty I worked with in the History and Gender, Women's, and Sexuality Studies Departments at Iowa. I want to acknowledge Leslie Schwalm, who helped make my work more intersectional and is the best advisor possible. I'm so lucky to have worked with her. My writing group of Jo Butterfield (who was my first friend in graduate school and a constant source of support), Anna Flaming, Colleen Kelley (who has read various drafts of this manuscript), and Angela Keyser were the perfect group to work with and still influence how I think and write about history. Christy Clark-Pujara, Heather Cooper, Karissa Haugeberg, Sylvea Hollis, Katherine Massoth, Caroline Radesky, and Heather Wacha have also been important to this project. Jeff Bennett, Jennifer Harbour, Jennifer Hull, Kevin Mumford, Andy and Pam Murray, Sharon Romeo, Johanna Schoen, Jennifer Sessions, and Denise Pate Spruill significantly helped shape my research and writing.

At UTEP I have been fortunate to have a supportive department and colleagues that have helped me navigate my life as an assistant professor. I want to thank Michelle Armstrong-Partida, Karla Carrillo, Brad Cartwright (who has also been a tremendous influence on my teaching), Sandy Deutsch, Robert Diaz, Diana Gonzalez, Cathe Lester, Cheryl and Charles Martin (who have served as mentors and friends), Lowry Martin (my brunch buddy, friend, and never-ending source of encouragement), Alana Nevarez, Richard Pineda, and Larisa Veloz. Larisa was hired the same year I was and made learning the ropes so much easier and more fun. She and Heather Sinclair were my pandemic lifelines: our Zoom meetings enabled us to write and talk.

Finally, I want to thank four individuals who are tremendously important to me. Marilyn Olson has shared an interest not only in history but also in travel and musical theater. I look forward to returning to New York City for our yearly marathon of cramming in as many Broadway shows as possible in a brief visit. Isaac West has always been there for me when I have needed him, offers me no-nonsense advice, and is the reason I signed up for that first graduate class in history. Phil Voight, who has been my closest friend for more than thirty years, has traveled to multiple archives, assisting me with research, and been there for me in good times and bad, most recently providing the emotional and pragmatic help I needed after the death of my mother during the pandemic. Finally, I want to acknowledge my brother, Chuck Stanfield. The best big brother in the world, Chuck is always supportive and interested and has faith in my abilities. He asks good questions, offers helpful suggestions, and since I was a child has made me believe I could achieve anything.

I write about many women in this book, but two captured my imagination and helped me rethink gender and citizenship during the antebellum era. Lydia Maria Child was the biggest surprise to me. I thought I knew about her, but after delving into her correspondence I was struck by her humor, wit, dedication to social change, and fierce argumentative skills. Don't judge her by her books—she is so much more than that. Sarah Forten (Purvis) allowed me to think of the antislavery women of the 1830s as both individuals and activists. Forten's letters exhibited the eagerness of the early Garrisonian abolitionists—the optimism that change could happen and the willingness to write, petition, attend lectures, and support antislavery fairs—all from the vantage point of a young woman of color in her teens and early twenties. Sarah wrote of the excitement of meeting traveling lecturers in Philadelphia (who often visited her home), proudly published poetry and essays in *The Liberator*, and was a member of the Philadelphia Female Anti-Slavery Society (PFAS). I only wish as many of her letters were preserved as those of Catharine Beecher, Lydia Maria Child, Sarah Douglass, and Sarah Hale.

My mother passed away at the end of 2020. She was excited when I signed the contract, and I'm sorry that she didn't see the book in print. It is to her that I lovingly dedicate this book.

Rewriting Citizenship

INTRODUCTION

Gendering Rights and Racializing Gender
The Cultural Practice of Citizenship

Lydia Maria Child and her husband, David, had depended on her writing and work as an editor to stay financially afloat throughout their marriage. When her husband's signature was required for her will, she lashed out in a letter to her attorney friend, Ellis Gray Loring. "I was not indignant on my own account, for David respects the freedom of all women upon principle, and mine in particular by reason of affection superadded. But I was indignant for womankind made chattels personal from the beginning of time, perpetually insulted by literature, law, and custom. The very phrases used with regard to us are abominable. 'Dead in the law,' 'Femme couverte.' How I detest such language!" She ended her complaint by joking that she would take action in the afterlife: "I must come out with a broadside on that subject before I die. If I don't, I shall walk and rap afterword [sic]."[1] For many women in the nineteenth century, citizenship and civic standing were issues that went beyond the question of voting rights. Lydia Child wanted her voice heard on the issue, even, as she said, if it was from beyond the grave.

From the end of the colonial era to this day, individuals—regardless of their race, gender, economic class, or identity—have sought the status conferred by citizenship. Citizenship holds the promise of legal standing, a sense of national belonging, and a defined relationship with the state. For some, the creation of the United States meant a seamless transition from subjects to citizens, while others still wait for genuine political equality. Those who were politically responsible for the creation of the new nation—the white male elites who made up the Continental Congress, served as officers in the Continental army, or helped finance the American Revolution—always saw themselves as citizens. Perhaps those who were culturally responsible for bringing the new nation to life by writing broadsides and songs also saw themselves as citizens. Women who labored for the army and the government and nonelite white males and men of color who enlisted would also have seen themselves contributing to nation building. However, as federal and state governments evolved, those on the margins were not only barred from decision making but also only received the civic protections that elites were willing to grant.

As a newly independent nation, the United States lacked the traditional means for forging a national identity that was used by European nation-states. There were few generational ties to the physical space that was the United States. There was no monarch with a divine right to rule nor easy ways to reach across the landscape. The revolution had severed the colonies' tie to London. The new nation even lacked a shared state-sanctioned religion. Thus, in the wide expanse of territory that eventually became the United States, the people needed a unifying device to create a national identity that was distinct from Great Britain and that could serve as an access point for political recognition.

An emerging print culture helped create a shared identity between readers. The fiery orators of the revolutionary era might have been able to draw a crowd, but they only became renowned when their speeches were published as broadsides, tracts, or newspaper entries. During the eighteenth century, the mere act of publication added to the gravitas of an argument, and the printed word soon trumped the spoken. Because publication suggested permanence, ownership, and a class-based skill, the printed word was fundamental to the credibility of the author in the public sphere.[2] Although Black and white women and African American men were largely excluded from this original republic of letters, there were exceptions, and some members of marginalized groups, such as Prince Hall, Judith Sargent Murray, and Phillis Wheatley, wrote and published in the eighteenth century. Typically, however, the work of those at the margins did not carry a cultural cachet until the nineteenth century. Publication alone did not mean individual actors had entered the public sphere. For the printed work of a Black or white woman or an African American man to transition from novelty to civic discourse, political power brokers, such as abolitionists, had to profess interest. Or the discourse needed commercial appeal, such as that offered by cookbooks or women's magazines, which promoted the ideas of the marginalized individual because publication had a profit motive. This transition did not occur until the nineteenth century, when the market for printed material expanded. With the growing availability of the printed word, men of color and women found an opportunity to challenge narrow definitions of citizenship and new ways to perform their civic duty.

The ideology of "true womanhood" provided both commercial appeal and an opportunity for women to reimagine their civic participation. True womanhood was an antebellum value system in which women, typically white and middle class, were expected to embrace the virtues of piety, purity, submissiveness, and domesticity. Barbara Welter popularized the term in her 1966 essay, "The Cult of True Womanhood, 1820–1860," in which she identified those traits as being prominent in nineteenth-century print materials.[3] The phrase itself, or the more common "womanhood," was in popular usage in the nineteenth century. Unlike earlier American gender ideologies, such as the "good wife" and the "republican mother," true womanhood was created and promoted by the female print industry that emerged in the early nineteenth century. The power of the printed word to shape cultural norms for femininity also meant that women could use those same words to reinterpret femininity in political ways.

This book is a cultural history of how race and gender influenced nineteenth-century citizenship. While much has been written about the cultural marker of true womanhood as a gender ideology of white middle-class women, my research reveals that it served an even more significant purpose by defining racial difference and attaching civic purpose to the daily practices of women. Whether individual women precisely followed these codes is less important than how people viewed this ideal and how race and gender shaped civic standing. The prominence of true womanhood relied on a female-focused print culture. The act of publication gave power to the ideology and allowed for a shared identity among white middle-class women and those who sought to emulate them. Kathryn Kish Sklar revisited the idea of domesticity, the most significant trait of womanhood in print culture, more than fifty years after Welter's essay. "Domesticity is about intimate space," Sklar wrote, "but it is also about the location of that space in a wider world. Domesticity is about women, but it is also about men and children. It defines and limits behavior, but it also creates space for innovation. Above all, because it seeks to reproduce daily life, it is a malleable process, a set of relationships that are ever changing—along with the life course of those in its domain and their intersections with larger social forces."[4] Domestic literature created a national code for womanhood that was racially constructed and infused with civic purpose. By defining women's household practices as an obligation not only to their husbands but also to the state, women could reimagine themselves as independent citizens in their own right.

The cultural importance of true womanhood manifested in three ways. First, women found their everyday practices to hold a civic purpose because of the values promoted in antebellum print culture. It was not merely the female social reformers and political activists who argued that women should have influence on the state. Most women believed that they had a stake in claiming citizenship and recognized an obligation to the state. Second, while activist women tried to overturn legal curtailments (such as limited property rights and the inability to vote and hold office), nonactivist women took a more rhetorically difficult position working within those constraints. They saw their civic status as different from—although not inferior to—that of men. They made forays into the public sphere through print culture and actively redefined the private sphere by linking their domestic work to nation building. In this way, nonactivist women could fulfill culturally constructed ideas of femininity, thus maintaining the authority of their womanhood. Some of those women were propelled by the authority of their womanhood to sign petitions, attend political lectures, and organize fundraising fairs, all of which were based on a new understanding of their duties as women to the state. Finally, evolving interpretations of womanhood were not simply a reflection of the changing labor practices of middle-class women in the emerging market economy; those interpretations also linked femininity with class and race. Middle-class white women sought to differentiate themselves from immigrants, the working poor, and women of color by enhancing the significance of the home and by distinguishing between household labor and household management. Middle-class African American women also saw the persuasive potential of true womanhood. Not only did they use the politics of respectability to enhance their own status, but they also argued that their well-ordered homes proved that their husbands and fathers were patriarchs, just like white male heads of household, and therefore were worthy of citizenship and the vote.

In recognition of the fluidity of citizenship and identity, a new interpretation of womanhood, one that recognizes women's repurposing of print culture in pursuit of civic standing, is necessary. This interpretation rewrites our understanding of women's influence over definitions of citizens and citizenship in the nineteenth century. Such an interpretation also interrogates the intersections of Black and white constructions of true womanhood by applying a cultural understanding of citizenship as lived experience rather than relying on a strictly political or legal interpretation. Doing so reconceptualizes domesticity as a political force in the nineteenth century and explores how home, race, and gender transected to create individual identities of Americans as Americans. My research demonstrates that early iterations of citizenship depended on how individuals performed civic virtue within the public sphere.[5]

Regulations of performances of citizenship either by law or by cultural practice not only limited who was considered a citizen but also hampered the expansion of that civic status. The performance of citizenship is essential not only to fulfilling the obligations of citizenship but also to demonstrating "suitability" for citizenship. Participation in the public rituals of citizenship is important for inclusion. If cultural sanctions prevent individuals from performing their citizenship obligations, literally or ritualistically, then those individuals must either redefine what they do as an obligation or perform civic duties in a way that mirrors those who have the status of citizens.[6] Writing about enslaved women in Civil War St. Louis, historian Sharon Romeo explains that "citizenship is both a legal status and a cultural identity that forms its meanings through social practices in which people test the boundaries of their rights and obligations." For those who have few or no legal options, "embodied performance, such as hanging a picture of a head of state or flying a national flag, can play a part in establishing the cultural aspects of political identity."[7] Print culture, the creation of documents for organizations, and female participation in reform all helped women construct an embodiment of the citizen-woman.

Different approaches to citizenship or cultural codes for masculinity and femininity were critical to improving women's civic status. The doctrine of jus soli, included in the broader concept of birthright citizenship, was not constitutionally recognized until the Fourteenth Amendment was ratified in 1868. This meant individuals were left to state definitions or local enforcement for their civic status. As African Americans battled against colonization, this idea of being born in the territory was an important argument. Richard Allen, the founder of the African Methodist Episcopal (AME) Church, stated in *Freedom's Journal*: "This land which we have watered with our *tears* and *our blood*, is now our *mother country* and we are well satisfied to stay where wisdom abounds and the gospel is free."[8] Historian Rochelle Raineri Zuck explains that David Walker quoted this letter in his famous *Appeal to the Colored Citizens of the World* (1829) and that he and Maria Stewart used this same language when defending the rights of people of color as part of the nation.[9] Historian Derrick R. Spires describes the practice-based theory of citizenship that evolved during the antebellum era. For Black activists, citizenship was interpreted "not as a common identity as such but rather as a set of common practices: political participation, mutual aid, critique and revolution, and the myriad daily interactions between people living in the same spaces, both physical and virtual."[10] It is important to note that people excluded from the privileges of full citizenship did not passively accept their limited status. Instead, they found ways to challenge how civic virtue and standing were understood by expanding their exposure to and influence over the public sphere.[11] Indeed, white women and Black men and women challenged the denial of their citizenship status by using print culture to elevate the everyday practices of the home as proof of their fulfillment of the obligations of citizenship.

An overarching contribution of this project is the juxtaposition of these cultural understandings of what makes a citizen, particularly for women, with how citizenship would be interpreted by courts and state legislatures during the nineteenth century. Traditional interpretations of the characteristics of citizens, which emphasized the immutable categories of race and gender, forced white women and African American men and women to redefine the obligations and duties of citizenship. Through the use of print sources, women publicized their performance of these defined obligations and laid claim to citizenship on their own behalf. By contrasting cultural and political constructions of citizenship, we are able to develop a more nuanced understanding of how citizenship mattered in the everyday lives of Americans.

FROM NATION BUILDING TO CITIZEN BUILDING

The transition from subjects of King George to citizens of the new republic might have been politically momentous, but the transformation itself lacked concrete legal meaning. The Articles of Confederation explicitly defined who was a citizen: "The free inhabitants of each of these states, paupers, vagabonds and fugitives from justice excepted shall be entitled to all privileges and immunities of free citizens in the several states."[12] However, that clarity was short lived, and the new Constitution was vague in terms of who qualified for citizenship and how this status would be distributed. Both the states and the federal government wielded that authority. State citizenship was often more clearly defined and was where many of the rights and duties of citizenship were carried out.[13] Although the Constitution may have been silent about who was a citizen, the early work of the federal government suggested that lawmakers understood citizenship as racially constructed and influenced by gender and class. Recognizing the shifting nature of identity categories, historian Matthew Frye Jacobson plays upon Simone de Beauvoir's famous observation about women by noting that "Caucasians are made and not born."[14] The early U.S. federal government proved this claim by codifying race in such a way as to give legal birthright to the white male citizen and by defining others against this norm. The 1790 Naturalization Act set the stage for coding citizenship as a privilege of white men. This act made it difficult for people who were non-European immigrants to become naturalized citizens. Women, unless they were single or widowed, seldom sought naturalization on their own because it offered few tangible benefits in a world of coverture.[15] Also in 1790 the government conducted the first U.S. census. It recorded the name of each head of house and then counted the number of free white males over and under sixteen, free white females, all other free persons, and finally the number of slaves. Clearly, when counting individuals, race and gender mattered. By 1798 the Naturalization, Alien, and Sedition Acts redefined the process of naturalization, demonstrating that citizenship was not just a question of political standing but also a fact of partisan divide, much as it is today.[16]

The meaning of citizenship and its application can be understood in multiple ways. Some scholars and historical actors use the term as a basic geographic designation of residency. Thus, each time a marginalized individual refers to himself or herself as a citizen it does not necessarily mean they are making an argument about their political identity. Other scholars describe citizenship as a legal status by defining the relationship between individuals and the state. Finally, some scholars explain citizenship as an identity that is internally constructed. For those who fall outside the net of recognized legal status, the third category of citizenship, an identity, is formed and practiced as a means to eventually become a legally recognized and protected citizen.[17] Although she is focused on twenty-first-century women of color, Melissa Harris-Perry explains that "citizenship is more than an individual exchange of freedoms for rights; it is also membership in a body politic, a nation and a community. To be deemed fair, a system must offer its citizens equal opportunities for public recognition, and groups cannot systematically suffer from misrecognition in the form of stereotypes and stigma."[18] Fulfilling gender norms such as true womanhood in the nineteenth century became one access point for civic status.

That gender was important in determining who was and was not a citizen is clear, but how the practice of citizenship was gendered is more difficult to isolate and frame. If cultural gatekeepers defined the practices of citizenship as inherently masculine, then female access to that status would have to be reimagined or remain unobtainable. For example, when historians examine the political emergence of nineteenth-century American women, they typically offer one of two narratives. Some focus on individual women who boldly entered public debates about women's status or political issues of the day. Other historians celebrate the "great silent army" of women who joined organizations that promoted abolition, benevolence, and moral reform and were more remarkable as a group than as individual actors.[19] Both narratives emphasize social practices rather than everyday structures and thus view citizenship as wholly overt and political. This book challenges those traditional interpretations. During the antebellum era many women followed a third path to the creation of a civic identity: they redefined the domestic world where most middle-class women dwelled and charged everyday practices with civic significance.

The modern and the historic are two perspectives for interpreting citizenship. The modern shapes our evaluation of historic discourse, but it is important not to lose sight of what historical actors thought of citizenship for themselves. Clearly for women, both Black and white, the construction of the law shaped their lived experiences as "Americans," but because the law was not always concrete in defining who was a citizen, there was room for women to resist cultural norms and expand the idea of citizenship to claim rights. In deconstructing laws, it became clear to those denied civic status just how fluid requirements for citizenship were. Federal, state, and local governments shifted the meaning of citizenship to reflect their current needs and prejudices. Although modern scholars recognize that citizenship has a "civil, political, and socio-economic dimension," the fact that it is "fundamentally a term describing a social status" would not have been a surprise to the eighteenth- or nineteenth-century woman. By the early nineteenth century, women were engaged in claiming citizenship through "a diversity of practices" that allowed for civic recognition without challenging cultural constructions of femininity.[20] Despite the limitations created by true womanhood, especially when viewed through the lenses of the twenty-first century, women's acceptance of those tenets did not mean they rejected their own civic importance.

THE GENDERED CITIZEN

In order to achieve a nuanced understanding of citizenship, gender is an important instrument of analysis in this study. As a relational term, gender, according to Joan Scott, means "knowledge of sexual difference." It is "the understanding produced by cultures and societies of human relations" between men and women. Scott emphasizes the importance of interrogating *how* hierarchies "of gender are constructed or legitimized" through rhetoric or discourses.[21] The core of her interpretation is that these categories are culturally created, based on power and hierarchy, and interpreted through rhetoric and discourse, which suggests strategy and intent. Of course, it is important to determine not only how hierarchy is created but also how it is used in the construction of power. This approach is central to understanding how citizenship evolved in the United States in the late eighteenth and early nineteenth centuries. Gender influences how citizenship has been understood, particularly how it has been both claimed and denied based on race. As practiced, citizenship is a designation without the same meaning for all holders of the status. Although a legal construction of the term would suggest it is a cut-and-dried test (one is or is not a citizen), in the reality of the nineteenth century there were degrees of citizenship and civic standing that were intertwined with the intersections of race, class, and gender.[22] Even today citizenship involves the attainment of a variety of rights based upon individual identities marked by race, class, gender, ethnicity, sexual orientation, marital status, ability, religion, age, and other possible markers. In comparison to the normalized standard of rights, a variety of binary categories have been created: women versus men, Blacks versus whites, gays versus straights. Cultural interpretations of identities shape the lived experience of individual citizens, often despite legal status. For example, although no one would question Georgetown student Sandra Fluke's or Florida teen Trayvon Martin's position as citizens, how Fluke exercised her speech rights and Martin his right to occupy a public space was challenged based on their gender and race. Dr. Christine Blasey Ford, Philando Castile, Sandra Bland, Eric Garner, George Floyd, Breonna Taylor, #MeToo, and #BlackLivesMattter demonstrate how fraught cultural citizenship is more than 150 years after the ratification of the Fourteenth Amendment. These twenty-first-century examples are shockingly similar to how women and Black men were treated in the early nineteenth century. Melinda Chateauvert concludes that these evaluations of civic standing are then wrapped within a familial relationship: "A person's citizenship status has historically been defined by his or her membership in a family or relationship to a household. Family relationships, consisting of sexual and genetic ties (conjugal and consanguineal ties) to the (male) head of household, automatically conferred a set of rights and responsibilities upon subordinate members."[23] Thus the approach to claiming civic status taken by antebellum women, both Black and white, revolved around how women functioned within the home and family. For those not protected by full citizenship, their claims became a way to demonstrate equality (and sameness) with the normalized home, which was believed to be upheld by standards of whiteness and the middle class.

The link between domesticity and citizenship was forged in the early nineteenth century, and because this was a transitional moment in the construction of women's domestic roles, female citizenship was ripe for redefinition. The rise in female literacy coupled with the emergence of an American publishing industry resulted in women accessing printed household advice produced for a distinctly American market for the first time.[24] The cultural, social, and economic importance of women's domestic labor was magnified in published works in part to justify the selling of household advice, which previously had been transferred free of cost from neighbor to neighbor or mother to daughter. The emergence of a female print culture allowed everyday practices to take on a civic meaning; books, magazines, and newspapers provided an opportunity for domestic work to take on a shared cultural meaning. Much like Benedict Anderson's description of the shared ritual of reading the morning papers and its replication across the land, women's reading of domestic advice created a shared identity of citizen-women despite the fact that individual women remained unknown to one another.[25] Domestic advice was a significant portion of nineteenth-century women's print culture. Authors of advice literature prescribed a role for nineteenth-century women that allowed them to exert their influence in the national arena without physically entering the public sphere. From a location that was not exclusively private yet not quite public, many white middle-class women began to develop a uniquely female civic identity. Instead of accepting that their "material, productive, domestic [and] reproductive relationships" prevented them from meeting the Aristotelian definition of "citizen" embraced by the founders, women could "deny that the relationships are negative components of citizenship" and thus reconceptualize their domestic duties, according to historian J. G. A. Pocock.[26] It is not simply because household labor changed at the dawn of the nineteenth century that womanhood was reconsidered and defined. The process of redefining the civic significance of domesticity not only began in the nineteenth century because of the separation of "home and work" but also was in part a response to legal definitions of citizenship on the federal level.[27] It was the shift in the cultural construction of the home that permitted women to perform their obligations not just as wives and mothers but also as citizens.

As the electorate expanded beyond propertied males (even while constricting along lines of race and gender), women more aggressively sought to establish their own relationship to the state. Instead of rejecting traditional enactments of femininity, many women followed the advice provided on the pages of books and magazines and reinterpreted their role within the home and their submission to their husbands and fathers as a fresh imagining of civic duty. Furthermore, a discourse of domesticity emerged that shaped the cultural meaning of the term. In other words, women's domestic labor was no longer a practice based on individual households, as it was throughout the seventeenth and eighteenth centuries. Instead, a discourse of domesticity evolved that was collectively interpreted as a cultural practice. As long as domesticity was synonymous with a private female sphere, it could be used to exclude women from the public sphere. However, this collective interpretation could also be subverted by women as a means for claiming their role within the state.

THE PUBLIC/PRIVATE DIVIDE IN GENDER HISTORY

Gender historians have been engaged in a debate about the meaning of the public and private for decades. Some have argued that the split between the "spheres" is merely ideological rather than a meaningful spatial divide of home and work. Others have tried to debunk the idea altogether by noting all the ways that women entered the public sphere.[28] Both positions are true, however. The split between men and women was suggested through cultural constructions such as true womanhood, and many (if not most) women also transgressed this divide at different points in their lives. The success of women's entry into the public sphere often required an apparent acquiescence to its exclusion of women. Whether women consciously appropriated the trope of womanhood as a justification for citizenship and a public voice or whether women internalized the ideology of true womanhood and then believed that it demanded certain types of public action is at some level immaterial. Either way, the tenets of true womanhood—piety, purity, submissiveness, and domesticity—were deployed by women in service to benevolence, mutual aid, antislavery work, and moral reform, which served as evidence of their role in nation building.

What makes the study of citizenship in the nineteenth century more complex is that the public/private divide was not only gendered but also racialized.[29] Antebellum free people of color faced both de facto and de jure segregation, and both forms of segregation limited their access to the public sphere. For example, the northern urban race riots that occurred from the 1820s through the 1840s often targeted places where African Americans congregated. These riots became a powerful barrier to African Americans' access to the public sphere. When the African American community constructed separate buildings for schools, churches, and assembly halls, even if they remained safe from the mob, their physical separation limited their challenges to the public sphere. That is why print culture was and is so important. For example, nineteenth-century print culture served the same function that social media serves today. Whereas activists today might rely on Reddit or Instagram to share stories and Twitter or more politicized sites such as Parler to organize protests, nineteenth-century families, friends, and neighbors shared subscriptions to *The Liberator* or the *National Era*, passing along issues by hand or through the mail. During the nineteenth century, print culture provided a means to make public the claims of those who were otherwise denied access to the public sphere. Newspapers and pamphlets provided the rhetor the shelter of physical distance from an angry mob and a powerful channel for communication across locations and social standing.

Much like the category of gender, public and private spheres are also relational terms and misunderstood when seen as only oppositional. Some critics claim that by eschewing the binary and embracing the relational aspects of the public and private, the creation of hierarchy is less likely.[30] With this relational approach, ideas are viewed as more public or less public rather than as an either-or proposition. Antebellum women's concepts of the public and private likely embraced the ideas relationally, although that does not mean the hierarchy vanished. On the basest level, men—through tradition and the law—were patriarchs of the private sphere, while women often provided a moral balance to the public. Women envisioned their private duties as influencing the public, and when domesticity and morality were not enough, women found ways to challenge the wider public sphere.

THE RACIALIZED CITIZEN

The significance of women's performance of citizenship increased as domesticity allowed women to make a reciprocal claim upon the state. If the building of households was tantamount to building the nation, domesticity allowed women to be more than passive recipients of the bounty of the state. The cultural elevation of domesticity meant that women, like men, fulfilled obligations to the state in order to receive the rights of citizenship. Beyond the seemingly contradictory idea of creating a "civic" role from a "private" zone, domesticity also served to solidify boundaries based on race and class. Free women of color strategically embraced the whiteness of domesticity to claim political empowerment for African American households. For the emerging antebellum African American middle class, domesticity provided one of the few options for Black women to claim citizenship and served as a means for whites to view African Americans as potential citizens. Historian Leslie M. Harris explains that "in the eyes of whites, citizenship for New York City's blacks was tied to the conduct of black women, despite republicanism's and the black community's emphasis on manhood as the basis of citizenship."[31] Although it was a heavy burden, the promotion of womanhood within the Black and white press gave women of color an opportunity to promote the respectability of their households.

As significant as the changes in white domestic labor were during the first half of the nineteenth century, this moment ushered in even greater changes for African Americans as labor became racialized. The emerging market revolution particularly stratified the experience of Black and white workers. When coupled with gradual northern emancipation, the shifting economy resulted in significant changes in African American civic status as working-class whites tried to preserve their own employment opportunities. The market economy's promotion of a distinct middle class that was romanticized as the emblematic national identity also served to minimize the civic identity of African Americans. To counter white imaginings of middle-class family life in a changing economy, Black women promoted their own civilizing work by creating homes; thus, domesticity became central to African American claims to not only respectability but also citizenship. Black families functioned, in theory, like their white counterparts. In practice, however, the performance of idealized domesticity was often difficult. The lack of disposable income, time, and single-family homes made the middle-class ideal life nearly impossible for some women to embrace in totality. Many women of color (as well as white working-class women) had to pick and choose which aspects of domesticity to perform. Despite this challenge, as documented in the African American press, Black women embraced nineteenth-century standards of domesticity and womanhood not only on their own behalf but also on behalf of their families and communities. A well-ordered and stable home demonstrated the independence of a household, the key to the republican citizen family. An examination of the antebellum print culture of domesticity demonstrates that authors actively redefined the function of the home in a way that permitted Black and white middle-class women to enact their citizenship from within the private realm of their own kitchen hearths. As the market economy replaced many of the productive aspects of households, the home gained a strong symbolic purpose.

For African Americans, attaching claims of citizenship to domesticity was problematic from the beginning. Whether on the pages of the Black and antislavery press or in the numerous censuses conducted by advocates for people of color, emphasis was placed on employment, education, and the creation of a respectable infrastructure of churches, benevolent societies, and locations of racial uplift when the African American population was described. Although making an argument of similarity to middle-class whites would appear to offer justification for civic standing, this approach ignored the fact that obtaining that status was much more difficult for African Americans because of structural discrimination. This approach to citizenship and status in the 1830s became the go-to trope for future generations and diminished natural rights claims to civic status.[32]

Throughout the antebellum era, female claims to citizenship were most influenced by the relationship the men in their families had with the state. For example, white women imagined citizenship much like their husbands, fathers, and brothers. Citizenship was a singular identity guaranteed through the fulfillment of individual duties and obligations. Because whites as a racial category were not excluded from citizenship and its benefits, civic status was determined by individual rather than group behaviors. As a result, white women equated their individual domestic behaviors as proof of their personal entitlement to the protections of citizenship. Racial difference, however, influenced how Black women interpreted citizenship as collectively held by families and a shared identity. While historian Elsa Barkley Brown describes the Reconstruction era vision of voting rights as "a collective, not an individual possession," this vision began much earlier.[33] Due to gradual emancipation in the North there was not a level playing field among free people of color. This, coupled with the fact that northern emancipation did not come with the legal backing of a constitutional amendment, meant that class played a larger part in demonstrating civic belongingness. Kimberlé Crenshaw's idea of intersectionality captures the unique problems antebellum women of color faced. Black women were not merely disadvantaged twice because of their race and gender; instead, they encountered a cumulative force that limited their rhetorical strategies.[34] Because their civic standing was restricted based on race, gender, and often economic class, African American women had fewer opportunities to transgress boundaries because they faced multiple rather than singular barriers. Women of color had to redefine rhetorical spaces to create their own space within the public sphere. The rhetoric of racial elevation reflected performances of middle-class values for the enhancement of all African Americans regardless of their sex, and women carried the burden of proving civic suitability for their entire race. The whiteness of true womanhood served to emphasize its privilege, echoing the often unspoken class component of citizenship.[35]

OVERVIEW AND CHAPTER SUMMARY

This book focuses on the antebellum era, roughly 1820–60, and examines how women viewed their citizenship from the vantage point of the private sphere. Too often scholars conflate women's interest in their status as citizens with the quest for female suffrage. This approach leads to privileging Elizabeth Cady Stanton's *Declaration of Sentiments* and the 1848 Seneca Falls convention as the sum total of the story of antebellum women's rights. While few scholars would disagree that this particular movement represented only a small percentage of the population, particularly during the period before the Civil War, it does imply a lack of political awareness by the remaining population of women. Many women did, however, question their status before the public call for the vote in 1848. These women exerted their political voice, as demonstrated by the creation of benevolent and moral reform societies and, more significantly, by the thousands of women who signed antislavery petitions during this period.[36]

My source base draws upon the publishing market newly directed toward women during the early nineteenth century and examines domestic literature, including cookbooks, novels, household manuals, newspapers, magazines, and sermons, as well as more traditional archival resources such as diaries and letters. This new print market provided women with both an outlet for publishing and, more importantly, a source for materials authored by women. A close reading of these sources reveals a greater depth of purpose than is typically attributed to antebellum women's print culture and gender norms. The often-overlooked subtext of these works, fiction and nonfiction alike, reveals a justification for domesticity, the need for women's expertise within the household, and a call for recognition of women's contribution to nation building. Court decisions and legislative debates are another important source base and are seldom read alongside women's writing. These debates provide a foundational understanding of the racialized and gendered interpretations of citizenship at the legal level. They also provide a context for the arguments women responded to in their domestic manifestos, novels of misfortune, and poetry dedicated to both womanhood and the abolition of slavery. Because antebellum women had less access to the public sphere, their political voice took a different form from men's but reveals an equal desire to engage in a discourse about the nation.

As a cultural history, this project is geographically broadly based. Unlike social histories that occupy a specific physical space, by their very natures, cultural histories tend to cast a wider net. Although the place of both the production and the (imagined) consumption of this literature varies, the primary spatial location is within the middle-class homes of Blacks and whites in towns and cities. The urban home had not only access to markets but also timely exposure to ephemeral print materials (e.g., newspapers and magazines) and functioned primarily as a place of consumption rather than production. The importance of markets to the cultural transformation at this time cannot be overemphasized. In particular, the ability to purchase goods would be central to the evolution of a consumer model for the American housewife. Because a comparison of Black and white deployment of true womanhood is central to this project, cities with significant free African American populations have been emphasized.

Chapter 1 explores the status of Black and white women as citizens and potential citizens by examining their civic status, voting rights, rights to property ownership, freedom of movement, and, most importantly, opportunities to engage the public sphere. Among the ways to understand the construction of civic status at this time is to examine legislative debates, regulatory laws, and state and federal court decisions. As political activism by women increased during the nineteenth century, courts and legislatures responded with more precisely defined rights based on race and gender in hopes of quelling demands for civic recognition.

Chapter 2 examines the rise of a female and Black print culture. Print culture expanded the opportunities for marginalized groups to engage each other and the public sphere to advocate for their rights and status. The rise of women's magazines, Black-edited and antislavery newspapers, pamphlets, novels, and advice material provides a marketplace and outlet for counterpublics and challenges to the political establishment and elite interpretations of citizenship.

Chapter 3 moves the study of womanhood to the community-building work of middle-class free people of color. The establishment of schools, churches, and cultural associations created spaces for women of color to practice the white incarnation of womanhood and to demonstrate respectability. Beyond the practice of womanhood, these spaces allowed Black women to create counterpublics that challenged the national narrative of racially defined citizenship.

The final two chapters examine the lives of five women who engaged the public sphere through print culture and the enactment of womanhood. Chapter 4 examines the writing, politics, and lives of Sarah Josepha Hale, Catharine Beecher, and Lydia Maria Child, three of the most prominent white women of the antebellum era. They wrote novels, household advice, and political tracts and shared a commitment to true womanhood. Despite different political agendas, each of these women used respectability to cloak political ideas and wielded influence on behalf of and in spite of their sex. Beecher and Hale provide a particularly complicated interpretation of the role of domesticity to enhance the civic standing of women, since they actively sought to minimize women's public engagement. Chapter 5 examines Sarah Forten and Sarah Douglass, Black women who were published authors and influential within their communities. Both women also espoused the ideology of womanhood to demonstrate their own respectability, as well as serving as exemplars for their race. The double jeopardy they faced being Black females required careful navigation of the public sphere, and like their white counterparts, they found it difficult to balance their public and private personae. The biographical approach taken in these two chapters illuminates the strategies and goals of these women by reading their lives and work comparatively.

A cultural history of citizenship provides a more nuanced understanding of how women and African American men engaged the state to claim civic status. The emergence of an American print culture in the nineteenth century was necessary for those who were largely excluded physically from the public sphere to both critique the state and provide evidence for how they fulfilled the obligations of citizenship. The ideology of true womanhood was one way women attached a civic purpose to their daily practices of domesticity. Although true womanhood was typically viewed exclusively as a white identity, women of color emulated the prescribed practices of true womanhood in hopes of claiming some of the civic privileges of whiteness. By analyzing how Black and white women reinterpreted their domestic duties to justify their inclusion within the state, we can better understand how citizenship was challenged and inscribed during the nineteenth century.

CHAPTER 1

The Expanding Female Sphere
Creating the Citizen Woman

The political stirrings experienced by our nation's white male founders were not theirs alone. Women, like men, expressed political desires before the American Revolution. In 1768 Phillis Wheatley, a young enslaved female, composed a poem in which she acknowledged "the favours" of the Stamp Act repeal by the "British king" and concluded, "A Monarchs smile can set his subjects free."[1] Did the final line of this poem hold a double meaning, or should it be taken at face value? Was she celebrating the end of a hated tax? Regardless of which interpretation is preferred, Wheatley was undeniably politically engaged with the events of the day. A few years later Abigail Adams corresponded with her husband, a member of the Continental Congress in Philadelphia, and famously requested that in the move toward independence, politicians would "remember the ladies." Not receiving an adequate response, a month later Abigail Adams followed up with a second, more forceful letter: "We have it in our power not only to free ourselves, but to subdue our masters, and without violence, throw both your natural and legal authority at our feet."[2] Both Wheatley and Adams used the written word to express their interest in current affairs and to reflect on their political status. While these are well-known examples of eighteenth-century women's political writings, there is no reason to suspect that their expressions were unusual or remarkable. Women reflected on the world around them both within the home and beyond the threshold.

In the postrevolutionary era, women and African American men sought to define their role within the nation as citizens rather than as dependents. Those who fell outside the confines of citizenship first made natural rights claims to equality under the law. When that approach failed the challenge became how to reimagine citizenship and redefine its obligations. Women considered their reproductive labor to hold significance. Domesticity, as illustrated in nineteenth-century advice literature (cookbooks, household advice manuals, novels, women's magazines, and newspapers), demonstrated the cultural construction of womanhood and the whiteness promoted through the expanding antebellum print culture. Historian Lori Ginzberg argues that by "the 1850s, the written word had long constituted an essential means by which women assured their place in civic life. Many women who wanted their views heard in the realm of public discourse wrote tracts, articles, fictional short stories, and novels, as well as authoring and presenting political speeches."[3] Antebellum print culture allowed women to creep into the public sphere in unexpected ways, and because other women had access to these materials, print culture allowed women to also see their roles as citizens.

The nineteenth-century construction of womanhood was central to how Black and white women performed their duties as citizens and demonstrated their suitability for that status. Black men, by serving as patriarchs of well-ordered homes and husbands of true women, demonstrated their similarity to white males and fitness for citizenship. The early republic and antebellum eras were ripe for defining citizenship and creating national identity. While the federal Constitution was quiet on the issue, courts and state legislatures stepped in and declared who received the rights and performed the obligations of citizenship.[4] Those excluded from citizenship countered these claims with fresh interpretations of civic identity. Print culture provided the best means for those excluded from the public sphere to exert their rights, challenge power, and expose others to their arguments for civic inclusion.

The American Revolution and the subsequent adoption of the U.S. Constitution resulted in a change in status for residents of the former British colonies. When white male subjects transitioned into citizens, a defined civic identity emerged. Although it was believed that economic dependents "could never develop civic virtue," if a man was free, white, over twenty-one, and a property owner, in most states he met the requirements for fulfilling the primary duty of a citizen: participation in the government through the ballot. Suffrage would become an unofficial litmus test for citizenship.[5] Not all states initially limited the franchise based on race or even gender. However, as economic barriers to voting declined, racial restrictions increased.

After the revolution, many newly minted male Americans had already fulfilled another recognized obligation of citizenship, military service, which excluded women and was racially segregated. Initially, free men of color were prohibited from service, although eventually a shortage of soldiers permitted enlistment. Men who were either too old or too young for active military service during the revolution could meet that obligation during the early republic by drilling with their local militia.[6] When called upon, military service not only is an obligation of citizenship in most nations but also provides a fast track to citizenship for groups previously denied that status. African American participation in the U.S. Civil War and the participation of French women in the resistance during the Second World War helped secure their voting rights.[7] Thus, discussions about women being deployed in combat, "don't ask, don't tell," and debates over trans individuals and military participation are all important political, legal, and citizenship concerns. Serving on juries, paying taxes, and avoiding vagrancy were other obligations of citizens that men of the federal era fulfilled in their daily lives.[8] Throughout this period, American males demonstrated their status as citizens of a republic by engaging in civic discourse that was shaped by race and gender, further entrenching the image of the U.S. citizen as a propertied white male and making it more difficult for women and African American men to enact a positive civic role in the new nation.

Despite Abigail Adams's request that her husband "remember the ladies," everyday life after the revolution offered no meaningful expansion of women's civic standing. The shift from royal subject to democratic citizen was not as seamless for women as it was for men. Despite this lack of status, the emergence of a feminine republican identity preserved women's cultural, if not political, standing. During the federal era, women's civil obligations were to the male head of household, fulfilled through domestic service and their biological function of reproduction. Unlike men, who directly interacted with the state, women were removed by at least an additional step from the government.

Since at least the 1970s historians have debated the civic status of women emerging from the revolution. Some have argued that women inhabited a separate citizenship, one based on sexual difference.[9] Because men and women entered the social compact differently—white men with political autonomy and women encumbered with the obligations of coverture (or the potential for marriage and coverture)—citizenship was influenced by sex.[10] By virtue of common law, a married woman's first allegiance was to her husband. A woman's obligations to the state were performed through her duties as a wife and thus by proxy by her spouse. Coverture, an English legal principle, stripped a married woman of her legal identity. William Blackstone writes in *Commentaries on the Laws of England* (1765–67) that in "marriage, the husband and wife are one person in law; that is, the very being or legal existence of the woman is suspended during the marriage or at least is incorporated and consolidated into that of her husband, under whose wing, protection, and cover she performs every thing."[11] Historian Linda Kerber maintains that the "legal tradition that substituted married women's obligations to their husbands for obligations to the state" might have eroded "by the late twentieth century"; however, "it remained a central element in the way Americans have thought about the relation of all women, including unmarried women, to state power."[12]

Despite the legal confines of coverture, some historians have described the colonial era as being a freer time for women because there was little government intervention to enforce power hierarchies, and home-based production gave significance to women's labor. The exemplar women of these arguments tended to act in tandem with a spouse as a deputy husband, or these women acted independently because they were widows. Independent women entrepreneurs, be they married or single, were in the minority.[13] The heavy hand of coverture meant that married women (regardless of individual ability or economic standing) as a class had no legally recognized political voice. In return for a husband's economic support and protection, a wife supplied her husband with domestic labor, sex, affection, and, potentially, children.[14] Instead of first proving allegiance to the state, a woman was expected to serve and experience citizenship through her husband. Without legal standing it was thought that women had no need for an individual civic status.

Coverture limited women's standing not only within the home but also in the broader society. For example, coverture could render a woman stateless if she chose to marry a foreign national. It was the twentieth century before married women could maintain an independent relationship to the state. *Mackenzie v. Hare* (1915) upheld a congressional statute that deemed a woman's marriage to a foreign national as voluntary expatriation. The Cable Act of 1922 began to rectify this problem, but loopholes remained.[15] Coverture limited women's ability to enter contracts, meaning women could not control their own wages or property, and the marriage contract would always be between unequal partners. The public sphere also served to regulate women's political influence. The British practice of coverture, transferred to the colonies, was still in use during the early national period and laid the groundwork for denying women citizenship. Vestiges of coverture continued to haunt women well into the twentieth century with protective labor legislation, the inability to obtain credit, and the lack of protection from marital rape. Despite modern women's legal status as citizens as a class, individual women continue to face the traditions of subordination through marriage, the wage gap, and limited access to status and power.

Coverture was not the only way civic status was defined by sex. Political festivals and parades provide a particularly potent example of the difference race and gender made in an individual's participation in the public sphere, demonstrating power and access. During the federal era, society largely relegated women to a spectator's role, and their political participation either remained on the periphery or was symbolic. For example, a festival held in honor of President Jefferson guaranteed the seclusion of female participants before and after the event was held. A newspaper announcing the celebration declared, "Private houses are engaged for all the Ladies who may honor the occasion with their company."[16] The public spaces of parades and festivals were segregated based on both race and gender, further reinforcing that the public sphere was for white men whether they were elite or not.[17] Cultural practices prescribed the female political voice to be an echo of nationalistic platitudes rather than one engaged in partisan politics. Women brought virtue to political gatherings because of their assumed lack of interest in the practice of politics.[18] Historian Mary Ryan explains, "The wives of the new nation were heralded not as citizens but as republican helpmates."[19] Eighteenth-century female authors who entered the public sphere through words rather than actions still faced disapproval and social sanction. The celebrated early American feminist Judith Sargent Stevens Murray explained in the preface to one of her first publications, "When a female steps without the Line in which custom hath circumscribed her, she naturally becomes an Object of Speculation."[20] Ironically, while the nation appropriated the physical form of the female body in the figure of Columbia, it relegated flesh-and-blood women to a dependent status. Women might have had a *republican* identity, but without the ability to fulfill their duties as citizens, they lacked a political rationale for civil rights.

Republican motherhood, the duty of women to raise and nurture the future citizens of the nation, was the prescribed method for women to engage in service to country during the era of the early republic. Kerber writes that "Republican Motherhood provided the justification of women's political behavior.... This new identity had the advantage of appearing to reconcile politics and domesticity; it justified political education and political sensibility."[21] Essentialist to its core, republican motherhood provided women, mothers, or potential mothers a means to situate themselves within the nation. Murray extolled motherhood and argued in many of her essays that it was a responsibility of women to ensure the well-being of the new nation through effective mothering.[22] In 1798 she described the daughters of Columbia, the young women of the new nation, as "sensible and informed," "companionable and serious," and "blest with competency—and rearing to maturity a promising family of children."[23] While believing women had the right to a voice in government, Murray removed women from the public sphere by locating their political voice to minisalons, held in their homes.[24] The ideology of republican motherhood offered a mixed bag of both benefits and impediments for women. Although Murray, Benjamin Rush (a member of the Philadelphia elite), and others used the importance of motherhood to call for improvements in education and literacy for young girls, motherhood did little to solidify the status of women within the nation and further tied their civic identity to biology and the domestic sphere. Education alone would not lead to equality. By inculcating republican values in their sons, women were merely the conduit for a strong nation. According to this ideology, the nation's future depended on the next generation of republican sons rather than on the mothers themselves. Throughout the early republic, women remained symbols of national identity rather than actual citizens. It was not until the nineteenth century that being a homemaker served to fulfill an individual obligation as citizen.

The chaos of the American Revolution provided enslaved African Americans with a variety of opportunities to pursue freedom and seek citizenship. Historian Christy Clark-Pujara explains that "enslaved people dealt a major blow to the institution of slavery in the North and South—they fled." She estimates that "one hundred thousand slaves, one out of every five, in British North America escaped during the American Revolution."[25] Wartime conditions destabilized systems of slavery in both the North and South and gave cover to those who fled their status. Like white women, African Americans found that the natural rights language of the Declaration of Independence did not come to fruition with the rights to people of color. The war itself presented the opportunity for the emancipation of slaves and indentured servants who fought for the British, and a significant number of individuals seized this opportunity. Enough slaves fled across British lines to create two distinct Black regiments, Clinton's Pioneers and Lord Dunmore's Ethiopian Regiment. Dunmore's soldiers fought wearing badges that read "liberty to slaves."[26] Despite initial restrictions on the enlistment of African American men in the Continental army, by 1778 New England states more consistently allowed Black enlistment, and in Massachusetts African American men were subject to the draft. In all, an estimated twenty thousand African Americans participated in the American Revolution. The decision to enlist and even the opportunity to flee slavery were typically options for men. Female prospects for wartime freedom were much more limited.

Many of the limitations upon white women within the public sphere were also placed upon African American men and women during the early national era. The participation of Black men in parades and festivals was largely segregated and viewed by white powerbrokers as spectacle rather than political engagement. During the first decades of the early republic, northern state legislatures began adopting gradual emancipation laws. Although African Americans thought freedom would be synonymous with citizenship, whites saw citizenship for Blacks more like emancipation, a gradual process. While gradual instead of immediate emancipation was enacted in large part to meet the economic needs of whites, policy makers also argued that former slaves needed time, training, and experience before they could become citizens.

While Abigail Adams engaged in her now famous discussion of rights in private letters, Phillis Wheatley explored similar questions publicly in her published poems, allowing for a wider audience. Much of her poetry was a reflection of the time in which she wrote. Wheatley often addressed her writing to grieving individuals and important community figures, and her poetry offered reflections on religion. However, she also composed political observations cloaked within the generic constraints of eighteenth-century poetry. Her poetry was bold, given Wheatley's status as a slave. In colonial Boston, however, her writing was considered a novelty, the political overtones often overlooked. Born in Senegal, Wheatley was sold into slavery and brought to Boston at the age of eight, causing some whites to question if an African slave could produce such works. Her book of poetry, originally published in 1773, included a note to the public verifying authenticity: "We whose names are underwritten, do assure the world that the poems specified in the following page were (as we verily believe), written by Phillis, a young negro girl, who was but a few years since, brought an uncultivated barbarian from Africa, and has ever since been, and now is, under the disadvantage of serving as a slave in a family in this town."[27] Wheatley's poetry is an early example of the power of print culture for those on the margin. Her growing fame even managed to draw Thomas Jefferson into the debate over the authenticity of her work. In an oft-quoted excerpt from *Notes on the State of Virginia*, Jefferson attacked the quality of Wheatley's poems instead of their authorship: "Religion, indeed, has produced a Phyllis Whately [*sic*]: but it could not produce a poet. The compositions published under her name are below the dignity of criticism."[28] Despite the speculation and criticism she faced in the United States, Wheatley generated a following in England, particularly after her visit there in 1773. Because of her talent and intellect, she was often used as an example of the inhumanity of slavery. She also served as an example of the powerlessness of women of color even if they had a public platform for their rhetoric.

THE EVOLUTION OF CITIZENSHIP IN THE EARLY NINETEENTH CENTURY

Historian Joan Hoff writes that "citizenship is a form of power."[29] White women and African Americans, without civic standing, remained politically powerless throughout most of the century. As women entered the nineteenth century, they searched for their own means to perform the duties of citizenship in a republic. The shifting political landscape of "Jacksonian Democracy," which expanded the white male franchise, coupled with evolving cultural norms and the emerging market economy, conspired to limit women's ability to claim a political role. As the economy industrialized, the perceived value of household labor both in real dollar terms and in social importance diminished.

There was little the market economy did not change, including the function of families. The antebellum family was no longer a "little commonwealth" that produced goods and interacted with the community as a commercial unit. Instead, the white nineteenth-century family focused on consumption rather than production and became economically separated from their neighbors and more closely tied to the market.[30] This change was even more pronounced for African American families. Because Black men were often banned from the professions and lacked opportunities for apprenticeship or education, most Black male heads of household were vulnerable to the instability of day-labor wages. This placed economic burdens on women of color, separating them from the practice of womanhood and nation building. The industrialized market constructed a middle step between consumption and production. The exchange of Black women's labor for wages meant that Black and white interactions within the market economy were inherently unequal. These economic shifts impacted the civic standing of women. Concurrent with these changes was the evolving definition of the work of men.

Instead of linking work to the production of goods, it became synonymous with the creation of wealth or receiving wages. "Work was a source of moral instruction, economic success, and political virtue," further distancing women from valued labor.[31] Historian Jeanne Boydston explained that "civic republicanism [which encompassed both the idea of republican motherhood and other aspects of male and female political status] was a transitional gender ideology, bridging old notions of rural patriarchy and industrial ideologies of the male breadwinner."[32] Although republican motherhood appeared to "reconcile politics and domesticity," this configuration of female citizenship forced the nineteenth-century woman to place the household at the center of her civic identity.[33] Mary Beth Norton explains that the home became the center of feminine political activity and created a need to redefine the concept of domesticity, making the female's "public" role one that was enacted from the private home.[34] Mary Ryan describes this process more boldly, declaring that the home was the "imperial center, the mother country, from which women launched their vast social influence."[35] While these historians emphasized gender often at the expense of race, it is critical to remember that economic changes also impacted Black families often differently and more severely, which means these findings cannot be generalized across race. Because the labor of African American men and women was compensated differently from their white counterparts, the positive cultural changes brought forth by the market passed by Black families. Inequalities in wages and labor were magnified because emancipation and gradual emancipation in the North came just prior to industrialization. Thus, there were new waged workers entering into a saturated market with too few unskilled jobs.[36] This meant that a rising class of African Americans had to embrace the cultural evolution of the early nineteenth century without the economic benefits of the market revolution.

CIVIC DOMESTICITY AND THE POLITICAL SIGNIFICANCE OF THE HOME

The result of these cultural, economic, and political shifts was the emergence of the ideology of true womanhood, a cultural creation that limited a woman to the private sphere while also elevating her position within that sphere. First identified by Barbara Welter in her influential article "The Cult of True Womanhood, 1820–1860" (1966), true womanhood was embodied through the virtues of piety, purity, submissiveness, and domesticity, elements that shaped societal expectations of women.[37] Welter isolated these virtues as central to antebellum gender discourse through an examination of print material directed toward women.

Although academics debate whether this shift in cultural definitions of womanhood was restricting or if it ultimately enhanced women's political status (as was argued by many nineteenth-century authors of those texts), the limitation of almost all of these discussions is that they only examine the role of *white* middle-class women. African American women certainly faced similar difficulties in defining their political role in the United States; however, the addition of race into the equation magnified their struggle. How African American women sought to define their role as citizens in terms of both race and gender (and its intersections with class) is a more problematic question. Nineteenth-century constructions of womanhood reflected each of those three categories, often placing female "types" in opposition to each other. Stereotypes magnified by white publications served to exclude Black women from the ranks of true womanhood and, more importantly, the civic status it promised.

Race was an ever-present, although often ignored, factor in the construction of nineteenth-century womanhood. The African American middle class used womanhood to demonstrate its similarity to the white middle class. African American demonstrations of respectability were an implicit call for equality. In contrast, white women deployed womanhood in part to define who they were not, making whiteness an aspect of their construction of the middle class, much like seventeenth-century colonists used gender to define racial difference.[38] Historian Shirley Yee explains that "racist and sexist imagery of womanhood had become standard perceptions in the eyes of white society," and these stereotypes became "mutually reinforcing images, not simply opposites."[39] Regardless of economic standing and social respectability, Black families occupied a middle class different from that of their white counterparts: it was always separate and never included the same opportunities available to whites.

Central to the construction of true womanhood was print culture, in particular the emerging market in domestic advice literature, as it helped to entrench a unified vision of femininity. Unlike republican motherhood, which argued that "good sons" were the future of the nation, the new domestic advice manuals located women as the center of both the household and a strong country, a crucial difference that is often ignored. The nineteenth-century domestic manual was not a new idea or even an American invention. Household manuals had existed in Europe for centuries, and colonists brought British domestic handbooks with them as they established new homes. However, during the nineteenth century, the first uniquely American manuals began to be published. Beginning with Amelia Simmons's *American Cookery* (1796) and extending throughout the nineteenth century, authors of these handbooks argued that the U.S. household required advice that was different from that offered to homes across the Atlantic. While the genre began as cookbooks, providing recipes for the American diet (utilizing foods uncommon in Europe), before long they evolved and dispensed advice about all aspects of household management, providing a philosophy of the home, its work, and the importance of the domestic sphere. Domesticity crept into the public discourse in a variety of ways. Popular novels, short stories, and essays reflected the importance of the home to the market economy and the political imaginings of the nation.[40] This transition was significant: it represented the shift in the beneficiary of a woman's domestic duty from the patriarch of the household alone to that of the husband and the nation. By creating a form of domestic nationalism, household manuals allowed women to engage in cultural citizenship and nation building without ever physically entering the public sphere.

The abolitionist, temperance, and other moral reform movements, as well as occasional political activities, began to lure some women beyond the private sphere during the antebellum era. Activist women often anchored their public work to morality and religion to soften their "unfeminine" action. For example, the Boston Female Anti-Slavery Society adopted a resolution supporting the public speaking of Angelina and Sarah Grimké because "God has so signally sustained and blessed their efforts" and concluded that it should afford "strength and encouragement to all women through the world, who may feel called to advocate publically any cause of humanity."[41] Although the number of female public speakers remained limited through the antebellum era, the support they received from other women helped expand political opportunities.

The decade before the Seneca Falls convention included many ways for women to take political action. They not only used the printed word but also turned to political petitions. Antislavery petitions signed by women were both the height of political activism and the essence of an "appropriate" feminine response. The signature on a petition represented the endorsement of a political opinion that would be forwarded to Congress and hopefully acted upon. Petitions also served to cloak women's political voice. A signature, perhaps provided in private as opposed to in a public location, shrouded within the language of motherhood, religion, and morality, was seen as a more appropriate form for female activism. Petitioning was a particularly important political act for women of color. Their signatures did not necessarily serve as a marker of race, and petitioning was a way to engage in activism without risking the scorn and backlash of whites. The convention movement of the 1830s encouraged petitioning, and Black activist Maria Stewart specifically called for people of color to sign petitions ending slavery in the District of Columbia.[42] A Connecticut woman of color wrote a call for women to petition that was originally published in the Hartford antislavery paper, the *Charter Oak*, and reprinted in the *Pennsylvania Freeman*: "Free women of Connecticut, (for I speak not now to slaves, to the servile minions of pride, selfishness and prejudice) have you this fall signed the petitions in behalf of the dumb, and entreated *all* the women in your town to do the same?" The author concluded her call in an almost militant fashion: "Up my sister, speak while there is time. Millions are perishing, victims of your delay."[43] Interestingly, despite her public call for signatures and action, her essay is merely signed "a Colored Woman." Was this an attempt to conceal her identity, or did she wish to highlight her race? Regardless of the reason, this essay emphasizes the link between the printed word and civic standing. The significance of antislavery petitions is difficult to overstate. Not only did they provide an outlet for women's political expression, but petitions in general called upon legislatures to "introduce the petition submitted to them, read them aloud, and formally receive them. From there the legislative body could decide to table a petition (ostensibly for further consideration) or refer it to a committee for investigation and recommendation."[44] The sheer number of antislavery petitions put a physical strain on Congress, and women realized they could influence Congress if not by persuading then by slowing the legislative process.

AFRICAN AMERICAN CIVIC IDENTITY

African American men first supported their claims for equality through natural rights, a key component of the Declaration of Independence. During the revolutionary era, New England African Americans petitioned for emancipation based on the claims white colonists were advancing for independence from Great Britain. This link between independence and emancipation continued into the nineteenth century. For example, after West Indies emancipation (1833/1834), African American rhetoric often portrayed Great Britain as the land of liberty rather than the United States.[45] Men of color such as Benjamin Banneker and Absalom Jones laid claim to an equal citizenship based first on natural rights and then contributions to the nation. Jones and seventy additional African Americans petitioned Congress to revise the Fugitive Slave Act of 1793. Jones, the author of the petition, wrote of the "natural right to liberty, and the protection of our persons and property from the oppression and violence which so great a number of like colour and national descent are subject to."[46] The natural rights approach flowed from the Enlightenment philosophy that influenced the rhetoric of the revolution. Natural rights claims did not require proof of military service to the nation or a particular suitability for citizenship; rights claims stood alone. Most importantly, natural rights would recognize citizenship for white women, people of color, and immigrants. If this approach had been respected by white elites, it would have been the most efficient route to citizenship and would not have required debates about civic status throughout the nineteenth century. Unfortunately, those elites only recognized natural rights as belonging to their own kind.

African Americans actively wrote themselves into public documents as citizens. The African Society, founded in Boston in 1796, published the "Laws of the African Society" in 1802. The opening paragraph described the mutual benefit organization and inscribed citizenship on its members, writing that they were "true and faithful citizens of the Commonwealth in which we live."[47] The Brotherly Union Society of Philadelphia, founded in 1823, began the preamble of its constitution with the following: "We, the subscribers, coloured men, of the county of Philadelphia, citizens of the Commonwealth of Pennsylvania and the United States of America."[48] The language of both documents suggests the use of "citizen" more broadly than merely designating residency. Instead, these documents projected an identity as citizens because members were active participants in their state and nation.

African Americans published documents that demonstrated their civic status. Publication ensured an expanded audience beyond their organizational membership and access to the public sphere with a counternarrative that challenged or at least supplemented the largely white-authored narrative of abolition, emancipation, and slavery. The number of published tracts was fairly limited in the late eighteenth century and early nineteenth century. However, with the birth of the antebellum Black press in the 1820s and a greater number of printers, the number of Black-authored publications increased exponentially.[49] Newspapers such as *The Liberator* and the *Pennsylvania Freeman* provided public space for notices of Black activism in white-edited newspapers. Publication of club documents not only provided notice of activities but also conveyed personal pride in an organization, demonstrated members' civic engagement, and encouraged others toward activism. By setting aside "ladies' pages," these newspapers encouraged women of color to publicize their activities and promote racial elevation, all with an eye toward expanding their civic standing. Despite the publication of natural rights claims, this approach was not successful. The nineteenth century ushered in new impediments to citizenship for those on the margins, resulting in the creation of new ways to make rights claims.

REGULATING CITIZENSHIP:
THE IMPORTANCE OF PROPERTY

From the first days of the new nation, property ownership was an important indicator of one's fitness for citizenship. Being a landholder granted an individual independence, which made for a "pure" civic actor beholden to no one. Given formal sanctions against married women's landownership and de facto restrictions upon free African Americans, it is clear that these groups were never imagined as civic actors at the time of the nation's founding. Rowland Berthoff explains that "property did not make him virtuous, but it freed him to choose the path of civic virtue: only men thus free to sustain the commonwealth ought to be citizens—not their dependent wives, children, tenants, employees, servants, or slaves."[50] Landownership ensured independence and thus the ability to cast an independent ballot.

Women's right to own and transfer property depended on their marital status. Coverture limited women's civic standing in a variety of ways, but relegating married women to a propertyless status kept them from being defined as virtuous citizens. The Litchfield, Connecticut, lawyer and educator Tapping Reeve explained in *The Law of Baron and Femme* (1816): "The husband, by marriage, acquires an absolute title to all the personal property of the wife, which she had in possession at the time of the marriage: such as money, goods or chattels personal of any kind." Providing no leeway for women to eventually regain their property, Reeve concludes, "By marriage, [a woman's possessions become her husband's] property, as completely as he purchases with his money; and such property can never again belong to the wife, upon the happening of any event, unless it be given to her by his will; and in case of the death of the husband, this property does not return to the wife, but vests in his executors."[51] In New York, like most states, women were provided dower rights, also known as the widow's third, that gave a woman the right to approve the sale of land that a woman had the chance to inherit.[52] The shift from the practice of coverture to granting married women property rights, a near universal practice by the decade after the Civil War, was a critical improvement in women's status, although it did not accompany the ballot or formal political participation.[53]

During the antebellum era, the right of married women to control property became more commonly debated. Eleven years prior to the passage of New York's Married Women's Property Act (1848), the *American Ladies' Magazine* published a lengthy essay calling for women's right to control their own property. Situated well within the template of true womanhood, the essay argued that women needed property rights (and the right to control wages) to protect them from intemperate husbands and to promote domestic tranquility. The anonymous author even suggested that women might be better suited for financial management even if they did not "handle the chisel, the pencil, or the pen, so well as men."[54] For African Americans, whether male or female, the ability to own property was even more difficult than it was for white women, who largely inherited the property they wished to claim. Influenced by the inability to procure permanent employment or loans, segregation, and the often murky status of being somewhere between free and enslaved, property ownership was only available for elite African Americans.[55] Property ownership was one sign of not only respectability but also, more importantly, stability. The Friendly Society of St. Thomas's African Episcopal Church (Philadelphia) required the treasurer of this benevolent society to "be of good character and reputation, possessed of freehold property, and on entering on the duties of his office, he shall give such security for the faithful discharge of his trust as a majority of the Committee shall require."[56] The organization also made the provision for excess funds with the plan to either loan the money or purchase property for the use of the society. *The Anglo-African* reported a list of homeowners in Patterson, New Jersey, "who by industry and economy, have accumulated considerable property." These achievements are even more significant because "although Patterson is noted as a manufacturing city, colored people are generally excluded from the various mills, silk, cotton, & c."[57] Although no longer universally a requirement for voting, property ownership was still an important marker of status. Newspapers and other documents highlighted those who owned property to publicize the individual and a rising community of free people of color.

EMANCIPATION AND CIVIC STANDING IN THE ANTEBELLUM NORTH

As the parameters of the white male franchise expanded in the nineteenth century, voting rights grew more closely related to defining a citizen.[58] For this reason, African Americans strategically considered what citizenship meant and whether or not it required the ability to vote. In a somewhat "chicken-and-egg" analysis, African Americans wanted to prove that their lack of voting was not prima facie evidence of their lack of citizenship; instead, their citizenship provided justification for their suffrage rights. Since emancipation did not guarantee citizenship or a civic standing during the early nineteenth century, people of color looked for ways to claim cultural citizenship. The *National Era* reported before the *Dred Scott* decision that "there is certainly nothing in the Federal Constitution which forbids the rights of citizenship to persons of color, or that confines such rights to persons of a white complexion." The paper compared the murky status of free Blacks to that of white women, arguing that "the privilege of voting and the legal capacity for office, are not essential to the character of a citizen, for women are citizens without either."[59] Defining against another "other" would be an African American strategy for claiming rights throughout the nineteenth century. Women's suffrage activists would use a similar strategy in the decades before the Nineteenth Amendment was ratified. Notoriously, Susan B. Anthony and Elizabeth Cady Stanton deployed increasingly racist claims against men of color and immigrants not only to justify white female suffrage but also as a scare tactic. Access to services such as schools, the ability to find employment, and the availability of housing would all need to be protected before free African Americans could achieve a modicum of social equality, with or without civic status.

The end of slavery came to the North in fits and starts, beginning with immediate abolition in Vermont's constitution in 1777 and Pennsylvania's gradual emancipation law in 1780. After the American Revolution, other states followed suit. Rhode Island, a northern state where slavery was essential to the economy, offered emancipation for those born after March 1, 1784, but soon revised the law due to the financial burdens placed on communities to pay for the upbringing of freed children. The revised law allowed children to remain enslaved until they reached adulthood.[60] It is important to remember that northern emancipation was a slow process. In 1810 there were twenty-seven thousand slaves in "free" states, and gradual emancipation meant that it often took a generation before individuals were completely free from slavery.[61] Delayed manumission and the reality that bondage was often replaced with lengthy terms of indentured servitude meant that northern slavery continued (albeit in a much more limited form) well into the nineteenth century, in essence as a legal anachronism. Because of their unclear and variable status during the early national period, legal and cultural codes affecting African Americans were evolving.

CHANGES IN VOTING RIGHTS

When voting rights became racialized, women of color who could not vote due to their sex were further separated from the state when their male heads of household lost political standing. States that had previously defined voting rights based on residency and economics began revising state constitutions during the antebellum era. New York provides a good example of this changing status. The state constitution of 1777 placed significant property requirements on voting based on the importance of the position. It required higher economic standing to vote for governor than it did for a member of the assembly.[62] The New York constitutional convention of 1821 debated Black male suffrage, ultimately deciding to place race-based sanctions on voting rights, as opposed to directly adding the word "white" as a qualification.[63] One delegate justified restrictions on Black males based on not fulfilling the obligations of citizenship, but he ignored the fact that they were typically barred from performing those obligations. This was a claim often made against women. Either they failed to meet the obligations of citizenship despite cultural and legal sanctions, or the male head of household served as a woman's liaison with the state.

Despite prolific engagement by free Blacks in social and political activities and the liberalization of voting rights for white males, the 1830s were a time of diminishing rights for African Americans as discriminatory practices moved from custom to law. While the number of Black men who voted was relatively limited, legislation was either passed or debated in most northern states to curtail basic civil rights of free men of color.[64] Some whites expressed conspiratorial fears, including that wealthy abolitionists would purchase the land in a congressional district, open it to Black settlement, and then those Black voters would elect a man of color to Congress.[65] Such claims explain why voting rights for African Americans were so important to some whites. The "misguided" liberalism of one state could potentially impact the entire nation by changing the racial dynamics of Congress.

The result of the heralded nineteenth-century expansion of the electorate, "Jacksonian Democracy," was the replacement of economic qualifications with racial restrictions on voting. Pennsylvania provides a particularly vibrant example of the evolution of white thought about Black male suffrage and rights. In 1790 delegates to the Pennsylvania state constitutional convention "voted down a proposal to expressly limit citizenship to whites"; however, by 1838 Pennsylvania had revised its state constitution and officially revoked free Black male suffrage.[66] This legal codification merely reflected a social reality of many years: few eligible African American men voted at this time in Pennsylvania because of social customs and a fear of violence at the voting station. The ambiguity of the term "freeman" in the pre-1838 state constitution meant that Black male voting rights were left to the whim of county officials, who often argued that the term "freeman" was synonymous with "white man" and thus excluded Black men from the vote. For example, at one point, Philadelphia County (with the largest African American population in the state) did not assess taxes on Blacks, resulting in their disenfranchisement.[67]

The drafting of the new Pennsylvania state constitution cannot be understood in isolation. The Panic of 1837 hit Philadelphia particularly hard because the city was a center for banking, and delegates to the state constitutional convention were not exclusively considering the legal status of free African Americans.[68] Initially, Black voting rights were a periphery issue, with banking and judicial reform taking center stage. Despite the fact that African American suffrage was not central to the ensuing debates in Harrisburg, during the new constitution's drafting process both antislavery activists and leaders of the African American community searched for ways to reverse this pending state decision. Petitions were read supporting both sides of the issue. On December 30, 1837, memorials (or, in contemporary language, petitions) were read calling for religious tolerance and the right of trial by jury for all human beings, and there were two memorials from Bucks County calling on the prohibition of "negroes from the right of suffrage," as well as memorials from Montgomery and Philadelphia Counties "to prevent all amalgamation between the white and colored population in regard to the government of this State." All of these petitions were tabled without discussion.[69] January 1 brought additional memorials in the same vein, and once again they were tabled. On January 3 the antiamalgamation petitions numbered four, but five petitions were entered on the record "praying that no change may be made in the existing constitution, having a tendency to create distinctions in the rights and privileges of citizenship based upon complexion." As was the practice the previous two days, all of the memorials were tabled.[70]

The amendment to restrict voting rights based on race was initially voted down by delegates at the Pennsylvania reform convention in June 1837. A second vote in January 1838 resulted in the adoption of the "white" Amendment 77-45.[71] As the enfranchised citizens of Pennsylvania prepared to vote on the newly drafted constitution, the Pennsylvania Abolition Society commissioned a census of the free Black community of Philadelphia. The goal of the census was to gather statistical data to prove the respectability of the free African American community.[72] Philadelphia African Americans also shaped the suffrage debate. Robert Purvis, a wealthy biracial Philadelphian, published "Appeal of Forty Thousand Citizens, Threatened with Disfranchisement, to the People of Pennsylvania" in 1838. The appeal was printed in the *Colored American* and in a stand-alone pamphlet. Purvis urged the voters of Pennsylvania to reject the reform constitution through a variety of appeals, including the large number of "industrious, peaceable, and useful."[73] Despite the strength of the demographic and socioeconomic evidence found in the census and the publication of speeches and essays, enfranchised Pennsylvanians ultimately voted to ratify the new constitution, thus rejecting Black male suffrage. The decline in Black voting rights throughout the North in the 1830s served as a warning that the rhetoric of natural rights would not be enough to change white attitudes toward African American citizenship or voting rights for women. Without the ballot, African American households lacked the political means to redress wrongs.[74] The growth of the Black press and the rise of antislavery organizations opened the way for men and women to create counterpublics and challenge white attitudes toward Black citizenship.

Public debate about female suffrage tended to be less volatile because it was typically an expansion of rights, as opposed to the constriction that Black men faced. While white policy makers were no more interested in women gaining the vote than Black men, the issue was addressed with amusement rather than alarm. Extending the vote to mothers, wives, and daughters wasn't yet seen as a threat to household power dynamics. During the early republic the civil standing of women was not always clear and seldom included a discussion of voting rights.[75] For example, the requirements for voting were vague in early New Jersey constitutions. The first state constitution in 1776 granted all inhabitants who were otherwise qualified the right to vote, which meant that single women who were property owners potentially had the right to vote. In the 1790 constitution, "the franchise was conferred upon voters referred to as 'he or she,'" removing the ambiguity of the previous constitution.[76] This modification clearly indicates intentionality in the state's construction of suffrage requirements. By 1807 female suffrage was specifically abolished, leaving property-owning single women without a political voice.[77]

As the nineteenth century progressed, support for female suffrage slowly grew. Soon after the 1848 Seneca Falls "Declaration of Sentiments," female suffrage became a subject of more public debate, although there had already been limited discussion of female voting rights for decades. The 1853 state constitutional convention in Massachusetts included a relatively extensive debate about women's right to vote on the new constitution. One delegate opened his discussion by stating, "I maintain ... that the women of Massachusetts have a natural right to vote."[78] Challenging the principle of coverture, he compared the practice to the "autocrat of Russia's [use of] the same argument affirming that his domination is paternal in character and principle."[79] Another delegate argued that "these fair petitioners" lacked the number of signatures necessary to demonstrate that most women desired to vote on the new constitution. Invoking the popular arguments about domesticity and true womanhood, he claimed that women did not want the vote because they were influential in other ways: "The way that women exercise power, it is true, is not exactly by voting: it is the power which is far more omnipotent [than] that which they could acquire at the ballot-box."[80] The discussion was tabled until the following day, suggesting the importance of the matter to delegates and their willingness to give the issue a full hearing. When the debate continued the next day, it was argued that women were in possession of natural rights but that those rights were protected by their male head of household through coverture: "[T]he great sphere of woman, after all, is at home.... And if she wishes to increase and strengthen her influence in the community, and over society, there is a sure and direct road to that result, as it is entirely within her power to form and control those who are to be the makers, the interpreters, and the administrators of our laws."[81] The recognition of the importance of the domestic sphere is clear in his remarks. With the power women held within the home, there was no need for further protections. The report that rejected women's call to vote on the constitution was accepted unanimously sans one vote. The white male legislators of Massachusetts used coverture and the belief that the family unit provided a political voice to justify denying white women an individual vote. Interestingly, this status of the family as a political actor is what African American women aspired to as a way to legitimate their families so that their male heads of household could vote. In 1915 Massachusetts women helped to defeat a referendum on female suffrage, demonstrating that, despite a long history of promoting women in the antislavery movement and other moral reforms, even women could not agree on the value of the ballot in the early twentieth century.

Legislative debates over women's political rights, coupled with women's antislavery activism, opened the door for women to redefine their civic role. Authors such as Catharine Beecher, Sarah Josepha Hale, and Lydia Maria Child tried to create a female civic identity through domesticity. Although also concerned about civic identity, women of color largely remained focused on issues of race and how it was shaped by gender. Despite this evolving interpretation of the domestic sphere, overt activism was still largely frowned upon. The *Boston Courier*'s proclamation, "Think of a delicate lady in jack-boots, and the idea is less revolting than that of a female public speaker," was typical of the era.[82] Certainly, women were not completely excluded. There were women who publicly spoke out on social issues, such as Maria Stewart and the Grimké sisters during the 1830s and other reform women in the 1840s and beyond. Despite the exceptions, by and large, women were instructed that their sphere could best be mastered through undivided attention toward the domestic. The "good wife" did not seek public exposure but instead "enjoys herself nowhere so well as under her own roof, and while attending to her private affairs."[83] In magazines and domestic advice manuals, writers sanctified the home and women's place within it; however, some were careful not to overpromote female moral superiority to the extent that it might push women into public activism: "But woman's sphere is wider still. As a member of society, she has a character to sustain and duties to perform.... However exalted her sphere is allowed to be, it does not follow that it comprises all the duties of the other sex, in addition to those which are exclusively her own."[84] Women could engage, if not enter, the public sphere, but not at the expense of their private obligations.

FREEDOM OF MOVEMENT, TRAVEL, AND MIGRATION

The much-venerated transportation revolution of the antebellum era was a boon not only for markets but also for individuals. In particular, the ability for women to travel without the supervision of men opened opportunities for activism (such as antislavery conventions), economic opportunities, and an easier conveyance of ideas through print culture. Of course, white women experienced greater freedom of mobility. As gradual emancipation became the norm in the North, the rights of free Blacks declined on the federal, state, and local levels. Restrictions on African Americans had a variety of purposes, ranging from limiting their political and economic influence to humiliating them. Policing the movements of Blacks became a central goal of anti-Black statutes. Free-state legislatures worried less about fugitive slaves crossing state borders (federal law protected slaves in those instances) than they worried that an influx of free people of color would either create employment competition with whites or become a tax on city and county welfare and charitable relief. State legislatures in Illinois and Indiana created codes to limit Black migration into their states. These codes were overwhelmingly confirmed when put up for a statewide vote.[85]

The granting of passports was an important indicator of citizenship that was debated in the Black and antislavery presses throughout the nineteenth century. For women, the granting of passports remained an issue into the twentieth century. Linda Kerber notes that as late as the 1950s "some American women were denied passports" because they married foreign nationals "before 1922."[86] Passports had an impact on the freedom of movement of free African Americans, but the protection also offered by a passport to those traveling abroad pointed to a level of status in one's home country. The case of Robert Purvis was one of the first to come to the public's attention. Purvis planned to be in England for the celebration of West Indies emancipation on August 1, 1834, and sought a passport for his journey. Initially, Secretary of State Louis McLane denied the passport because Purvis was a "colored man." The State Department instead offered a special passport that described Purvis as a free person of color who if needed "was entitled to the protection of American officials abroad." Purvis fought the "special status" and was eventually granted what was probably the first passport issued to a person of color by the United States.[87] The new Pennsylvania Constitution prevented African Americans from that state from getting passports after Purvis. White abolitionist Sarah Grimké wrote a British activist, "As we were sitting at breakfast this morning Sarah Douglass mentioned that her brother had been refused a passport to England on account of his color, the Secretary of State alleging that by the new Constitution of Pennsylvania the people of color were not citizens and therefore had no right to passports to foreign countries."[88] Grimké's letter reveals that her activism was not limited to public words and deeds. Eating breakfast together reflects the intimacy of the Douglass-Grimké friendship, which went beyond paying formal afternoon calls. The success of Robert Purvis did not extend to other African American travelers. When other people of color pointed to Purvis as a precedent for their own passports, the State Department argued that "Mr. Purvis was a gentleman, a man of property, of scarcely perceptible African Descent."[89]

Class, color, and social status allowed for "flexibility" in the State Department determination of which Americans were protected by the government when abroad. In 1849 an African American applicant for a passport was told that "passports are NEVER granted under such circumstances and that the applicant ought to have known better than to apply for them."[90] Henry Hambleton, a free-born African American from Philadelphia, was informed in his rejection letter from the State Department: "I have to inform you, that passports are not granted by this Department to persons of color; and that protections are only given to them when they are in the service of diplomatic agents, &c., of the United States, going abroad. Hambleton's certificate of nativity is herewith returned."[91] The African American press focused on the "official" nature of this discrimination. In reality, passports were not required for foreign travel until the twentieth century; however, the denial of passports demonstrated the statelessness of all free Black Americans.[92] The State Department began issuing passports to African Americans in 1861, finally reversing the decades-old policy of exclusion.[93]

The ability to travel was important to antebellum Americans. Historian Elizabeth Stordeur Pryor writes that "travel made American freedom visceral and thus lubricated the cogs of citizenship."[94] While antebellum white women faced social sanctions for traveling alone, African American women faced that sanction and often were denied access to transportation altogether. Even when allowed to travel, African Americans faced discrimination. The state took no role in protecting individuals from discrimination; thus, corporations, particularly railroads, could segregate passengers based on their race.[95] Sarah Douglass, an activist and woman of color from Philadelphia, weighed in with a published essay on a pending bill in the state legislature that would restrict "the travel of free people of color into and out of the state."[96] African American travelers found that even if they purchased a first-class ticket, they could still be removed to the segregated car.[97] Frederick Douglass (no relation to Sarah) reportedly resisted such treatment, and "on a few occasions he clung to his seat and refused to be dislodged, until the conductor and his assistants ripped him and his seat from the railroad car and threw them out together."[98] Elizabeth Jennings, who was removed from a streetcar, successfully sued for damages. A sympathetic newspaper editorialized that "railroads, steamboats, omnibuses and ferry-boats will be admonished from this as to the rights of respectable colored people." An article published in *Frederick Douglass' Paper* compared the respectability of women of color and that of European immigrants: "It is high time the rights of this class of citizens were ascertained, and that it should be known whether they are to be thrust from our public conveyances, while German or Irish women with a quarter of mutton or a load of codfish can be admitted."[99] As European immigration increased, people of color argued that respectability and true womanhood should be the markers for access to public conveyances rather than whiteness. However, despite the success of Jennings's lawsuit, during which she was awarded $225, women of color continued to face discrimination and removal from public transportation into the twentieth century.

When marginalized groups are denied access to the public sphere and public spaces, they must find ways to challenge the system from the outside. Counterpublics are one such method. From the vantage point of early African American print culture, Joanna Brooks explains that "counterpublics foster political and cultural activities that allow working-class and other disfranchised persons to reclaim a measure of subjectivity despite being positioned as the instruments, objects, or properties of the middle class."[100] The antislavery activities of African Americans functioned both within and outside traditional white power structures. As the movement began, most well-known abolitionists, as well as editors of antislavery newspapers, were white, and influential abolition societies typically had white leadership. Undoubtedly, performances of respectability were directed toward a white audience. Despite the cooperation of integrated abolition societies, African Americans, in both writing and organization work, challenged both governmental structures that allowed slavery and discrimination against people of color and the racist attitudes of white abolitionists, challenging the power within antislavery groups.

Women's access to the public sphere, crucial to their claim to citizenship, was limited by cultural assumptions of female propriety. During the 1830s, as the antislavery movement broadened to include women as either abolitionists or colonizationists, support for female public participation also increased. Despite an expansion of their public engagement, women were expected to adhere to the principles of true womanhood. Public speaking before a raucous or promiscuous (male and female) audience challenged notions of respectability and flew in the face of cultural constructions of the ideal woman. The *Pennsylvania Freeman*, a white-edited abolitionist newspaper, defended women's right to speak in public while raising the issue of propriety: "We have never believed in the propriety of women lecturing publicly to promiscuous assemblages, as a *general* custom; but if they think proper to do so, we shall not question their *right*." However, the paper recognized the moral authority of the women's cause, concluding, "They are as much entitled to think freely and act in accordance with their own judgment as are the lordly editors who seem to think that women are responsible to man alone, and not to God."[101]

Female lecturers remained less common in the 1830s and 1840s, even within the abolition movement. However, the presence of female speakers provided cover for the average woman who wished to engage political issues in a more female-gendered way, such as attending a fundraising fair, writing a poem, or signing a petition. In 1859 a young diarist from Oregon wrote that through the press women "can always deliver [their] sentiments to the world without any violation of delicacy," and they will receive "far more attention than they would if they were given to the world in the public lecture rooms."[102] The opportunities for female civic engagement increased during the age of abolition while simultaneously reinforcing the norms of true womanhood. It is with antislavery activism that U.S. women began to reimagine the implications of womanhood.

As women formed associations during the antebellum era they were more likely to engage in public performances of citizenship. However, public simulations of political participation were often seen as charming by men rather than as serving a critical function. For example, the account of a gathering of over nine hundred women celebrating the Fourth of July in Barre, Massachusetts, was reprinted in newspapers as far away as South Carolina. The article described the "fair creatures" toasting "old bachelors," "matrimony," and the "industry of young ladies."[103] Like the eighteenth-century African American celebrations of Election Day, public political play was acceptable if it remained play rather than legitimate political participation. As women developed their own print culture, organizations, and an identity based on their sex, they were actively engaged in creating a counterpublic.[104] Moving beyond play and theater, nineteenth-century women began a rehearsal of arguments that would challenge the assumptions of their civic status.

Despite assumptions that antebellum females were apolitical, women often engaged in political talk in their private writings. Louisa Adams Park, the wife of a navy physician at sea, reacted to the controversial election of 1800: "Bad news—the papers say Jefferson and Burr will have the votes."[105] Mary Ann Nelson's fiancé teased her about politics during the election of 1840: "Well Molly, what do you think of the election are you still a Locofoco or has William converted you?"[106] Adaline Lindsley reacted to the death of William Henry Harrison in both political and emotional terms: "For the first time the Republic is called to mourn the loss of its chief magistrate. Never since my remembrance has so great an excitement been caused as the initiation of Gen Harrison into office—not only before but since his inauguration—so much has been promised—so much was expected—that his demise has thrown all parties into consternation." At the end of this entry, Lindsley expressed her lack of confidence in Tyler: "The hopes of a nation are now blasted—and their only alternative now according to the laws of the constitution is to lift John Tyler to the evacuated seat."[107] Hannah Thompson Aldrich, with her husband and two young sons, had recently arrived in Wisconsin, the "far off West," when she wrote to her sister in New Hampshire about the 1856 presidential election: "He [her two-and-a-half-year-old son, Walton] has got some clothes pins and stuck a piece of leather on top and calls it his Freemont [sic] flag. He hurrahs for Freemont almost every day." Her family's isolation in Wisconsin meant they had to wait to hear election results: "Wish you would write us about the Election in New Hampshire, or send us the *Sentinel*. We are very anxious yet dread to hear the result. There are more Freemont men in this town than any other. Democrats are very scarce."[108] The arguments of white male elites that women were not interested in politics was clearly wrong. Private musings turned to published words as civic domesticity legitimated women's voices and civic engagement.

CONCLUSION:
THE *DRED SCOTT* DECISION AND
THE DENIAL OF CITIZENSHIP

Throughout the nineteenth century the meaning of citizenship was in flux. Politicians and jurists were constantly defining and redefining the concept of citizenship in order to control civic standing based on race and sex. Two nineteenth-century Supreme Court decisions attempted to clarify (or obfuscate) citizenship, which was constitutionally undefined until the Fourteenth Amendment. The *Dred Scott* decision removed African Americans from the ranks of citizens regardless of their status as enslaved or free.[109] Four years before the start of the Civil War and one day after the inauguration of James Buchanan as president, the Supreme Court, presided over by Chief Justice Roger Brooke Taney, weighed in on the question of citizenship and determined who was not included in the sweeping category "of the people." The court determined that people of color, free or enslaved, "were not intended to be included, under the word 'citizens' in the Constitution, and can therefore claim none of the rights and privileges which that instrument provides for and secures the citizens of the United States."[110] The court ruled not only that Dred Scott lacked the legal standing to sue in the courts but also that even if he had been determined to be free, he still lacked the status of citizen. The ruling did not equivocate. By stating that no Blacks could be considered citizens, the court went beyond the original question before it. The court concluded that "only whites, or persons of Caucasian race, can be such citizens; or, negatively, that no person of African or Ethiopian race can be such a citizen."[111] There was a strong reaction to the *Dred Scott* decision. Proslavery advocates, including those found in the North, embraced the majority opinion of the Supreme Court and used it to legitimate their agenda. Antislavery advocates saw the decision as a cause for concern, beyond the denial of citizenship to free African Americans. It was feared that the *Dred Scott* decision would be used to strike down emancipation laws in the North.[112] Lincoln's attorney general, Edward Bates, declared the status of Black citizenship unchanged by *Dred Scott v. Sandford* because "the Constitution contains not one word upon the subject." Bates believed that "anyone who was born on American soil was a citizen, no matter what," thus restoring "'birthright' as the basis of 'natural-born' citizenship."[113] Despite the lack of any real change to Blacks' legal standing based on the attorney general's proclamation, it did clear the way for the Lincoln administration to expand opportunities for African Americans.

The language that explained that citizens are those "who hold the power and conduct the government through their representatives" could arguably exclude women as well. *Minor v. Happersett*, decided after the Fourteenth Amendment was ratified, found that women were indeed citizens but that suffrage was not a guaranteed right of citizenship. In some states the political rights of white women were less than those of free African American men, although white middle-class women generally did not face the same risks of physical violence from strangers or economic instability. The concrete nature of the decision did not stop white women and African American men and women from creating and refining a performance of citizenship and seeking new ways of meeting "official" definitions of citizenship.

In the twenty-first century, race and citizenship continue to intersect. Representative Alexandria Ocasio-Cortez argued on Twitter that "the history of citizenship in the U.S. is the history of racism. It has been used as the legal enforcer of racism for most of U.S. history. Citizenship affords power & that's why citizenship of African Americans is as long denied—to both slaves & descendants."[114] The legal battle over the inclusion of citizenship status as part of the 2020 census and the chants at a political rally of "send her back" targeting women of color in Congress demonstrate that the nation still uses race in part to determine who is and is not counted as an "American." During the Civil War, Black and white women engaged in war work in hopes of earning political rights. African American men fought for the right to serve in military units at an equivalent status as white soldiers. Access to the printed word provided opportunities for these groups to challenge their status within the nation. Whether they directly challenged their status or instead sought to redefine their everyday activities as fulfilling the civic obligation, women and African American men served as their own agents. While the law might limit voting rights, print culture gave women and African American men the means to critique the law.

CHAPTER 2

Constructing Home and Nation
Household Advice and Civic Domesticity

> Since the domestic sphere is entrusted to our sex, and the proper arrangement and government of a household are so closely connected with our enjoyment and virtues nothing that involves the rational comforts of home is unworthy of attention.
>
> —Mrs. L. H. Sigourney, "On Domestic Employment"

These words, penned by popular writer and poet Lydia Huntley Sigourney, appeared in the first issue of the *Ladies' Pearl* (August 1841), a short-lived women's magazine published in Lowell, Massachusetts. Despite the title, "On Domestic Employment," Sigourney's essay contains no recipes for company meals, directions for removing stains from dark silks, or even suggestions for managing servants. Instead, Sigourney focuses on the cultural importance of the household and the need to respect women's profession. Lydia Sigourney, like other popular antebellum authors, promoted the importance of women in the home by moonlighting in the publication of domestic advice. This new genre expanded female readership and provided new outlets for paid writing for female authors. The antebellum era saw a rise in published materials for females, with the largest surge coming in the form of household guidance, which appeared in cookbooks, novels, magazines, and, perhaps most significantly, domestic advice manuals. Given the legal and cultural confines placed on women, the printed word provided a strategic way to claim civic status based on domestic duties.

Domestic literature published between 1796 and the U.S. Civil War offered advice that reflected the modernizing economy and provided an evolving political identity for women. Early cookbooks might give patriotic names to various recipes, but it took the emergence of American domestic advice manuals to attach a political significance to women's household labor. In particular, Catharine Beecher's *Treatise on Domestic Economy* (1841) provided a clear marker between the primarily apolitical early manuals and the more civically charged later advice books. Beecher's work, due to its popularity, was largely responsible for the development of this new genre. Given the social sanctions placed on women's public civic engagement, a cultural approach is the best way to reveal how middle-class women situated themselves within the state. A reinterpretation of antebellum womanhood emerges once cultural citizenship, the everyday practice of one's civic identity, is placed at the center of an analysis of early nineteenth-century U.S. domesticity by recognizing that civic engagement is not limited to public action.

Citizenship is a fluid term, particularly when examining those seeking the status of citizen. For individuals lacking the clarity of legal or politically recognized citizenship, defining their status through deeds, actions, and labor might be the only means to demonstrate a positive relationship to the state. Monika Swasti Winarnita explains that "cultural citizenship encompasses the intertwining concepts of aspirations for legal citizenship and everyday lived experience of citizenship."[1] Joke Hermes links cultural citizenship to "partaking of the text related practices of reading, consuming, celebrating and criticizing offered in the realm of [popular] culture."[2] Cookbooks, domestic novels, and other print materials allowed Black and white nineteenth-century women to redefine everyday life as fulfilling the civic obligation to the state.

The authors of domestic literature present the gendered labor of middle-class antebellum women as central to nation building. The first half of the nineteenth century served as a transitional moment in U.S. history, with sweeping changes in the economy, transportation, and print culture, all of which served to influence the construction and importance of gendered domestic roles. Many middle-class women, both Black and white, formed their "imagined communities" through the written word and developed a uniquely feminine civic identity.[3] Between authors and readers, the domestic realm acquired a cultural significance that permitted women to perform the obligations of citizenship. While white men could easily fulfill their civic obligation through voting, paying taxes, serving on juries, and a myriad of other public ways, the women of the early republic lacked opportunities to perform their citizenship.

White American women not only created a feminine means for enacting citizenship but also established a deeply raced female civic identity based on domesticity. African American women challenged this interpretation by appropriating the identity of the true woman and using it as an access point for their own civic engagement. Although domesticity and true womanhood have been central to many studies of nineteenth-century American women, most scholars have neglected to examine the inherent whiteness of antebellum "womanhood," as well as its political potential, regardless of the race of the woman practicing it. By placing claims for citizenship at the center of womanhood, this chapter demonstrates how groups marginalized by their race and/or gender were able to deploy domesticity strategically when making claims to civic status. It also recognizes that not all calls for civic inclusion entailed a direct claim for voting rights, particularly during the antebellum era. Recognizing citizenship itself and not merely suffrage as an end goal of middle-class women's gender identity provides a more nuanced interpretation of nineteenth-century femininity and civic identity. It also highlights how other marginalized groups use cultural performances of the everyday for inclusion within the nation. The evolution of a female print culture provided politically isolated women a means for creating communities of their own. This chapter examines women's use of published domestic advice from the vantage point of both authors and readers and argues that this literature contributed to the creation of a counterpublic actively deployed by women as a mechanism for claiming and proving their citizenship. Philosophy professor Nancy Fraser defines counterpublics as "subordinated social groups [that] invent and circulate counter-discourses, which in turn permit them to formulate oppositional interpretations of their identities, interests, and needs."[4] The creation of counterpublics provided those on the outside with a way to gather support and deploy their discourse of civil engagement in a way that recognized their political and social goals. Since women and African American men were largely excluded from the public sphere, they turned to their own print culture to challenge the dominant view of who was a citizen.

Domestic manuals in general and cookbooks in particular provide a vast array of demographic and social information about an era, from the use of standard weights and measures to the average size of households based on how many servings are supplied in each recipe. Even a casual perusal of early American cookbooks reveals the enormous amounts of individual ingredients called for in recipes, ranging from dozens of eggs to ten plus pounds of flour in a single recipe. This suggests not only larger families but also larger households that dined with the immediate family and a tendency to use recipes and fine baking for larger events as opposed to the average dinner.[5] Much like lifestyle magazines today, antebellum magazines and manuals represented aspirations rather than realities. Domestic advice literature provides historians with a deeper understanding of not only nineteenth-century domesticity but also how society coded the gendered experience of economic and social change.[6] The actual reproduction of recipes in the individual kitchen is less important than the status suggested by such foods, the confidence they inspired that one could perform the role of the middle-class wife, and the assurance that the role of homemaker was culturally and politically important. The publication of cookbooks and domestic advice served to nationalize food practices and give cultural authority to recipes and household advice. This newfound authority allowed writers and readers to envision an importance to their labor that extended beyond their individual kitchen.

Household manuals reveal the cultural impact of middle-class domesticity. Defining "middle class" is difficult during the antebellum era. Middle-class status can be determined by consumption patterns and sustainability of lifestyle and can serve as an economic and cultural marker. Because the ideologies of domesticity and true womanhood were a construct of the middle class, it is unlikely they would have evolved in its absence. For example, many British manuals were written for households with a large staff and a strict social hierarchy and did not necessarily address the female head of household. Published American domestic advice influenced a new vision of middle-class households and, in particular, the role of female heads of household. No longer wanting to be seen as just another laborer in household production, women adopted the identities of "wives" and "mothers" in this literature and ordained themselves managers of their own domain. This reconceptualization of the relation between women's and men's work—and, by extension, between home and market, private and public—was central in the creation of middle-class gender norms. Beyond this redefinition of the female domestic role, the fact that there was a steady increase in written domestic advice material during the first half of the nineteenth century suggests that the power of the average woman as a consumer had increased alongside women's literacy rates, which made the publication of such manuals profitable.[7]

U.S. domestic manuals stressed the need for women to learn to perform domestic duties for themselves. This departure from their British counterparts is significant because it demonstrates the economic diversity of the emerging middle class in the United States, conveying the reality that family fortunes could easily change. For example, an essay in the *American Ladies' Magazine* argued that mothers should train their daughters in the domestic arts because any home could fall prey to economic setbacks: "It is equally important that she instruct her daughter in personal neatness and the different departments of housewifery. As she knows not in what station of life she may be placed, it is best to look forward and prepare herself for the fulfillment of any duty that may devolve upon her."[8] A hidden transcript of manuals, essays, and domestic novels was the idea that a housewife was also a house manager. These publications argued that a woman must be able to train her socially inferior staff and monitor their work. By understanding the mechanizations of the home, the white female could assert an importance of her role that was not shared by her domestic servants.

"Literary domestics," or novels of domesticity, were popular during the antebellum era, providing a unique niche for the professionalization of women writers. These typically melodramatic novels stressed the importance of understanding household work even if others performed that labor. Catharine Maria Sedgwick, author of the popular *Hope Leslie; or, Early Times in Massachusetts* (1827), published the literary domestic *Home* (1835). The book provides a redemptive arc for the pampered daughter of a family that lived beyond their means. When their wealth disappears, the daughter, without complaint, learns to keep house for a frugal neighbor. In doing so, she not only avoids the county poorhouse but also ends up marrying one of the sons of that respectable home. *Home* went through twelve printings in the first two years of publication, and Sedgwick noted in 1841 that since its publication she had earned more than $6,000 from Harper and Brothers, and that amount did not include proceeds from her earlier books published elsewhere.[9] In 1837 Sedgwick published *Live and Let Live; or, Domestic Service Illustrated*, which shifted the focus from the daughter of a failing household to the plight of servants. This book tracked Lucy, a young servant, and her experiences in various households. Dedicated to "my young country women—The future ministers of the charities of home," Sedgwick emphasized the importance of treating household employees with kindness and respect. As she did in her previous book, Sedgwick argued that it is important to train middle-class girls in the domestic arts: "It is as consternate a folly to prevent an American girl to grow up ignorant of household affairs, as it would be to omit mathematics in the education of an astronomer, or the use of the needle in the training of a milliner."[10] Sedgwick, like other authors, believed that *American* women should be efficient managers of their households regardless of their economic standing.

In another antebellum novel, *Our Nig; or, Sketches from the Life of a Free Black* (1859), African American author Harriet E. Wilson repeatedly stresses the lack of domestic skills of the villainous white mother and daughter who overwork and abuse Frado, the young mulatto girl who is indentured to them.[11] Wilson seems to suggest that there is something unnatural—unwomanly—about a female who has no knowledge of the domestic. Only an "unnatural" woman could engage in the barbaric treatment of her household help that Mrs. Belmont inflicted on Frado. Both Sedgwick and Wilson used domesticity as a litmus test when evaluating secondary characters. The heroines of each of these novels appear as "natural" homemakers and thus are superior women despite their race and class.

The rise of the literary domestic helped cement the growing female print culture, providing an outlet for new authors. Another popular author of the genre, Caroline Howard Gilman, lived in Charleston and edited a children's weekly that ran throughout the 1830s, providing a rare southern perspective on domesticity. She published two household novels, *Recollections of a Housekeeper* (1834) and *Recollections of a Southern Matron* (1838), that provided fictionalized accounts of household management. Besides novelists such as Sedgwick, Wilson, and Gilman, there were many more authors who provided a steady stream of short stories for women's magazines. For example, Lydia Sigourney was a prolific writer for female audiences, with fifty-six books, including two conduct books, and an estimated contribution to "over three hundred different periodicals."[12] The antebellum woman had many formats to choose from when reading about domesticity.

In the nineteenth century the popularity of published domestic advice can be ascribed to a variety of factors, but most importantly to the perceived growing complexity of the home. Evolving standards of cleanliness provide a particularly good illustration of new norms for housekeeping for which the nineteenth-century woman would seek instruction. Authors such as William Alcott and Catharine Beecher and health reformers such as Sylvester Graham linked cleanliness and personal hygiene to good health and moral virtue.[13] In fact, a clean house might even keep a husband from straying, as one women's magazine explained: "Cleanliness costs nothing but a little extra labor—that is all. And if it makes a man love his home, and attracts him oftener to it, is not such labor well bestowed?"[14] Clearly, sanitary practices served pragmatic and cultural functions while modernizing the home.

Both cookbooks and domestic manuals included recipes for cleaning products, ranging from a solution for removing spots on white cloth to an "excellent paste for the skin." Catharine Beecher devoted five pages to the importance of clean skin to general health in her *Treatise on Domestic Economy*. In *The American Woman's Home*, coauthored with her sister Harriet Beecher Stowe, the cleanliness chapter was expanded by two pages and included four scientific diagrams of the skin, including hair follicles and nerves.[15] In 1855 Catharine Beecher published *Letters to the People on Health and Happiness*, which offered a wide variety of medical and general health advice. In particular, Beecher wanted to combat unhealthy habits of women that limited their ability to serve their domestic duties: "My heart aches when I see how the mass of women, by ignorance and by blind bondage to custom and fashion bring on themselves pangs innumerable and premature old age. Many a blooming bride at twenty, finds herself, at thirty, wrinkled and care-worn; unhappy as a wife, unreasonable as a mother, and almost useless as a citizen."[16] During the antebellum era, cleanliness was a marker of class; by the post–Civil War era, sanitary living was considered to be part of the "American way," a virtue that set "Americans" apart from the poor and immigrants.[17]

TRUE WOMEN AND THE NEW ECONOMY

The rise of the market economy changed the status of women's labor. The ideology of republican motherhood, the duty of women to raise sons to participate in a democracy, was the first incarnation of the citizen-woman in the United States linking reproductive biology to civic participation.[18] This ideology served as a bridge between the colonial goodwife and the nineteenth-century true woman. However, motherhood alone did not create citizenship, much less political equality, and even some proponents of the idea of republican motherhood admit that the legacy of the revolution was "ambiguous" for U.S. women.[19] Hence, the arbiters of nineteenth-century household advice, whether Catharine Beecher or *Godey's Lady's Book*, broadened the scope of female civic participation beyond republican motherhood to include women's work in the home in addition to child-rearing. By replacing women's former role in the economic production within the home with a civic function, the domestic sphere retained its importance, as well as its distinct status, for an emerging middle class.

The period of the early republic ushered out the ever-industrious colonial good wife and introduced the "angel of the home." The cultural construction of true womanhood and domesticity served an important rhetorical function. It provided value for the domestic sphere that was not tied to production or waged labor and allowed women to imagine political action based on their new roles as the creators of civilized homes. Women were repeatedly assured of their status as "the head of a little society" and their influence "from the circle of home into the rough highways of the world."[20] An article in the *Colored American* stated, "Let home be now your empire, your world!," and reprinted domestic philosophy from white-edited journals.[21] No longer was the middle-class woman seen as a partner in the economic output of the household; instead, she provided shelter for the man who worked for wages in the wider world. The *Ladies' Wreath* explained in 1846, "It is the enviable province of the wife, to soothe and cheer her husband, when he comes with fevered brow and ruffled spirit from his daily avocations, to enjoy for a few short hours, the delights of home."[22] Antebellum essays suggested that the home served as an antidote for the ills of the market revolution and allowed the wife to participate, albeit indirectly, in the family's financial success.

A reality of the market economy was the creation of a public/private dichotomy in American lives that excluded women from one sphere but promoted her reign over the other. This move from a subsistence economy to a cash-based market economy created gendered interpretations of work. Nancy Cott, a historian, explains that because of the "premodern aspects of women's household work," men increasingly "did distinguish women's work from their own, in the early nineteenth century, by calling women's 'sphere' a 'separate' sphere."[23] This shift in production was given cultural meaning, what historian Jeanne Boydston termed "the pastorialization of housework," with the idealized view of domesticity propagated through printed materials.[24] The publication of domestic advice demonstrates the dual importance of the women's market—women's power as consumers and their importance within culture. There was a surge in the production of women's journals during the first half of the nineteenth century, providing access to both advice and promotion of the home.[25] Whether or not an individual woman chose to embrace true womanhood, American societal attitudes shifted, and the sanctified home was culturally endorsed. Although women lost some of the power inherent in being producers, they gained influence in the market with their newfound role as consumers. More importantly, women claimed the cultural authority of the home as their own and parlayed that status into civic identities that influenced laws, cultural norms, and political reform. While the ideology of separate spheres was important, it was not always rigid, and women found ways to assert their claim to civic status beyond the home. Female antislavery activists used motherhood to mask their political rhetoric and to draw attention to the horrors of slavery. In the twentieth and twenty-first centuries women continued this rhetorical sleight of hand to provide shelter for more radical agendas. The Los Angeles chapter of Women Strike for Peace created fund-raising cookbooks in 1968 and 1970 at the height of their Vietnam War protests.[26] Mothers of the Plaza de Mayo, MADD, Moms Demand Action, and other groups merged motherhood and activism. Individual women such as Cindy Sheehan and Sybrina Fulton worked on behalf of their own children. The performance of motherhood has legitimized women's political engagement well past the nineteenth century by both elevating women and providing a shield for more controversial activism.

Household advice literature provides a particularly vivid rhetorical prescription for women's domestic sphere. Beecher's *Treatise on Domestic Economy* was the first book-length nonfiction work to begin the process of defining domesticity and the practice of true womanhood, thus providing women a specific role to perform within the household and, more importantly, within the nation. Barbara Welter looks at the "virtues" of piety, purity, submissiveness, and domesticity that shaped societal expectations of women.[27] While these "virtues" appear limiting from a modern vantage point, the responsibility of "civilizing" the new nation was, as Welter, tongue in cheek, explains, "a fearful obligation, a solemn responsibility which the nineteenth century American woman had to uphold the pillars of the temple with her frail white hand."[28] Middle-class women's roles experienced a radical transformation at this time, shifting from a place where women's labor spoke for itself to a world where domesticity was measured by cultural norms. For example, women's magazines enshrined womanhood within a rhetoric of spirituality: "Yet true womanhood, even though it may be darkened by disappointment and saddened by sorrow, has higher pleasures, as it has higher duties, holier ministries, calmer thoughts, and stronger affections, and that she may make her lot dignified, Christian and happy."[29] The average woman, then, could imagine her contributions as more than merely mundane housework and could envision herself instead as part of a larger mission both as angel of the hearth and savior of the nation.

The availability of domestic help and who fulfilled that position were also influenced by the shifting economy. The trading of female labor among families and neighbors as described by Laurel Thatcher Ulrich in *A Midwife's Tale: The Life of Martha Ballard, Based on Her Diary, 1785–1812* had largely disappeared by midcentury. In urban areas a shortage of domestic labor had emerged by the beginning of the nineteenth century.[30] An 1811 letter written by Mary Lee to Hannah Lowell underscores the scarcity of domestic help in Boston: "A good domestic in this land of liberty is, you know, a great treasure."[31] Meanwhile, the household account records of Mrs. Daniel Coxe suggest that while there was no lack of people to be hired, few remained in her employ for an extended period of time.[32] The difficulty in finding and keeping suitable domestic help expressed in these examples was influenced by the economic shifts that brought new opportunities for women to work outside the home, whether their own home or someone else's. With the spread of industrialization, the domestic labor shortage expanded. By midcentury, even women in rural areas began to bemoan the lack of available domestic help. The young women who previously provided domestic labor in neighboring homes prior to marriage began to find work in factories and teaching; thus, the available labor pool shrank.[33] Adaline Shaw was one of those young rural women. She resisted her father's request that she quit her factory work and return to Maine. Shaw wrote that she enjoyed her financial independence and then challenged the negative reactions to her employment: "I do not know why our friends have such an aversion to a factory.... [I]s it because they consider it disgraceful.... I cannot think that it is any disparagement to a girl to get an honest living."[34] The shift to factory work by young women created a push-pull effect on cultural norms. Books and magazines continued to encourage the importance of domesticity and the sanctity of the home, particularly for married women. The temporary nature of factory work, as well as the protection and oversight of the female mill workers, ensured that those women had not forfeited their right to eventually become true women.

As the domestic labor pool shrank, foreign-born help became the norm in the urban North. This changing workforce was reflected in the popular press as authors continued to lament the difficulty of finding good help. Many questioned the competence of servants, and as Irish immigrants began to dominate the job, complaints about the generic Bridgett or Biddy began appearing in the press. Harriet Beecher Stowe seemed resigned to the "blundering Biddy [who] rusts the elegant knives" and suggests that women who can't afford good servants cut back on their possessions, as they are likely to lose them anyway.[35] African American women also filled positions as domestic servants in large numbers because few other opportunities were open to them. It is estimated that in 1860 roughly 75 percent of Black female workers in Boston were household servants.[36] Throughout *Miss Beecher's Domestic Receipt Book*, Catharine Beecher's advice reflects this stratified view of domestic help that developed in the nineteenth century. She consoles the young wife by recognizing that the management of servants is the most difficult task she faces, but firm kindness will likely prevent problems. Her advice to servants encourages patience, as the employee likely has no idea of the trials facing the mistress of the house.[37] Obviously, the shift in who performed domestic labor influenced this bigotry among white employers. When a relatively powerless immigrant or a free woman of color, as opposed to the daughter of a neighbor, was engaged in domestic labor, the social differences became more entrenched. As the waged labor of women declined in cultural value, the unpaid labor of middle-class women as both keeping house and managers of others' labor increased in cultural importance.

It is important to realize that domesticity was not a singular entrenched dogma but instead a cluster of values that influenced cultural constructions of femininity and were performed in different ways for different ends across race, class, region, and, sometimes, politics. For example, the Garrisonians in part justified the immediate abolition of slavery based on its attack on "the virtue of slave women and the sanctity of slave families."[38] Although abolitionists might have seen true womanhood as providing women a free pass to practice politics, given the moral nature of their cause, not all proponents of this ideology viewed it this way. A New England minister who published his sermon on the duty and dignity of women as they were first engaging in public antislavery work explained that women should not "mingle in the fierce contests of strife, and war, and confusion," even on behalf of religion, because "their influence will be most salutary and efficient in their appropriate sphere." Adding the final stamp of authority, the minister explained that "Jesus our Master, and eminently the friend of the tender sex, never employed any of them in his mission as *messengers*."[39] Under this interpretation, the important work of womanhood remained within the private home. It was women who changed the meaning of their own labor.

Nineteenth-century print media sought to reify the ideas of womanhood while providing a nationalistic significance to these traits. For example, manuals stressed a mother's duty to raise the next generation of good citizens and proceeded to instruct her in how the proper maintenance of the home could achieve this. These claims demonstrate the shift from republican motherhood, from raising sons to be responsible voters, to raising daughters who would shape home and nation. Amy Kaplan explains that the "ideology of separate spheres configures the home as a stable haven or feminine counterbalance to the male activity of territorial conquest," an argument that was played out in magazines and books throughout the antebellum era.[40]

A review of two of Catharine Beecher's books emphasized her nationalistic purpose, noting that "they are calculated to instill into the mind of the reader lessons of patriotism and domestic virtue."[41] Despite the legal realities of female subordination, "the will of the mother is the supreme law of the little community over which she presides."[42] Indeed, authors repeatedly sought to amplify the national significance of women through domesticity. The dedication to Catharine Beecher and Harriet Beecher Stowe's *American Woman's Home* reads: "To the women of America in whose hands rest the real destinies of the Republic, as moulded by the early training and preserved amid the maturer influences of the home, this volume is affectionately inscribed."[43] The mavens of household advice maintained that women's domestic influence was central to the strength of the nation.

The sanctification in print of household labor was also carried out in the lives of women. Good housewifery, whether accomplished alone or with the aid of servants, was a skill to be praised and admired. Lydia Sigourney wrote a close friend, "I think with particular pleasure of your health and actively of your nice and excellent housekeeping" and later in the letter recognized "the faithful, affectionate domestics who keep every wheel going with clock-work regularity."[44] An 1848 condolence letter also illustrates the importance of domesticity, as the author notes, "Thy beloved wife was one whose many domestic virtues must make her loss a great blank in the home circle."[45] While women's domestic abilities were often the topic of praise, they were also subject to criticism. Mary Ann Nelson, a young woman from Columbus, Ohio, found herself the target of such criticism in 1841 when another young woman wrote that "she could not recommend" Nelson "to any gentleman as *a wife*." According to a Miss Dilworth, Nelson was "entirely destitute, of a knowledge of domestic affairs [and] household duties."[46] Mary Ann Nelson replied to her fiancé that she "felt a little hurt at the unkind remark of Miss E.

Dilworth" and wondered where she "has had the opportunity of judging of my qualities as a housekeeper." After repeating and then responding to several of the charges against her domestic abilities, Nelson concluded her letter on a more positive note: "My imagination tells me now that I should not only consider it duty, but also a source of great pleasure to keep a neat house for one to whom my heart is most devotedly attached."[47] Clearly, the standards of true womanhood, publicized in female print culture, were experienced in everyday life. Domestic manuals trained women to create that "stable haven" whether it was intended to shelter men from the rigors of the public sphere or to "civilize" frontiers through the comforts of hearth and home. The market economy and the emerging print culture in the United States not only launched the ideology of true womanhood but also quickly permeated how members of the middle class interpreted this ideology in their daily lives.

PRINT CULTURE, DOMESTIC ADVICE, AND A GENDERED CIVIC IDENTITY

In the eighteenth century there were relatively few books authored for a primarily female audience. However, by the mid-nineteenth century, books produced for women had become commonplace. Writing a memoir for her niece in 1853, novelist Catharine Sedgwick highlighted this shift when she exclaimed, "My dear Alice, would you like to know what were the books of my childhood? You, of the present time, for whom the press daily turns out its novelties, for whom Miss Edgeworth has written her charming stories, and Scott has simplified history, will look upon my condition as absolute inanition."[48] Nineteenth-century women's diaries and letters are full of references to books and reading. Fourteen-year-old Connecticut schoolgirl Zeloda Barrett's diary entries for January 1804 are peppered with references to what she was reading, interspersed with mentions of the weather, the school day, and knitting.[49] Twenty-year-old Vermonter Pamela Brown's diary entries for a January thirty-two years later are similar to Zeloda's. Evenings were spent reading aloud, with a mixture of the classics, popular novels, and women's magazines.[50] Mrs. Daniel Coxe's Philadelphia household account book shows that she "subscribed to the Union circulating library in [on] Chestnut on the 10th of Dec. 1816 and paid in advance for 6 months."[51] Born and raised in Philadelphia, at nineteen Emily Wharton Sinkler married a southern planter and moved to South Carolina. In her letters, Sinkler often begged for more reading material to be sent. In 1847 she wrote, "We have succeeded in having a share of the Charleston Library which has slumbered in the family since it was founded transferred to us and I can get as many books as I want."[52] Unfortunately, Charleston was forty miles away by train, so the subscription library was not a permanent solution to her reading needs. For the mid-nineteenth-century woman, significantly more books over a broader number of subjects were available compared to what was available to her mother or grandmother. Some families had enough wealth that they could purchase reading materials on a regular basis. Many women had to find other ways to access books and magazines, whether at libraries (public and private), reading rooms, or churches or simply borrowing books from friends.

The newly educated antebellum woman expected people to have broad tastes in reading, with interests beyond the Bible and moral philosophy, the mainstay of literate women a century before. Adaline Lindsley of Middlesex, New York, was unmarried and in her early twenties when she kept her diary (1840–43). A graduate of a female seminary, Lindsley often wrote about continuing her education on her own as she contemplated the importance of a vigorous intellectual life. Unfortunately, Lindsley did not always find this mental engagement in her daily life. For example, after a round of social calls she complained, "His acquaintance with—literature is scarcly [sic] beyond the science of the Bible. I do not know when I have spent an evening so monotonously as I did there."[53] In a letter to his daughter who was attending a female seminary, Ely Burchard urged her to pursue a wide range of studies, and he asked her, "What are you reading and what are you engaged in?"[54] The expansion of publishing in the mid-nineteenth century created an interest in and market for women's reading materials. Females of all ages turned to books to educate themselves, broaden their worlds, and ultimately change how they were seen as citizens.

Whether women read for improvement, advice, or some form of escapism, books became a key channel for transmitting information and cultural ideals and allowed women to create imagined communities. During the first fifty years of nationhood, most books purchased in the United States were British imprints. By the 1850s, however, Americans authored 80 percent of books purchased domestically, a 50 percent increase since 1820.[55] Books served both female readers and female authors. For women largely excluded from the public lectern, authorship provided a communicative outlet.

Household advice, beginning with cookbooks, became an important informational outlet for women. Amelia Simmons's *American Cookery* (1796) was the first domestically written cookbook published in the United States.[56] In 1742 Williamsburg, Virginia, printer William Parks published an American edition of the British *Compleat Housewife*. Parks's edition of the book merely excluded recipes that contained ingredients not available in British North America and made no attempt to adapt or add recipes that were uniquely American.[57] Simmons's work was the first to take this second step by producing something exclusively for an American audience. In her study of women and cookbooks, Janet Theophano locates Simmons's place in American culture: "Simmons's cookbook, which asserted a national identity, was as much symbolic as practical. This first printed American culinary voice provided recipes in a vernacular idiom for food preparation in the New World."[58] Simmons's book included the first published recipes for items such as pumpkin pie and Indian pudding. It was the first cookbook to provide recipes that used pearl ash to chemically induce the rising process and the first to introduce terms such as "cooky" and "slaw" into the English language. In the second edition of her cookbook, Simmons engaged in a little cultural nation building by including recipes for "election cake," "independence cake," and "federal pan cake."[59] These colorful titles fit the author's self-proclaimed title as an "American" orphan.

It is clear from the full title, *American Cookery, Adapted to this country, and all grades of life by Amelia Simmons, an American orphan*, that this book reflects a distinct voice. Perhaps drawing from her own experiences, Simmons prefaced the cookbook with the recognition that though it was written for "the improvement of the rising generation of *Females* in America, the Lady of fashion and fortune will not be displeased." In an early justification for the importance of domestic skills, she explained that her book provided "more general and universal knowledge of those females in this country, who by the loss of their parents, or other unfortunate circumstances, are reduced to the necessity of going into families in the line of domestics, or taking refuge with their friends or relations, and doing those things that are really essential to the perfecting them as good wives, and useful members of society."[60] The introduction is unusual because it recognizes the need for women without the protection of family to have a skill with which to support themselves. Simmons went on to explain that "the orphan must depend solely upon *character*" and cautioned that "every action, every word, every thought, be regulated by the strictest purity."[61] Although *American Cookery* predates the advent of true womanhood, it still argues for the importance of female character, particularly for women lacking male protection.

The influence of Simmons's book can be seen in nineteenth-century manuscript cookbooks, which demonstrate the transmission of printed materials into the everyday lives of women. Manuscript cookbooks are created when recipes are handwritten or clipped from other sources and kept together in a booklet, thus creating a new personalized collection for an individual. In essence, they are culinary scrapbooks. Manuscript cookbooks are telling of everyday preferences because they are filtered through individuals based on their own interests and choices rather than through an editorial staff at a publishing house. For example, the antebellum woman was unlikely to take the time to reproduce a recipe if the ingredients were beyond her financial means or not available locally. Was the creator of the manuscript cookbook the primary person responsible for daily meals, or was her presence in the kitchen limited to fine cooking when entertaining? The type of cooking the antebellum housewife engaged in influenced the recipes she collected. Often, manuscript cookbooks included evaluations of recipes. Jane Hassler's 1857 Philadelphia cookbook included notations of "good" or "excellent" after the title and listed the source for a recipe.[62] Manuscript cookbooks included a variety of recipes, but desserts in general and cakes in particular made up the largest category for collected recipes.

Nineteenth-century manuscript cookbooks continued Simmons's use of patriotic titles for recipes. Abigale Wellington Townsend's (ca. 1840), Mrs. Samuel Leeds's (1856), and Jane Hassler's cookbooks all included recipes for Washington cake, and other manuscripts included recipes for Franklin cake and for Mrs. Adams's mincemeat.[63] Amelia Simmons's federal cake appears in several manuscripts, with Jane Hassler including multiple variations of the recipe. The recipe for Wiggs in Simmons's *American Cookery* had become Whigs by the time it had reached Mrs. Leeds's collection. This is somewhat ironic, given that the recipe appears in 1856, the same year that Republicans supplanted the Whigs as the second leading political party in the United States. By midcentury, manuscript cookbooks revealed a political purpose to women's baking.

It would be thirty years after the publication of Simmons's *American Cookery* before an advice manual with a larger scope would be written and published in this country. While the general cookbook remained standard, the 1820s, 1830s, and 1840s ushered in an upswing of celebrity chefs, (such as Hale and Child) and regional cookbooks. Philadelphia-born Emily Wharton Sinkler began her manuscript cookbook in 1855, nine years into her marriage. Her cookbook includes recipes from *The Virginia Housewife* (1824) and *The Carolina House-wife* (1847), suggesting that these books were not part of her personal collection but borrowed from elsewhere. Once Sinkler became the lady of her own house, she clearly desired to replicate regional cuisine.[64] Lydia Maria Child's *American Frugal Housewife* (1828) was among the first of these manuals that went beyond the traditional "receipt book" by offering advice about cleaning, marketing, and health to the American household. Child was also among the first of the celebrity chefs in this country. She was already a published author and an emerging national figure, so her name attached to a cookbook would be noticed (despite the fact that her previous work did nothing to demonstrate her expertise as a cook and homemaker). Child did not glorify the cultural role of the housewife to the same extent that later manuals would. In fact, in many ways her book was a throwback to the colonial era, when household production guaranteed a home's ability to function independently. Child's approach was less gendered, as it did not differentiate between men and women, unlike the manuals that would follow it in the next few decades.[65] Child did, however, emphasize the importance of a wife's frugality to the household's fortunes both spiritually and economically, and she advocated that all family members be engaged in economic production.[66]

Child's departure from the emerging doctrine of a woman's sphere is puzzling. Child describes almost none of the cultural trappings of the home, unlike later authors who would fixate on them. Historian Jeanne Boydston explained that early antebellum households were "mixed economies," which she defines as "economic systems that functioned on the basis of both paid and unpaid labor and were dependent on both."[67] Child's introduction is a reflection of this mixed economy. When looking at Child and Catharine Beecher's *Treatise on Domestic Economy* side by side, it is difficult to remember that little more than ten years separates their publication. The authors seem to be advising women who lived more than a hundred years apart, as Child's advice is still centered on *household* production, while Beecher's addresses the *home*. These two books are examples of how the shift to a market economy occurred differently nationwide, but by the 1830s and 1840s new advice for households was expected.

The advice literature that followed Child was shaped by the social and economic transformation of the middle class. Although the manuals of the 1830s emphasized frugality, they did so while discussing issues of class and station and how to best maintain that status. In other words, the home began to take on a cultural function as opposed to a purely economic one. Creating a home rather than a house was now a defining characteristic of the middle-class families of this era.

Sarah Josepha Hale's *Good Housekeeper* (1839) is a bridge manual between Child's *Frugal Housewife* and Beecher's *Treatise*. Hale, the editor of *Godey's Lady's Book* (1837–77), was already a national figure when her book was published, and she was considered by readers an arbiter of style and good taste. Hale had written a negative review of Child's *American Frugal Housewife* in the *American Ladies' Magazine*, a precursor to *Godey's*, in which she complained about Child's unseemly preoccupation with frugality.[68] This critique of Child reflected the evolution of household manuals during the 1830s. By the end of the decade the middle-class homemaker was interested in maintaining both a lifestyle and a home. Despite the economic downturn of 1837, artful consumption remained a goal of the middle class. In the preface to the second edition of her cookbook, Hale tried to further differentiate herself from Child. A standard complaint about *The American Frugal Housewife* had been that its advice was based on "old ways," with little to offer the city-dwelling woman; Hale claimed that her book met the needs of a wider audience, being "practical for all classes—for the rich and poor and the dweller in the city, and the country household."[69] Hale's advice points to her vision of the home as a place of comfort rather than Child's view that it was a place of production. Another manual, Frances Harriet Green's *Housekeeper's Book* (1837), was geared toward the young bride who was new to keeping house. While Green preached household economy in the introduction to her manual, she also wanted the young wife to keep an eye on best fulfilling the status she could maintain: "While she is fitting up her house a young woman would do well to consider the number and sort of servants she can afford to keep and regulate the style of the house accordingly."[70] Beyond discussions of taste and status, the primary subject of Green's introduction was health and nutrition, an issue that had become more popular due to the water cure and other health reforms. Modern housekeeping and health advice was central to Catharine Beecher's writing published in the next decade. Even more importantly, Beecher's household advice embraced a new ideology of womanhood and the female role in nation building.

CATHARINE BEECHER AND THE CREATION OF CIVIC DOMESTICITY

Catharine Beecher's *Treatise on Domestic Economy* (1841) was among the first books during the antebellum era to move beyond recipes and to introduce a wider philosophy of the home. Beecher's book is distinct from those that precede it and clearly influenced the manuals that followed it. Beecher's *Treatise* legitimized domesticity in the new economy, culturally encoding women's transition from producers to consumers. Beecher and other advice authors provided a means for women to practice cultural citizenship—the everyday lived experience of citizenship—through household chores and child-rearing. By creating a form of domestic nationalism, household manuals allowed women to engage the state as citizens and practice nation building without ever entering the public sphere.

A Treatise on Domestic Economy was the standard for domestic advice until it was replaced by Beecher's own *The American Woman's Home* (1868), coauthored with sister Harriet Beecher Stowe. Catharine Esther Beecher (1800–1878) was the eldest child in the famous Lyman Beecher family. While brother Henry Ward Beecher achieved fame through his ministry (and scandal), sister Harriet Beecher Stowe through her novels, and half-sister Isabella Beecher Hooker as a women's rights activist, Catharine at midcentury was "one of the most famous women in America."[71]

At first glance, the reader of Beecher's *Treatise* can see that this book offers a unique approach. While most manuals and cookbooks of the day offered a few general words of wisdom in a brief introduction or opening chapter, Beecher bucked this norm with a lengthy polemic on "the peculiar responsibilities of [the]

American woman." Arguing that "the principles of democracy, then, are identical with the principles of Christianity," Beecher blended the tenets of republican motherhood with religion, presenting her belief in the moral superiority of women.[72] Much like a lawyer drafting a brief, Beecher laid out her argument for the appropriate role of women. First, she explained how hierarchy and subordination were part of the natural order, but what made democracy unique was that "each individual is allowed to choose for himself, who shall take the position of his superior." According to Beecher, women were not excluded from this process, as "no woman is forced to obey any husband but the one she chooses for herself; nor is she obliged to take a husband, if she prefers to remain single."[73] Beecher continued, "Women have equal interest in all social and civil concerns; and that no domestic, civil, or political institution, is right, that sacrifices her interest to promote that of the other sex." Beecher believed that for women to secure those privileges, "in the domestic relation, she [must] take a subordinate station, and that, in civil and political concerns, her interests [must] be entrusted to the other sex, without her taking any part in voting, or in making and administering laws."[74] Beecher supported her claims by extensively quoting from Alexis de Tocqueville without interspersing any of her own commentary.[75] Beecher primarily focused on Tocqueville's take on the United States' cultural tradition of public and private spheres and concluded this excerpt with his claim that the strength of America is due to "the superiority of [its] women."[76] Making the private sphere central in maintaining the public sphere, Beecher then summarized her interpretation of the benefits of what Welter identified as the cult of true womanhood. According to Beecher, American "women are raised to an equality with the other sex; and that, both in theory and practice, their interests are regarded as of equal value." While women may be subordinate to their husbands, "by custom and courtesy, they are always treated as superiors. Universally, in this Country, through every class of society, precedence is given to woman, in all the comforts, conveniences, and courtesies, of life."[77]

Beecher's elaborately constructed argument for the proper role of women provides an insight into the views of mid-nineteenth-century white America. When compared to previous manuals, the *Treatise* seems like an unusual forum for such arguments. However, by coupling politics with useful household advice, Beecher found an ideal outlet for propagating her vision of civic domesticity to her target audience. Essays in women's magazines published after Beecher's *Treatise* followed a similar argument thread. Women were promoted as being both different from men and equal to them: "It is universally conceded that women have a dignity and value far greater than themselves or others had previously imagined, and that their talents and virtues place them on a footing of perfect equality with the other sex."[78] For Beecher, equality came from morality and virtue rather than the civic power found in voting, office holding, and political influence beyond the home. However, that does not mean Beecher thought that women did not have political capital; instead, women spent their capital differently from men.

When leafing through Beecher's book, it is clear that the material is very different from its predecessors. Beecher's *Treatise* is unique because she broadened the scope of domestic advice beyond cooking and simple instructions for cleaning. Instead of including recipes, Beecher focused on providing advice about how to manage a healthy home, including the need for cleanliness and exercise. She introduced a sense of science and professionalism to household management that not only modernized domestic advice but also further separated her *Treatise* from earlier books such as Child's *American Frugal Housewife*. Not content to offer recipes for herbal medicines or folk remedies, Beecher instead provided diagrams of the human body. Along with this medical information, Beecher included chapters on the care of domestics, infants, children, and the sick. She wrote about domestic manners and social duty, as well as household construction and how to perform typical household tasks efficiently and sanitarily. Beecher's inclusion of architectural plans and diagrams of the well-ordered kitchen demonstrates an awareness of the importance of space and how it controls the gendered labor of women.[79] This also suggests that Beecher viewed her audience as the middle-class woman who would have the desire and means to build a modern home.

As the market economy began to condense female production into her labor in the kitchen, Beecher expanded the importance of woman's role as wife and mother to include her service in the interpretation of her production. For example, Beecher stated that any man who observed the work of a "well educated and pious woman" managing a large household would conclude that "no statesman, at the head of a nation's affairs, had more frequent calls for wisdom, firmness, tact, discrimination, prudence, and versatility of talent, than such a woman."[80]

Beecher not only justified the importance of woman's role within the household but also enhanced woman's authority by reinforcing the home's complexity. In order to accommodate such a range of topics, Beecher's *Treatise* is substantially longer than its predecessors in the genre. Referring to its breadth of information, one reviewer wrote: "If from this time forth there exist anymore discomfort or mismanagement in any of the thousand important concerns embraced within the subjects of the 'science' of Domestic Economy, it will certainly not be Miss Beecher's fault."[81] The popularity of the book was based on both the information it provided and its politicization of domesticity. By making household management (as opposed to production) a civic responsibility, women felt compelled to master the necessary skills. Beecher's text demonstrated the complexity of the nineteenth-century home, complementing the idea that the home was at the center of the nation. Her glorification of the middle-class home inspired women to embrace modern housekeeping.

With its inclusion of emerging household technology, as well as its emphasis on the middle-class urban household, Beecher's *Treatise* replaced the manuals that came before it and shaped the manuals that were to follow. For example, after the publication of Beecher's *Treatise*, printings of Child's *American Frugal Housewife* drastically decreased.[82] In the years after the publication of the *Treatise*, Catharine Beecher followed up her success with a recipe book (which she presented as a supplement to the *Treatise* in recognition of the public's interest in cooking alongside other aspects of household management), essays on health, and further writings on education and the role of women.[83] Other authors joined the discussion Beecher began. Harriet Martineau's *Household Education* (1849) focused on the need to continue education within the home for all household members and provides a guide to meet that goal. In the preface to the 1851 edition of William Alcott's *Young Housekeeper or Thoughts on Food and Cookery*, Alcott echoed some of the sentiments expressed by Beecher. He wrote that the "duties and destinies of the housekeeper are too important to be misunderstood. The elements of the nation, nay, the world itself, are prepared, to a very great extent in our nurseries, and around the domestic fireside."[84] While this work was more of a cookbook than Beecher's *Treatise*, Alcott's opening chapter is titled "The Dignity of the Housekeeper," in which he promotes the importance of the role played by the female head of household. Eliza Leslie, a popular author of children's books, novels, and cookbooks, joined the household advice market in 1850 with the publication of *Miss Leslie's Lady's House-Book: A Manual of Domestic Economy*. Her first cookbook, *Seventy-Five Receipts for Pastry, Cakes and Sweetmeats* (1828), was largely based on the curriculum at the first cooking school in the United States. Located in Philadelphia, Mrs. Goodfellow's Cooking School has been described as a "'finishing school' for upper-class ladies in the domestic arts."[85] Leslie's cookbooks were popular, but by midcentury the discerning housewife required more than recipes and sought information for the management of her modern home.

RACE, CITIZENSHIP, AND TRUE WOMANHOOD

While domestic advice manuals focused on the middle-class woman, it is important to note that the authors envisioned their audience as white. Whether one reads between the lines or simply looks at the illustrations of the harried white housewife and the contented white family gathered around the fireside—content, of course, because the wife followed the offered advice—domestic advice manuals equated domesticity with the white middle class. It is difficult to determine the exact role manuals played in the racialization of the domestic sphere and womanhood. Clearly, this was contested terrain. As Bonnie Thornton Dill writes, "A dominant image of black women as 'beasts of burden' stands in direct contrast to American womanhood: fragile, white, and not too bright."[86] The product of emancipation in the urban North, a growing African American middle class emerged by the 1820s and 1830s in cities such as Philadelphia, Boston, and New York. An independent Black press also developed to provide, in essence, a guide to life for the African American middle class. During the antebellum era, members of the African American community sought to claim true womanhood for themselves as a means of demonstrating respectability to the white middle class. Historian Patrick Rael argues that many of the tenets of true womanhood espoused by the white middle class were also embraced by the Black middle class. Articles were reprinted from white sources preaching domesticity and the unique qualifications of women to make a house a home. Black authors, both male and female, generated similar articles.[87] Much like essays in the white press at this time, prescriptions for feminine behavior often took the form of cautionary tales, proclaiming disastrous outcomes for women who did not follow the norms of true womanhood.

Antebellum Black women also wrestled with the whiteness of womanhood in their fiction and nonfiction writings. Whether creating the image of the Black Madonna, suggesting that African American women were also pious and pure, or featuring the "tragic mulatta," who was "beautiful and more refined than white-skinned women," these works reveal a desire to capture the cultural ideal of domesticity and womanhood. Lydia Maria Child's *Romance of the Republic* (1867) is a particularly good example of this genre.[88] Although the sources of domestic advice might have been segregated, the desire to achieve true womanhood crossed racial lines. Hartford, Connecticut's Ann Plato, through the help of her church, published a collection of poetry and biographies of young women of color who exemplified the traits of womanhood.[89] Free African Americans saw domesticity and true womanhood as a means for racial elevation and thus greater civil rights. For whites, who typically defined and enforced the contours of domesticity and womanhood, these ideologies added a racial and cultural component to their economic standing and an air of exclusivity to middle-class status.

The absence of domestic advice books authored by African Americans is curious, given the growing print culture among Blacks during the antebellum period. The development of publishing houses and the expansion of the Black press, which often devoted itself to discussions of domesticity and gender roles, would seem to provide a prime environment for publishing domestic advice manuals. Yet despite the existence of this infrastructure, no manuscripts devoted to providing domestic advice to average Black households and homemakers were published. Instead, domestic advice for African American women appeared in newspapers and tended to focus on female behavior and not specific domestic practices.[90] This approach by the African American press demonstrated in part that the performance of womanhood by free women of color was strategically more important than the actual practice of domesticity. Only two books offering domestic advice were published by African Americans before the Civil War, and they were joined by a cookbook published shortly after the war. Rather than focusing on the private home, however, the two advice books were authored by men and were directed toward those employed in domestic service, demonstrating that not all household manuals emphasized a gendered civic domesticity.

The House Servant's Directory (1827), a how-to guide for those new to domestic service, was written by Robert Roberts, a butler in several upper-class households.[91] *The House Servant's Directory* is often cited as being the first Black-authored book published by a commercial press. The book followed the British standard of male-authored advice for elite households, although it was briefer than its English counterparts and more focused on the workers themselves. Roberts sought to professionalize domestic service. In many ways this can be paralleled with Catharine Beecher's desire to increase the complexity of the home without the focus on gendered civic status. If domestic labor was all that was available to those on the margins (due to either race or gender), then it makes sense to promote that labor by making it more specialized. The book begins with an introduction from the publisher that provides credentials for Roberts. While providing credentials was not unusual in domestic advice books, they were typically merely a sentence or two when the author was presumably white, anonymous, and without a national reputation. Household advice manuals or cookbooks authored by African Americans often included lengthy credentials, in which white elites vouched for the Black authors' expertise and respectability.

Tunis G. Campbell, author of *Hotel Keepers, Head Waiters, and Housekeepers' Guide* (1848), is better remembered today for his Reconstruction era political activities. Campbell, who was born in New Jersey, received some formal education as a young man and was a sometime minister prior to his work in hotels. Like Roberts, Tunis Campbell was also an activist for abolition and the promotion of free people of color; thus, he likely saw domestic service as a means to an end and as a higher-status job. Also, like Roberts's book, Campbell's book served as a training guide primarily for young men and was "intended for hotels and private families."[92] This dual focus suggests that the households Campbell provided training for were those with a large enough staff to create a chain of command among the employees. Campbell emphasized a mutual dependence between employer and employee that gave dignity to the work and justified a living wage.[93] Despite their focus on men, both of these advice manuals demonstrate the status ensured by domestic knowledge.

Until fairly recently, the designation as the first cookbook written by an African American belonged to Abby Fisher's *What Mrs. Fisher Knows About Old Southern Cooking* (1881). The book was published in San Francisco by the Women's Cooperative Printing Office, and Fisher's recipes reflected the cooking style of antebellum southern homes. Culinary historian Jan Longone then received what is believed to be the only extant copy of *A Domestic Cookbook by Mrs. Malinda Russell* (1866) from a vintage book dealer. Russell's book is short, only thirty-nine pages, with simple descriptions reminiscent of Amelia Simmons's *American Cookery* in style.[94]

Malinda Russell's book is important for more than the recipes. She provides a lengthy narrative of her past and her credentials that reflects antebellum values despite its postwar publication. Russell provided her own credentials, unlike Robert Roberts, who turned to the white elite to provide his bona fides. The book opens with "A Short History of the Author," in which Russell revealed that she was born free in Tennessee, the descendant of slaves. Russell tells of her attempt to migrate to Liberia, which was thwarted after she was "robbed by some member of the party with whom she was traveling."[95] Russell offered an older affidavit that she used for her planned migration to Liberia to introduce herself to her reader and demonstrate her respectability: "We, the undersigned, have been acquainted with Malinda Russell . . . and certify that she is a girl of fine disposition and business-doing habits. Her moral deportment, of late, has been respectable; we have little doubt, should she reach Liberia, in Africa, in which place she is now bound, that she will make a valuable citizen."[96] The claim of "her moral deportment of late" is intriguing; however, nothing more of Russell is known beyond this short introduction. Russell described her brief marriage and widowhood, her work as a laundress, and the difficulty of raising her son, "who is crippled." She explained that she has been "called by my maiden name since [her husband's] death."[97] At the end of her introduction, Russell offered her credentials as a cook. She ran a boardinghouse in Tennessee for those who "came to the Springs for their health." She "kept a pastry shop for about six years, and by hard labor and economy, saved a considerable sum of money for the support of myself and son." However, this money was taken from her by a party of marauders in January 1864, which resulted in her need "to leave home, following a flag of truce out of the Southern borders being attacked several times by the enemy."[98] Next, the cookbook included a section entitled "Rules and Regulations of the Kitchen," which called for cleanliness and offered further credentials and her motivation for writing the book: "Being compelled to leave the South on account of my Union principles in the time of the Rebellion and having been robbed of all my hard-earned wages which I had saved; and as I am now advanced in years, with no other means of support than my own labor; I have put out this book with the intention of benefiting the public as well as myself."[99] While Roberts and Russell both offered credentials in their books, their approaches were different. I suspect the reason behind the different approaches lies with the authors' unique purposes and audiences. For those interested in domestic employment, Roberts provided information not available elsewhere. Russell's goal was to sell herself. Despite her assurances of culinary expertise, the book itself is unremarkable. The recipes are brief, typically less than three sentences in length. With the proximity of the publication date so close to the end of the Civil War, it is surprising that the book is devoid of political labels beyond a recipe for Washington cake. There are items named for unknown cooks: Sally, Elizabeth, Kate, and Eve are all recipe sources. This book looks in many ways like other mid-nineteenth-century manuscript cookbooks in the brevity of the descriptions, the random listing of the recipes, and the preponderance of desserts.

Given the number of free African Americans in upscale catering and other food production in the urban North, it would seem that published cooking advice would follow the explosion of white-authored cookbooks at midcentury. In her analysis of twentieth-century Black-authored cookbooks, Rafia Zafar argues that "Black women and their cookbooks come across as less 'high culture'" than their published counterparts.[100] There are claims for social status made in each of these books, but instead of basing it on the sanctity of the private home, it is based on the service provided in someone else's home. For antebellum women of color, domestic advice would come from the Black press or texts that assumed a white audience. There are many reasons why middle-class women of color were omitted from this growing market of domestic advice. However, African American women's attention to the ideology of true womanhood in the Black press, in the antislavery movement, and in their own writing demonstrates the strategic value of making the ideology their own.

CONCLUSION

Like many antebellum women, Clarissa Warner pondered her future role as a homemaker as she prepared to marry. Her letter to her fiancé was not preserved, but one can imagine the anxiety she expressed that resulted in his reply: "I hope your imaginable incompetency in domestic affairs will never cause you one unhappy thought. I think your attainments in Domestic Economy equal and in theory superior to most of the young ladies at the present day & it would be most ungrateful in us who profess to love each other not to be willing to extenuate each others imperfections, and to do all in our power to render each other honorable."[101] The typical antebellum bride did not just commence "keeping house" but instead managed the home that shaped the fortune of her family and ultimately the nation. Household manuals attached cultural meaning to everyday practices that shaped what it meant to be white and middle class in antebellum America. The antebellum Black press tried to include free women of color in this world of domestic whiteness by prescribing appropriate behavior and recognizing their participation in political events such as conventions and antislavery fairs through their domestic labor.[102]

There are many explanations as to why the genre of domestic advice manuals grew in popularity in the United States during the nineteenth century. Certainly, increased literacy rates played a role, the complexity of new household technology required women to learn new skills, and even the mobility of the population meant that young wives often did not live near mothers, grandmothers, or sisters and would have to consult nonfamily sources of information. All of these factors and more would contribute to the necessity of the genre. However, as much as changing cultural dynamics called for the genre, the genre also shaped the culture by providing the public with new lenses through which to view and interpret the ramifications of industrial change. Catharine Beecher shaped the genre of domestic manuals by providing women with new information, in essence "professionalizing" the role of the housewife. Through cultural coaching, Beecher and other antebellum advice authors instructed women on being better housewives, "true women," and, most importantly, worthy citizens.

This lithograph illustrates the stages of a white middle-class woman's life from cradle to grave by focusing on her life within the domestic sphere. Courtesy Library of Congress.

AMERICAN COOKE

OR THE ART OF DRESSING

VIANDS, FISH, POULTRY and VEGETABLES,

AND THE BEST MODES OF MAKING

PASTES, PUFFS, PIES, TARTS, PUDDINGS, CUSTARDS AND PRESERVES,

AND ALL KINDS OF

CAKES,

FROM THE IMPERIAL PLUMB TO PLAIN CAKE.

ADAPTED TO THIS COUNTRY,

AND ALL GRADES OF LIFE.

By Amelia Simmons,

AN AMERICAN ORPHAN.

PUBLISHED ACCORDING TO ACT OF CONGRESS.

HARTFORD:

PRINTED BY HUDSON & GOODWIN.

FOR THE AUTHOR.

1796.

Published in 1796, *American Cookery* was the first cookbook written for an American audience. Courtesy Library of Congress.

The first church building for the African Episcopal Church of St. Thomas, Philadelphia, was built in 1794 and located at 5th and Adelphi Streets. Courtesy Historical Society of Pennsylvania.

CONSTITUTION OF THE
BOSTON FEMALE ANTI-SLAVERY SOCIETY.

PREAMBLE.

Believing slavery to be a direct violation of the laws of God, and productive of a vast amount of misery and crime ; and convinced that its abolition can only be effected by an acknowledgment of the justice and necessity of *immediate emancipation*,—We hereby agree to form ourselves into a Society to aid and assist in this righteous cause as far as lies within our power.

CONSTITUTION.

ARTICLE 1st. This Society shall be called, The Boston Female Anti-Slavery Society.

ART. 2d. Any lady may become a member of this Society, by subscribing to the sentiments contained in the Preamble, and paying fifty cents annually. Any lady paying five dollars at entrance will be considered a life member.

ART. 3d. Its funds shall be appropriated to the dissemination of TRUTH on the subject of Slavery, and the improvement of the moral and intellectual character of the colored population. The opinions of the members, as to the best means of effecting these purposes, will be freely given at the meetings. Questions relative to the business of the Society may be decided by a vote of two thirds of the members present, or such decisions may be transferred by them to the Board of Officers.

ART. 4th. The government of this Society, shall be vested in a Board of Officers, consisting of a President, whose duty it is to preside at all meetings of the Society. A Vice President, to supply the place of the former, in case of absence. A Corresponding Secretary, who shall keep all communications addressed to the Society, and manage all the correspondence with any other bodies or individuals, according to the direction of the Society, or officers. A Recording Secretary, who is to keep a record of transactions, and give notice of the time and place for all meetings of the Society. A Treasurer, authorized to receive subscriptions, donations, &c. and to pay the bills of the Society ; and five Counsellors, to advise and assist the other officers. In case of the absence of both President and Vice President, a presiding officer may be chosen by vote. Two thirds of the officers shall constitute a quorum.

ART. 5th. An annual meeting of the Society shall be held on the second Wednesday in October, at which meeting the reports of the Secretaries and Treasurer shall be read, and officers chosen for the ensuing year.

ART. 6th. Quarterly meetings of the Society shall be held on the second Wednesdays of January, April, July and October, at which time the Secretary shall report the proceedings of the Society, and such other business shall be transacted as circumstances may render necessary. If for any unforseen reasons, other meetings become advisable, the President is authorised to summon the other officers, and they may give notice to the members of the Society.

ART. 7th. If any vacancies occur in the Board, during the intervals of the regular meetings, the Board shall have power to fill such vacancies, *pro. tem.*

Women's antislavery societies published their constitutions in newspapers such as *The Liberator* and as individual tracts to both spread their message and claim the authority of print culture. Courtesy Library of Congress.

Seal used by many female antislavery societies, including the Philadelphia Female Anti-Slavery Society. There are many different versions of this seal. This image is often credited to Elizabeth Margaret Chandler. Courtesy Historical Society of Pennsylvania.

Published in *The History of Pennsylvania Hall* (Philadelphia: Merrihew & Gunn, 1838). Courtesy the Library Company of Philadelphia.

4. Private Schools.

	Established in	Number of Scholars on roll
Sarah M. Douglass, Institute Building, Lombard street above Seventh,	1835	30
Margaretta Forten, 92 Lombard street,	1850	10
Amelia Bogle, 12th street below Spruce,	1841	17
Adam S. Driver, Barclay street above Sixth,	1850	37
Elizabeth Clark, corner Fifth and Gaskill streets,	1850	40
Emeline Higgins, 4 Raspberry street,	1840	30
Ada Hinton, 6 Locust street,	1849	20
Sarah Gordon, 9 Rodman street,	1849	30
Diana Smith, Prosperous Alley,	1836	15
Emeline Curtis, 62 Gaskill street,	1850	12
Sarah Ann Gordon, Bonsall street above Tenth,	1852	20
Ann McCormick, Brown street above Fourth,	1854	30
George W. Johnson, Lombard street above Seventh,	1854	40

Summary of the Day Schools.

	Total.	Average Attendance.
Public Schools,	1031	821
Charity Schools,	748	491
Benevolent and Reformatory Schools,	211	
Private Schools,	331	
	2321	

S. M. Douglass teaches higher branches than are taught in Public Grammar Schools. The Managers of the Institute in whose building her school is kept, have made an arrangement with her by which she will at all times have 25 girls preparing for admission into their school.

M. Forten and A. Hinton teach branches similar to those taught in Grammar Schools, the former being the only one that takes boarding scholars. All the others teach nothing more than the elementary branches. The proprietors of female schools all teach plain sewing, and most of them add ornamental kneedle work, and knitting.

5. Evening Schools.

Raspberry Street Schools commence on the first Monday in October and continue five months. Five sessions are held each week.

Mens' School, John W. Stokes, Principal, and three male assistants. Total 138; average attendance 50.

Womens' School, Mary Roberts, Principal, and four assistants. Total 255; average attendance 63.

Apprentices and Young Men's School at the New Institute commences on the first Monday in November and continues four months. Charles L. Reason, Teacher.

The Raspberry Street Schools were established many years ago, and were formerly conducted by voluntary teachers. They always enjoyed a large share of the public confidence, but since the paid system of

This illustration appeared in the March 1850 issue of *Godey's Magazine and Lady's Book*. Courtesy New York Public Library.

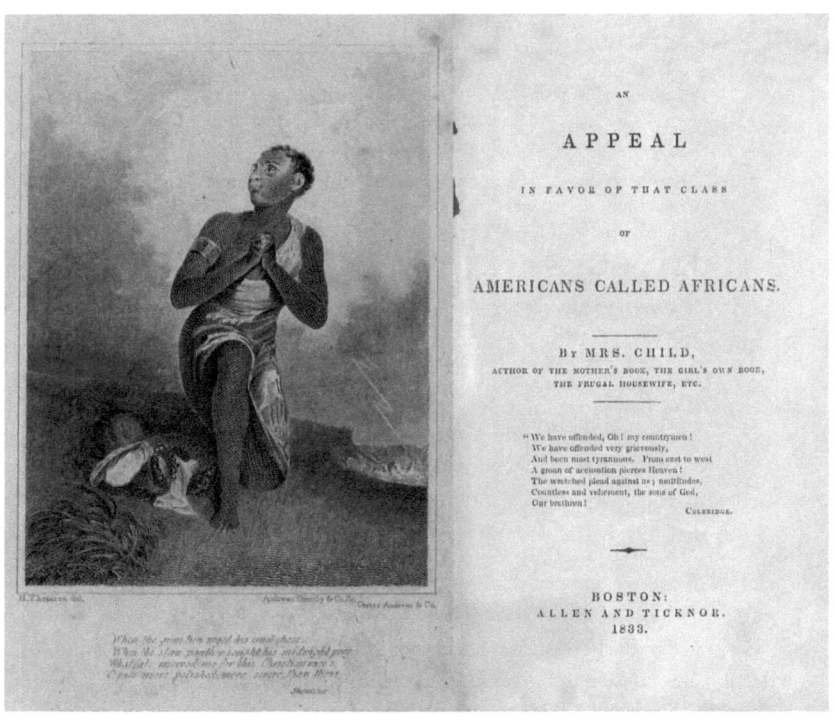

The title page of Child's book emphasized her authorship of more traditionally domestic books.

Illustration by Sarah Douglass for Amy Matilda Cassey's friendship album.
Courtesy the Library Company of Philadelphia.

CHAPTER 3

The Infrastructure of Race

Citizenship, Gender, and
African American Public Culture

At the age of nineteen, Jeremiah Sanderson had just begun his life of activism, serving as the secretary of New Bedford (N.Y.) Colored Citizens. Writing in 1840 to the more established Black abolitionist speaker William Cooper Nell, Sanderson acknowledged the centrality of appearance when demonstrating racial elevation: "I shall not soon forget how very kind and politely I was treated... especially when I consider the circumstances under which the visit was made. Rude and unpolished in manner, rough in appearance." Sanderson recognized his potential mistake, noting that "a genteel external you know is an item of no small importance in the establishment of claims to respectability by a stranger."[1] While he likely exaggerated his "rude and unpolished" manner, the importance of appearance cannot be overestimated. Even the most sympathetic white activists made distinctions and passed judgments about the people of color they encountered at antislavery events. Isaac Post's sister-in-law Mary Robbins Post described some of the participants at an abolitionist meeting she attended in a letter to Post: "There were very many colored people and many appeared like a superior class both in appearance and conduct."[2] In the decades before the Civil War, both Black and white antislavery activists recognized the importance of propriety, appearance, and refinement for free Blacks in the success of the abolition cause. As African Americans made more rigorous claims to civic standing, racial elevation was preached, and the politics of respectability were practiced.

It is no coincidence that these strategies evolved in tandem with the rise of true womanhood, as forms of respectability, albeit shaped by both race and gender, were a shared trope among people seeking to raise their civic standing. The practice of true womanhood and civic domesticity served as a form of civic discourse. Respectability was appropriated by Black and white women as justification for entering the public sphere. Yet womanhood also demonstrated the status of men as patriarchs of their own homes, especially for those on the margins due to race and/or class. The use of domesticity by white women, in large part, emphasized the sanctity of the middle-class home and promoted women's centrality to that institution. It also served to create a white identity. As the middle class became more stable as a social identity, whites considered it important to define who shared that identity and, even more importantly, who did not.[3] This made claims of respectability even more important to a rising class of African Americans.

For African American women, the benefit of promoting domesticity emphasized racial elevation by highlighting their adherence to white gender norms. Many free people of color and their white advocates linked citizenship to both class and race, implicitly differentiating between the newly emancipated and the more established person of color. The ability to enter into the ranks of the middle class allowed African American men to demonstrate independence and self-sufficiency, already key components of the masculine American identity. Middle-class status and respectability were also often measured by female gender norms because domesticity became a visible way for men to demonstrate their authority as heads of household. To have a wife with the ways and means to practice true womanhood and to be in possession of a home were how African American men could publicly perform their masculinity and economic status, thus demonstrating their worthiness for citizenship and the vote and enhancing the civic status of their entire household.

During the first half of the nineteenth century, white women found that the infrastructure necessary to practice true womanhood was already in place. During the antebellum era, the education of white females and female participation in church groups initiated by the Second Great Awakening became commonplace. Moral reform societies provided white women a fledgling, although gender-segregated, political voice. Calling forth the women of Pennsylvania, an antislavery pamphlet proclaimed, "Say, our sisters, is it a time for *us* to keep silence? Is it a time for *woman* to shrink from her duty as a citizen of the United States?"[4] Clearly, some women began to entertain the belief that they had a moral duty to exercise a political voice, even if their activism was reined in by gender norms. Whether white women were part of the middle class or striving to join its ranks, they had multiple platforms for performing piety and purity. Print culture in the form of magazines, advice books, and novels instructed women in the fine art of domesticity. Because white male patriarchal status was firmly entrenched within law and culture, one of the tenets of womanhood, submissiveness, was assumed to be the natural status of the proper white woman.

For Black women, however, the tools for performing true womanhood were not readily available. From the early national period through the antebellum era, communities of free people of color needed to construct the organizations and opportunities necessary to sustain an emerging middle class and the promotion of racial elevation. Unfortunately, racial elevation and respectability was a double-edged sword. To be tolerated by some members of white society, African American leaders and their families had to demonstrate education, taste, and propriety. Among other whites, however—those who might compete with African Americans for economic and social resources—the goal of African American racial elevation was mocked and often provoked violence.[5] For African American women, like their white counterparts, the act of performing citizenship was located within domesticity. African American women, however, experienced this performance differently due to the racial overtones of "womanhood" and the need to promote citizenship not just for themselves but for all members of their household. Kabria Baumgartner describes women of color as engaging in "purposeful" womanhood, which called for them to be "resilient, enterprising, and active—a proud seeker of knowledge." While this ideology did not free women of color from the confines of true womanhood, it still offered "a more capacious definition of domesticity, piety, and activism since it was specific to the experiences, actions, words, and thoughts of African American girls and women."[6] Women of color might perform civic domesticity as proof of productive citizenry, but purposeful womanhood allowed them to seek opportunities for themselves and uplift for their communities.

This chapter examines the legal and social status of African Americans in the urban North and the creation of a unique Black infrastructure that included churches, schools, and a print culture used to establish a Black middle class. Because equality did not always translate into opportunity, separate institutions were needed before racial integration could become the primary goal. The acceptance of white gender norms was central to the legitimization of a Black middle class and was seen as the gateway to civic standing. The social backlash free northern Blacks faced made their claims to citizenship all the more crucial. For example, schools were seen as a necessary step in claiming greater rights. Whites and Blacks alike worked to create educational opportunities for African American children. Formal schooling, however, did not necessarily translate into economic opportunity, and the establishment of African American schools became a flashpoint for violence. This chapter concludes that claims of racial elevation and true womanhood were the primary rhetorical strategies used to promote not only abolition but also the rights of free Blacks throughout the nation. African American women were crucial to this process because they not only served as markers of middle-class status but also demonstrated the fitness of Black men to serve as citizens of the United States. Even more importantly, African American women actively engaged in a dialogue of citizenship within the parameters of true womanhood and provided much of the intellectual and physical labor needed to sustain the political work of both abolition and the creation of antebellum Black communities. By reconstructing the stories through "ladies' pages" and the African American press and organizational records within churches and the wider community, as well as women's professional experience within schools, it has been added more fully. True womanhood and civic domesticity were markers of both citizenship and nineteenth-century middle-class femininity.

THE CREATION OF AN AFRICAN AMERICAN MIDDLE CLASS

Despite being relatively ignored in the larger narrative of American history, there was a rising African American middle class during the antebellum era. They, like their white counterparts, grappled with the construction of a feminine identity and how it impacted the civic role of women. However, defining middle-class status for nineteenth-century African Americans is difficult because the markers that are typically present for whites are not readily apparent for free Blacks. Issues of status are influenced by the implications of racial discrimination. Contemporary writer Joseph Willson struggled with the definition of "upper class" and ended up providing a fairly broad interpretation that would include both the upper and middle classes: "What, therefore, I would have the reader understand by the designation 'higher classes,' as here applied consists of what portion of colored society whose incomes from their pursuits or otherwise, (immoralities or criminalities of course excepted,) enables them to maintain the position of house holders, and their families in comparative comfort."[7] Emma Lapsansky has studied African American elites in Philadelphia and argues that the process of achieving middle-class prominence was accomplished differently by Black and white males. "Official public service was not an option for African American men," she notes, "and often they were both 'elites' and working class, unlike their white counterparts. They may experience prominence, but not power."[8] By and large, African American men lacked the same opportunities to break into the middle class as white males. Unless a man was already wealthy (e.g., Robert Purvis inherited wealth from his white southern father), owned a successful small business, or was an ordained preacher, elite status was difficult to come by.

The wives, mothers, and sisters of African American men followed a road toward elite status that was also shaped by whites' denigration of their race. Like white women's, Black women's prominence was largely achieved through their choice of a spouse. However, racial segregation in employment affected not only their husband's but the entire family's ability to perform a middle-class status recognizable beyond their own segregated community. Inadequate employment opportunities for Black men meant their wives would likely be engaged in waged labor as domestics or laundresses or in some form of temporary employment. Despite these overwhelming economic struggles, the antebellum African American press embraced many of the tenets of true womanhood as espoused by the white middle class. Black-edited newspapers reprinted articles from white sources, preaching domesticity and the unique qualifications of women to make a house a home. These reprints were not just filler; instead, they served to demonstrate elite behaviors, provide an awareness of other places, and improve basic reading skills. Nazera Sadiq Wright explains, "Reprinted articles and stories steeped in moral judgment suggested that cultivating black readers' conduct would provide alternative solutions for black families' disenfranchisement."[9] Not all of those stories were reprints; Black authors—both male and female—also generated domestic advice.[10]

The antebellum Black press, as well as other forms of African American discourse, added a racial dimension to the discussion of domesticity and childrearing. Bostonian Maria Stewart, a prominent African American author and orator during the 1830s, argued for an expanded political role for women because of their position as mothers of the race, making motherhood not only an issue of republican concern but also a component of the evolving ideology of Black nationalism.[11] For free women of color, domesticity served a dual cultural function that was critical to the simultaneous construction of both gender and racial identities. W. E. B. Du Bois in *The Souls of Black Folk* describes the concept of "double consciousness" as a "sense of always looking at one's self through the eyes of others, of measuring one's soul by the tape of a world that looks on in amused contempt and pity. One ever feels his twoness, —an American, a Negro." For free women of color, the difference central to her gender would add another dimension to a conflicted identity.[12] This different experience was significant. For white women, true womanhood went hand in hand with middle-class status, while for free Black women, it was an additional hurdle to overcome when entering the ranks of the middle class.

Antebellum African American books, newspapers, and pamphlets promoted middle-class standards within the Black community and demonstrated those standards to an external white audience. Of course, this was not a completely new rhetorical strategy; programs for "moral elevation" had been a goal for antislavery whites for decades. Late eighteenth- and early nineteenth-century abolitionists stressed that newly emancipated Blacks could, with the proper instruction, become morally suited for freedom. Being suited for freedom, however, did not necessarily mean that early national abolitionists supported full citizenship for emancipated Blacks. Early white abolitionists argued that programs for racial elevation must be established before free people of color could be considered full citizens of the nation.[13] By the 1830s African American leaders had also adopted this strategy, actively promoting racial elevation for poor and working-class people of color as evidence of their suitability for citizenship.

Antebellum African American society in Philadelphia was different from other Black communities in the urban North. The strength of antislavery organizations in the city made the free community more visible: the stability and early development of Black institutions such as churches and schools helped create distinct neighborhoods in Philadelphia before they clearly emerged in other cities. Finally, despite extreme poverty among many in the free Black community, there was also great wealth. The 1838 census demonstrated that "the black community might be seen as 14,000 poor people juxtaposed to upward of 1,000 economically 'substantial' black citizens."[14] A thousand "substantial" citizens was not an inconsequential number, and Philadelphia had a middle- and upper-class free Black population that rivaled the size of the entire free African American population in other urban areas.

THE DEVELOPMENT OF AFRICAN AMERICAN INSTITUTIONS

The key component to establishing stable free Black communities during the nineteenth century was the development of a distinct African American infrastructure. This institution building was an instance of necessity being the mother of invention. Despite the relatively slow pace of gradual emancipation in northern states, opportunities and protections for free men and women opened up even more slowly. During this era, often in direct response to discrimination, African Americans meted out benevolence, mutual aid, and self-help. These mutually reinforcing institutions also provided outlets for political activism necessary for the performance of cultural citizenship. African American women were important in the establishment of benevolent organizations that in turn influenced the growth of churches and schools. Permanent Black institutions provided a market for a distinct Black print culture and often financially subsidized African American newspapers and publishing houses. Organizations provided people of color with a political and social platform for claiming rights and demonstrating their fitness for citizenship. Given African Americans' exclusion from the public sphere based on race (and the addition of gender for free women of color), distinctly African American institutions were critical public forums that encouraged oratory and created spaces for gathering crowds. These institutions promoted a distinct Black public sphere, as well as counterpublics that challenged the political narrative of the status quo. The evolution of a Black print culture from these institutions allowed African Americans to make inroads into national debates about race and citizenship that included the participation of women.

THE EVOLUTION OF BLACK CHURCHES

Whether they were separate congregations affiliated with predominantly white denominations or independent African American denominations, Black churches were the first and most significant contribution to a Black infrastructure in large urban areas such as Boston, Philadelphia, and New York. Philadelphia was the epicenter for the movement. Beyond providing religious instruction and a place for burial—which was often denied Black parishioners of white churches—Black churches served a variety of secular and nonsecular functions. For example, African American churches provided a willing pool of donors to abolitionist causes both local and national. The financially struggling New England Freedom Association went to the Black churches to secure monetary support for a fugitive mother and child, raising an additional $23.19 for the cause.[15] Congregations proved to be receptive audiences for such pleas and pitched in to provide funding for schools and mutual aid societies as well. African American churches provided women the opportunity to connect in settings beyond their immediate neighborhood and form organizations that otherwise might have been difficult to establish.

The African Episcopal Church of St. Thomas (organized in 1792; it became a member of the Episcopal Church in 1794) housed several women's organizations within its congregation. Church vestry minutes report that the Female Benevolent Society paid for the interment of women on several occasions and that the Female Association of St. Thomas requested to "place their surplus funds in trust with the Vestry ($45.00)."[16] The Benevolent Daughters of St. Thomas, composed only of unmarried women, filed articles of incorporation with the state of Pennsylvania in 1825. Article 8 of their constitution called for providing relief and support for sick members in good standing, and article 9 stated, "When a member dies it shall be the duty of the Committee (if so requested) to have her buried in a plain and decent manner, at the expense of the Society."[17] The purpose of the Benevolent Daughters provides a poignant reminder of the difficulties faced by single women of any race, but particularly African American women who might not have family with the means to provide the most basic assistance. The constitutions of the Female Benevolent Society and the Benevolent Daughters both refer to the membership as citizens of the Commonwealth of Pennsylvania. Whether this was merely their understanding of their status, a claim of residency, or a more pointed rhetorical ploy for inclusion in a legal document as citizens is not clear. Regardless, women self-identified as citizens in their official organizational literature, and what citizenship might entail would develop over time.

There were significant, practical, and tangible benefits to building structures to house African American churches and schools. Churches served not only as houses of worship but also as political meeting places and locations for cultural events otherwise off-limits to people of color in segregated cities. Churches provided women with economic opportunities that would be difficult to claim in the broader community. For example, African American women could turn to churches to rent space for their home or business. In 1828 Susan Thomas paid one year's rent, twenty-four dollars, for her singing school to be held in the basement of the African Episcopal Church of St. Thomas. Mrs. Marie Osborn rented the parsonage as living space for several years at the rate of twenty-four dollars a quarter when the church lacked a permanent rector.[18] This type of financial arrangement was mutually beneficial. It provided the church with an influx of cash, it gave women like Susan Thomas some form of income and independence, and it provided the community with increased opportunities for entertainment and cultural uplift. Finding a place for large groups to meet was often difficult. Even sympathetic white owners of lecture halls and auditoriums often barred Black groups from holding meetings because they feared the financial liability of a violent mob. Locating events in churches owned and operated by African Americans was one solution to such challenges.

Given Black people's limited opportunities for social and economic advancement, membership in independent Black churches became an important way to obtain status, particularly during the first years of the nineteenth century. Early African American leaders were typically linked to Black congregations. Absalom Jones founded an African American Episcopal congregation in 1792, the first independent Black church in Philadelphia, and in 1804 he became the first African American ordained as an Episcopal priest. Under his leadership at St. Thomas, two schools and an insurance company were founded.[19] Before the creation of his new congregation, Jones worshiped at St. George's Methodist Church, an interracial congregation that practiced segregation within the sanctuary. As Black congregants began to resist this segregation, Jones and Richard Allen founded the Free African Society, a nondenominational mutual aid society that served as a safety net for Blacks leaving St. George's, as well as demonstrating that an independent African American organizational structure could thrive.

Instead of following Jones to St. Thomas, Richard Allen founded Bethel Church in 1794 and saw a steady rise in its membership from approximately forty congregants when the church opened its doors to nearly four hundred by 1810.[20]

Allen felt it important to establish a church that was independent not only of the white St. George congregation but also of the white Episcopal Church hierarchy. The political and social benefits of this move were not lost on Allen, as he argued that an independent Black church provided members with the opportunity to "build each other up."[21] An independent church also served to demonstrate independent thought and spirituality, useful in the development of African American political movements. Boston was about a decade behind Philadelphia in the creation of independent Black churches. In 1805 the African Baptist Church, originally called the African Meeting House, was organized with Thomas Paul installed as pastor, and an AME church was founded in 1818. By 1860 there were a total of six African American churches in the Boston area.[22]

Black congregations provided leadership opportunities for women as well, most notably Philadelphia's Jarena Lee and Maria Miller Stewart of Boston. Lee was the first female preacher in the AME Church. Stewart was a public speaker and author who often lectured on religious topics, although she was not a preacher. Lower-profile opportunities were also encouraged among female congregants.[23] Despite the fact that there were more female than male members, Richard Allen's AME Church initially did not formally license or ordain female preachers, even though the church was independent from larger and less flexible denominational hierarchies. Despite the lack of an official role in the early church, women were not universally discouraged from active participation.[24] The Daughters of Conference was formed from the gathering of women who provided service to the church at the meeting where the denomination was established in 1816. These women performed more traditional domestic rather than religious duties, such as mending and laundering the clothing of the male delegates in order to enhance their status and appearance while visiting Philadelphia.[25] Mary Still, an antislavery activist, spoke out about the importance of women to the AME Church: "We are sometimes told that females should have nothing to do with the business of the Church. But they have yet to learn that when female labor is withdrawn the Church must cease to exist."[26] During the early nineteenth century both Black and white women were largely prohibited from speaking in front of promiscuous (mixed-sex) audiences. Women therefore relied upon religious tropes and church platforms to justify their presence.[27]

The existence of Black churches became an important marker to whites of uplift and morality within free Black communities. The Philadelphia census taken at various times by Pennsylvania antislavery groups stressed the number of African American religious institutions. A survey of free Blacks in Washington, D.C., states that there were approximately seven thousand people of color in the city, two-thirds of whom were free. The article continued to stress that there were six churches whose evening congregations included close to two thousand members.[28] Abolitionists pointed to the piety of African Americans not only to demonstrate racial elevation in the North and to criticize slavery in the South but also to counter stereotypes of antebellum free people of color, particularly women.

Discrimination against Black congregants was one of the key reasons why new churches and denominations were formed. The indignity of segregation within a house of worship was the last straw for many free people of color. A letter signed "Ella" in an early issue of *The Liberator* described the humiliation of segregation: "Often as I have met the look of scorn and heard the whispered remark of 'This bench is for the black people,'—'This bench is for the people of color,' has the tear gathered in my eye, and the prayer ascended from my heart to God."[29] This racism from individuals who shared their religious faith was particularly painful. Separate seating at St. George's in Philadelphia led both Richard Allen and Absalom Jones to create new congregations.[30] As the nineteenth century progressed, denominations that were considered to be sympathetic to abolition and their African American members engaged in practices that were increasingly hostile toward integration within the church. For example, the Protestant Episcopal convention held in New York in 1850 declined to admit duly organized and qualified African American churches, even though they had been "admitted in Rhode Island, in New Jersey and else where."[31] Quakers also engaged in discriminatory practices within their own church despite an exemplary record on abolition. A British pamphlet that examined the Society of Friends in the United States quoted a free Black as saying: "In reply to your question, 'Whether there appears to be a diminution of prejudice towards us, among Friends,' I unhesitatingly answer NO. I have heard it frequently remarked, and have observed it myself, that in proportion as we become intellectual and respectable, so in proportion does their disgust and prejudice increase."[32] Even some of the most committed antislavery congregations did not equate emancipation with equality and perhaps felt more comfortable when their race work was done from a distance.

While Black churches provided a necessary space for African Americans to worship, organize, educate, and socialize, by the late 1840s a sizeable portion of the Black community began to question both segregated churches and schools. What was once seen as a source of independence became a location of exclusion. African American educator William J. Watkins articulated this argument in *The Liberator*: "In Boston there is a colored population of not quite 2000, and yet we have *five* colored churches. We voluntarily give aid and comfort to the enemy, by keeping alive these separate organizations, although a little sober reflection will convince us of the fact that they are a curse instead of a blessing."³³ Watkins was not alone in this opinion. At the moment when independent institutions were becoming truly established and stable, many activists began to see that success as a stumbling block to future integration. A distinct Black public sphere was no longer sufficient to pursue claims of equality. This dissension within the ranks was most vocally manifested in the debates over education.

SCHOOLS FOR FREE PEOPLE OF COLOR

Since the early national era, education and citizenship have been linked, providing the justification for publicly funded schools during the nineteenth century.³⁴ Beyond promoting the civic standing of free people of color, the founding of schools for African Americans was critical in the establishment of communities and networks among free Blacks in the urban North. Schools and churches provided both the physical spaces and intellectual links that were necessary precursors to more organized political activism. Although schools in particular provided the basic skills necessary to access print media, they also provided a platform for social activism. Males and females lobbied for improved educational opportunities, which often led to activism in other arenas.

While some African American men had been calling for civil recognition since the late eighteenth century, women's personal and more public activism often began with education and was performed both individually and in groups. In the first decades of the nineteenth century, African American women's groups raised money for education and provided clothing for children attending school. Individual women found education a worthy recipient of their legacies. For example, in 1825 Ann Flower willed the African Episcopal Church of St. Thomas, Philadelphia, $751.39 for the tuition of a certain number of boys (to be determined). The money was invested, with the proceeds earning thirty dollars a year.³⁵ Schools, whether they were sponsored by charitable groups, publicly funded, or supported by independent private institutions, were also important for women because they provided training and the opportunity for professional employment, which had previously been almost nonexistent for women of color. Schools demonstrated how whites and Blacks linked education and racial elevation and, on a broader scale, the cultural importance of respectability and how it could be obtained. Free schools offered poor African American children and adults (who had more limited access to education in terms of both years in school and days attending) literacy and basic writing skills that at least provided the potential for wider vistas of economic (and, by proxy, social) improvement. For the children of middle-class African Americans, education most likely began at an earlier age and if privately funded included the necessary curriculum that would allow students to participate in the political and leisure-time activities of the middle class as adults.

Education was seen as a central component for cultural advancement. *Freedom's Journal*, the first Black-edited newspaper created for an African American audience, claimed in one of its earliest issues that "the future respectability of our people will eventually rest on the education which our children and youth now receive."[36] Educating African American children had been an important goal of white and Black Philadelphians for decades, beginning during the process of gradual emancipation. Despite the popularity of the idea, public funding was often minimal, and the bulk of the burden was placed on both Black and white benevolence societies. Education was seen as the key to social mobility and thus equality. The 1838 census of the free people of color of Philadelphia, which was solicited largely to counter the movement to disenfranchise African American men in the new state constitution, touted both the public and private schools in the city. The same year a report by the Anti-Slavery Convention of American Women proclaimed, "The desire for education has greatly increased in the next generation, we trust it will be a very rare thing to find a colored person in the free states, who does not know how to read, write, and cipher; and this circumstance alone will do a vast deal toward the removal of existing prejudice."[37] The convention was integrated, although the delegates were predominantly white. This address reflects the typical sentiment of white activists that racial elevation would promote rights as opposed to seeing civil rights as promoting elevation.

Benevolence societies and churches typically sponsored the first African American schools in a town. However, by the beginning of the nineteenth century, public education became increasingly available to free people of color. Quakers had sponsored educational opportunities open to African Americans since the latter half of the eighteenth century. For example, the Society of Friends funded the first general curriculum Philadelphia school for African Americans in 1770 for the purpose of "religious and literary instruction as would qualify them for the proper enjoyment of freedom, and for becoming useful and worthy citizens."[38] Gradual emancipation, first adopted in Pennsylvania in 1780, created the impetus to provide both basic reading and writing skills, as well as manual (vocational) training in African American schools. Girls were instructed in sewing, and boys received industrial training, all with an eye to self-support once these children reached adulthood. In 1794 the American Convention of Abolition Societies called for instruction in "those mechanic arts which will keep them most constantly employed," concluding that such a plan for study would "less subject them to idleness and debauchery, and thus prepare them for becoming good citizens of the United States."[39] An 1830 history of the New York African free schools explained the more noble aspect of their mission: "The laws of the land might declare, that they should no longer be slaves, but it was only in the cultivation of the mind, that they could become truly emancipated and free."[40]

Urban abolition organizations recognized the importance of education for African Americans gaining their freedom. The Pennsylvania Society for Promoting the Abolition of Slavery (PAS) formed a committee on education in 1790 and subsequently established its own schools, helped fund previously established schools, and worked for the integration of the city's public schools.[41] New antislavery organizations founded in western locations followed the Pennsylvania model. For example, the Ohio Female Anti-Slavery Society urged local chapters to help raise funds "for the support of colored schools."[42] This support provided antislavery groups with a more tangible philanthropic focus and a pragmatic local solution to the question of "what next?" as slavery began to disappear in the North. As abolitionist societies became more established, they began tracking demographic markers of free Blacks as part of their political mission. Publisher Matthew Carey counted the various "schools for coloured persons in the city of Philadelphia & districts" in 1822 and reported that there were 240 boys and 184 girls being educated. In addition, there were 179 students in ten schools "taught by coloured teachers—located primarily in the Cedar Ward."[43]

One of the problems of leaving the administration of schools to benevolent organizations was the lack of stability of nonstate actors. Some groups, such as the PAS, had long-term relationships with educational institutions, while others had more of a passing interest. For example, the minute book of the Clarkson Institute (the educational arm of the PAS) reported that the Association for the Instruction of Colored Women, by "the unanimous conclusion of the members present," decided that the "institution [had] ceased to be useful, it was therefor resolved to suspend any further exertions in the cause." The members of the association would present the "Clarkson Institute of Pennsylvania any and all the monies, goods & Chattels belonging to said institution on our behalf."[44] An entry two months later recorded the group's consideration of working with the newly formed Anti-Slavery Association of Philadelphia to share the burden of managing schools.

Despite the PAS's long-term support for education, the organization was unable to commit to a specific type of school. Clarkson Hall, established in 1812 as basically an elementary school for African American boys, had many incarnations over the years. The school served as a boys' school, rented rooms for a private girls' school, operated for a short stint as a high school, opened as an infant school for working parents, and offered an adult education annex. In 1820, perhaps in an attempt to cut their ties to education, the PAS offered the Clarkson building to the Philadelphia Board of Education to house the proposed public school for African Americans. The board turned them down, and the PAS continued to sponsor schools.[45]

Schools sponsored by African American benevolent societies faced an even more precarious funding structure than did those funded by white organizations. For example, the proceedings of the African Benevolent Society of Newport, Rhode Island, reveal a constant struggle over budget shortfalls. Established in 1808, the African Benevolent Society organized for the object of "the establishment and continuance of a free school for any person of color in this Town."[46] The all-male membership struggled with finances early in the venture. First, they dismissed the female instructor (leaving just a male teacher for the entire school) and then for the next term moved to an evening school, which would save money and help adults.[47] Next, they sought help from the Female African Benevolent Society, which apparently supervised a different school and also worked to provide clothing for students.[48] Finally, they began to collect subscriptions for the school and asked parents to help pay for their children's education. The combination of all these efforts allowed the group to cobble together funding for the school for over a decade.

For antislavery whites, African free schools were evidence that, given the opportunity, Black children could succeed intellectually. Reporting a public examination of students at New York's African free school, the *National Advocate* editorialized that the system of public education "proves that their intellect and capacity, when under proper regulations and discipline, are equally strong and energetic as those of other complexions." Students performed exercises in "spelling, reading, writing, arithmetic, geography and elocution, and of needle work in addition to these, on the part of the females."[49] White women who supported colonization began sponsoring schools in Liberia. Important female opinion leaders such as Sarah Hale, Catharine Beecher, and Lydia Sigourney supported colonization efforts and promoted schools, leaving the impression that activism for education was suitable for the woman's sphere.[50] While antislavery whites increasingly pointed to the success of African free schools to justify abolition, free Blacks used similar arguments to claim citizenship rights from the 1830s through Reconstruction.

Despite the growing support for African American schools in the urban North, some segments of the white population revealed an anxiety about the education of young girls of color and colleges for African American young men. Canterbury, Connecticut, provides a strong case study. In 1831 Prudence Crandall opened a female academy in Canterbury. A year later Crandall admitted Sarah Harris, a twenty-year-old African American woman who hoped to receive the education necessary to "teach colored children." In a letter penned by Crandall she described Harris as "a colored girl of respectability—a professor of religion—and daughter of honorable parents."[51] The negative reaction to this admission decision was swift. Locals complained, and parents threatened to remove their daughters from the school. Instead of submitting to pressure and dismissing Harris, Crandall decided to close the school in its current state and reopen it as a school for "young ladies and little misses of color." With the financial and political support of antislavery activists, Crandall reopened the academy in February 1833, with the first out-of-state students arriving in April.[52]

The decision to reopen the school as one exclusively for African American girls did not appease the white residents of Canterbury. Prudence Crandall described a town meeting held in February: "They appointed a committee ... [and] told me the meeting had resolved to do everything in their power to destroy my undertaking that they *could* do it *should* do it and what will be the result of this commotion I cannot tell."[53] By spring, the vague threats made in February had begun to take shape. Local merchants refused to supply the school, and much of the local community discouraged students from attending.[54] In June 1833 Crandall was arrested "for the alleged crime of instructing certain colored girls not belonging to the state of Connecticut."[55] Since the facts of the case were not contested, the trial was based on the constitutionality of the law. The advocates for the state argued that "the term 'citizen' had, in the constitution and laws of Connecticut, and in the Constitution of the United States, and in the laws of Congress, a technical and significant [meaning]—that Indians, Africans, or their descendants, although free or free born, were not entitled to the immunities or privileges of citizens." The initial trial, held in August 1833, resulted in a hung jury.[56] The second trial, held in December of the same year, concluded with the conviction of Crandall. The appellate court decision ended the dispute by dismissing the charges based on legal issues not central to the question of Black citizenship. This resolved the legal issues for Crandall but left the constitutionality of the law itself undetermined. Crandall recognized that after the legal issues were resolved there was no reason to continue the fight for a new school in Connecticut. In a letter written before her arrest, Crandall contemplated her future: "If this school is crushed by inhuman laws another I suppose cannot be obtained, certainly one for *white* scholars can never be taught by me. As for myself I think I shall fare well enough—I have sufficient property in my hands to pay my debts—to work I am not ashamed and to beg I do not fear the necessity."[57] Why was Crandall's school so controversial? Crandall, who was not from the area and who received financial support from well-known abolitionists, was seen as an outside agitator. However, race and propriety became an even bigger issue. Some whites objected to the curriculum, which taught middle-class skills rather than following a vocational approach. They viewed such skills as unnecessary for girls of color, and some feared that these educated young women might seek white husbands.[58]

Prudence Crandall was not the only white woman to encounter difficulties teaching young women of color, particularly if the school served to attract additional African Americans to the community. Myrtilla Miner's School for Colored Girls, founded in December 1851 in Washington, D.C., grew from six students to forty in just two years.[59] While the opposition to Miner's school lacked the same dramatic impact of Prudence Crandall's trial, locals tried on several occasions to have the school removed or thwarted fundraising campaigns that would have expanded student enrollment.[60] In a letter to the Ladies Anti-Slavery Society of Glasgow, Scotland, Harriet Beecher Stowe described the struggle and pluck of Myrtilla Miner: "A man one day called upon her and told her that a mob was organized to destroy her schoolroom.... 'What good will it do to destroy my schoolroom!' Was her reply. 'I shall only get another, and go right on.' 'But' said he 'we will frighten your scholars so that they will not dare to come to you' 'No you will not' said she. 'Wherever I dare to go to teach, they will dare to come learn.'"[61]

Teaching remained a respectable profession for young women of color who were seeking both middle-class status and a means to support themselves. In 1851 activist and author Frances Watkins Harper was the first female teacher at the Union Seminary (near Columbus, Ohio), a school on the manual training plan that had been sponsored by the AME Church. Watkins taught domestic science, despite her background in literature.[62] Charlotte Forten Grimké, a graduate of the Salem Normal School in 1856, eventually taught freed persons in Port Royal during the Civil War.[63] Women saw teaching as a suitable occupation before they married, although for many women of color teaching was a lifelong profession, whether they were married or single. Schools began to spring up with the mission of preparing African American women for a career in education, thus filling in the gaps where teachers were in short supply and providing respectable young women with occupations before they became mistresses of their own homes. In some Black communities, the education and employment of females were low priorities. The first cut made at the Newport, Rhode Island, school, after all, was the female teacher.

Despite the lack of stability in girls' schools, when they closed, coeducational opportunities often became available. The incoming correspondence files for the PAS indicate that African American women were interested in teaching positions. What is not clear is how often positions became available and if all interested candidates filed a letter of application. Most of the letters were short and to the point. In 1843 Eliza Newell wrote the PAS board of education: "I respectfully offer myself as a candidate for the situation of teacher in the Public School for Coloured Children. Any consideration on your part will be thankfully received."[64] Martha Holcomb was even more direct: "Gentlemen, I respectfully solicit the situation of Principal teacher in your school."[65] Some letters were longer, and applicants touted their areas of expertise, including the ability to teach both basics and sewing. Other letters offered respected references.[66]

While by midcentury more Black women were becoming educated, there were not substantially more employment opportunities opening up for them that required this education. Thus, for African American women who needed to work and also sought the status of "true women," teaching was the best option open to them. However, for some, while the work might have been desirable, the pay was not sufficient. Elizabeth Reynolds wrote to the board of education: "I have concluded to give up my situation as teacher of the school under your care, except you would judge it proper to raise my salary as I think it inadequate to the labor of the school."[67] Jane Stokley, an assistant in the infant school, requested a raise of $1.50 per month: "Where I now reside they have raised my rent one dollar . . . on account of getting the hydrant water in." She added that she was "not yet tired and feel a willingness to do the best that lays in my power towards the children."[68]

The growth of middle-class Black communities resulted in two different goals in the education of African American children. As Black communities became more established, some wanted separate schools in order to control curriculum and hiring practices and to create career paths for African American men and women. In contrast, others sought integration within local public schools. The establishment of Pennsylvania's Institute of Colored Youth (ICY) resulted in a more independent Black school system (despite maintaining ties to the Quakers) and served to unify several of the private schools in existence in the 1850s. Originally founded in 1837 after an 1832 bequest of $10,000, the ICY was first located outside the city limits and then reopened in Philadelphia in 1852. The school's curriculum included "in addition to the usual elementary studies, Composition, History, Algebra, Geometry, Mensuration [measurement of geometric quantities], Plane and Spherical Trigonometry, Surveying, and Navigation, natural philosophy, Chemistry, mechanical Drawing, and Drafting, Anatomy, and Physiology." Applicants were required to pass exams in "Reading, Writing, Spelling, Arithmetic as far as Fractions, and in the Geography of the United States."[69] Initially, the Philadelphia incarnation of the ICY only offered classes to boys; however, a female division was soon added. The ICY was seen primarily as an independent Black institution. *Frederick Douglass' Paper* editorialized about an opening at the school: "A number of applications have already been received from *white* Teachers but the Managers are not disposed to accept any of these, unless a competent *Colored Teacher cannot be found*. We hope one will be found, as there are those among 'our people,' amply qualified who are peradventure, 'wasting their sweetness on the desert air.'" Douglass urged his subscribers to "read the advertisement."[70]

The organization of African American schools in the antebellum North became a battleground over Black identity and how that identity could include a path to citizenship. Philadelphia had a variety of public and private schools for Black children, and the ICY was the pride of the African American community. Boston, however, provides a good opposing case study. The public school system in Boston had a segregated school within its jurisdiction. The Smith School, originally founded in 1808 under a different name and later operated through an endowment established by Abiel Smith, was a flashpoint of confrontation within the Black community. As early as 1842 a debate emerged over whether or not the school should continue or if Black children should be admitted into their neighborhood school. An article signed by "a Colored Man" appeared in the *Boston Courier*, arguing that "the colored school as it is conducted here, has a tendency more to degrade than elevate the colored population.... The colored school here should be done away with... and our children should have access to the schools in our respective wards."[71] Questions of identity and activism were central in this debate.

Despite the city's decision to keep the Smith School open, anger simmered into the 1850s. The increasing vulnerability of free northern African Americans certainly resulted in a more vigorous defense of their status as free individuals and caused many to question the value of moral suasion and uplift strategies.[72] William J. Watkins wrote in a letter to the editor of *The Liberator*: "We foster and keep alive a colored school, although we know its existence is the sole barrier to the admission of our children into the several schools in the wards where they reside. If the colored people unanimously resolve that this exclusive school shall die, how soon we would chant its funeral requiem."[73] The 1854 Boston School Festival, held in Faneuil Hall, recognized the achievements of two students from the Smith School and provided another public opportunity to question the segregated Boston schools: "How can colored children come to anything shut up in a pen by themselves?"[74] Some African Americans hoped that integration would achieve more than just a superior education for their children. Boston-based Black abolitionist William Cooper Nell wrote to Amy Post, a white abolitionist, that integration "*has* had and will have a decided influence on the *School Question*—for as you know this *Colorphobia* is not exhibited by children until their parents have had a wicked finger in the pie."[75]

In 1855 Boston integrated its public schools, allowing African American students to attend their neighborhood schools. Although this ended debate about the Smith School, integration did not mean Black students were entering a "color-blind" system. For example, African American parents reacted to integrated schools with a mix of appreciation and promises of "elevation" in the following resolution, published in *The Liberator*: "Resolved, that to attest our appreciation of the passage of this anti-colored school act, we the colored parents of Boston, do hereby pledge ourselves to have our children punctually at school, and neat in their dress, and in all other ways will aid their instruction in the task which has been assigned them."[76] To appease white reluctance to integration, claims of respectability were also needed.

Despite the large endowment for the education of African American youth, a vocal majority of the Black residents of Boston felt that integrated public schools were a better option for residents. While urban Blacks could debate the merits of independence versus integration, for rural families there were fewer options. Robert Purvis moved his family to rural Philadelphia County shortly after the 1842 Lombard Street Riot. Despite his family's status in the African American community and the purchase of a $13,000 estate in Byberry Township, the educational opportunities for the Purvis children were limited. After the children outgrew the local private Quaker school, the only option open to the family was the segregated county school, located nearby in the town of Mechanicsville. The school was housed in a "miserable shanty" and was only required to operate four months of the year.[77] Purvis responded to this situation in a letter to the county tax collector: "I object to the payment of this [school] tax on the ground that my rights as a citizen, and my feelings as a man and a parent have been grossly outraged in depriving me [of] . . . the benefits of the school system which this tax was designed to sustain."[78]

ORGANIZATIONS FOR ELEVATION

Because of the loss of civil rights for Blacks during the 1820s and 1830s, free people of color began expanding the number and types of public institutions in their communities. Churches and social concerns spawned some societies, and others developed independently. Organizations for African American women were not limited to large metropolitan areas. The African Female Benevolent Society of Troy, New York, was founded in 1833 as a self-help group that also likely provided mutual aid when required. The group was still going strong fifteen years later when Henry Highland Garnet served as the anniversary speaker.[79] The 1838 census of

Philadelphia's Black community found ninety benevolent or mutual aid societies in operation. While two of these organization were founded in the late eighteenth century, the majority began in the 1820s and 1830s to meet the needs created by urbanization.[80]

Literacy was an important component to racial elevation, and literacy rates were used to illustrate the potential of organizations that promoted education for children and adults.[81] Philadelphia was a city of libraries for both Blacks and whites. The Colored Reading Society for Mental Improvement was likely the first lending library for African American men in Philadelphia. It was established in 1828, and members paid an initiation fee and monthly dues. At weekly meetings members would check out and return books and even discuss what they had read.[82] Although membership was restricted to men, women in members' households also likely profited from the lending library. According to the 1838 *Census of Free People of Color of the City of Philadelphia*, there was one female literary society with a library and reading room attached.[83] The Minerva Literary Society, founded in 1834, contained fifty volumes in its library. The Philadelphia Female Literary Association (FLA) likely did not have a library, suggesting a class difference between the two organizations. The more well-to-do members of the FLA likely had family libraries in their own homes and did not need to spend association fees for reading materials. The books purchased by the FLA seemed more centered on supporting political issues. By 1856 there were four libraries for people of color in Philadelphia boasting over two thousand volumes. The ICY library housed thirteen hundred books checked out to 450 readers. This suggests that the school's library had a wider use than enrolled students.[84] Libraries were not the only community institutions that supported literacy: the Black press was also important to this endeavor, as were the benevolent societies that supported the Black press. Often, African American women's groups would send donations or subscribe to newspapers. In New York an organization formed to support Frederick Douglass's *North Star*. The group held a fair and also sought the support of similar organizations across the country.[85] Another group of New York women organized the Provisional Committee to provide financial assistance to Samuel Ringgold Ward's *Impartial Citizen* (Syracuse, New York). They also held a fair where they netted thirty-four dollars for the struggling newspaper.[86]

A variety of education-based societies were formed during the antebellum era to promote reading, writing, and public speaking skills. The Pennsylvania Augustine Society met at Bethel Church and promoted "the means of acquiring knowledge sufficient to read and understand the sacred Scriptures, and to manage with propriety, the ordinary concerns of domestic and social life."[87] The Banneker Institute, established in 1854, was a literary group that provided intellectual growth for African American young men who had completed their formal schooling. Newspapers outside Philadelphia advertised the institute's lecture series, suggesting that the press saw this group as a means to demonstrate racial elevation in practice.

AFRICAN AMERICAN PRINT AND PUBLIC CULTURE

Antebellum Black newspapers filled an important niche and are revealing of Black culture on many levels. Essays and editorials disclosed political thought, while advertisements provided a glimpse into the everyday lives of African Americans. Descriptions of meetings, letters to the editor, and even the ever-present poetry exposed how political thought was understood and acted upon by the average reader. The Black press was important because it served to create a racial identity within a white majority country, although racial identity did not result in a singular political voice. For African Americans, the ability to contribute to public discourse was central to achieving full citizenship.[88] Newspapers were particularly important because they were inexpensive to produce (and thus to purchase), easy to transport, and more likely to cast a wide net for potential readers. Both Blacks and whites passed along newspapers in person and through the mail to family and friends who lived far away. This suggests a longer "shelf life" for nineteenth-century papers. Not only did news travel more slowly, keeping individual newspapers relevant for a longer period of time, but editorials, community news, and the issues-oriented perspective of the press made newspapers interesting long after they had originally been distributed. The portability of newspapers and other forms of print ephemera meant that the public sphere became more malleable. Eighteenth- and early nineteenth-century print culture expanded the public sphere beyond the geographically anchored space identified by Habermas by linking individual African Americans and small communities scattered throughout the nation into a more cohesive whole.

African Americans have a long history of accessing print culture as a means for creating both a distinct Black public sphere and counterpublics that both critiqued and participated in the white public sphere.[89] This, coupled with the relatively inexpensive nature of print ephemera, allowed African Americans to develop a distinct voice to challenge white assumptions about the role of people of color within the nation. The founding of African American organizational structures led to the formation of publishing houses and newspapers. The AME Church established the first known African American publishing company in 1817, a literary magazine in 1841, and its own newspaper, the *Christian Recorder*, in 1852. Despite being backed by the AME Church, the *Christian Recorder* struggled financially. The paper suspended publication in 1856, although the church remained hopeful that the suspension would be temporary. The paper resumed publication in 1861 and remains in print today.

Freedom's Journal, the first Black-edited newspaper in the United States, had a two-year run from 1827 to 1829 and created the earliest "imagined community" among free people of color by promoting a sense of racial consciousness. Published in New York City, *Freedom's Journal* had a national readership that sought to circulate information and to shape behavior. The paper boasted having agents in over twenty cities, including southern towns and locations in Canada and Great Britain.[90] For readers, the dissemination of information was important. The paper promoted education for children and adults. In many ways, it worked as a conduct manual with advice about food, drink, and dress.[91] Recognizing the role of women in the goal of racial promotion, the paper often focused on behavior and being submissive rather than providing domestic advice and recognizing the activism that would be so important in the next decade: "We do not wish that women should implicitly yield their better judgment to their fathers or husbands but let them support the cause of reason with all the graces of female gentleness."[92]

The newspaper also served as an outlet for advertisements for the Black community and provided, in essence, a guide to life, making material culture visible to the free Black community. Advertisements in antebellum Black-edited newspapers familiarized African Americans with goods and services produced and provided by people of color beyond their own neighborhoods. An introductory editorial explained that the central mission of *Freedom's Journal* was the "dissemination of useful knowledge among our brethren, and to further their moral and religious improvement."[93] Over the next thirty years, the growth of a Black press, distinct from the antislavery press, continued to create a broad community among people of color in the urban North. Mastheads promoted the politics and goals of the Black press. Frederick Douglass's *North Star* proclaimed, "Right is of No Sex— Truth is of No Color," while *Freedom's Journal* stated, "Righteousness Exaulteth a Nation." Although newspapers owned and operated by African Americans continued to struggle, by the 1840s more papers had been launched, suggesting that the free Black community was growing more literate, prosperous, and politically active.[94] Coupled with informal partnerships with the antislavery press, African Americans claimed a more prominent presence in public culture by midcentury. The rhetoric of respectability used in the Black press was intertwined with claims of citizenship. While the goals of propriety and education were not gendered, domestic production and piety were left in the hands of women.

The affiliated white abolitionist press provided an outlet for informing interested Blacks and sympathetic whites about the activities of African American communities throughout the country. These papers circulated information about class-based and political activities of people of color, such as women's organizations, male and female literary societies, moral reform, school exhibitions, and the political work for civil rights. In particular, William Lloyd Garrison's *Liberator* served as a repository for organizational materials from African American groups, including constitutions, petitions, correspondence, and lectures, that otherwise would no longer be extant. Despite being primarily the political voice of Garrison, *The Liberator* received significant economic support from the African American community. James Forten not only provided early necessary financial assistance but also used his influence in Philadelphia to publicize the paper. In December 1830 Forten wrote that he had twenty-seven subscribers for the new paper and requested that Garrison "send on a few Extra Papers that I may hand them out to my friends."[95] A year and a half later, Forten again wrote to Garrison, suggesting that he send copies of the paper to local book sellers because "they would perhaps sell well, at any rate they would attract public notice." Forten also provided the good news that "your friends are not inactive in endeavouring to obtain subscribers. Mr. Purvis has already 70, on his list."[96]

The antislavery press and Black-edited newspapers provided women, both Black and white, a literary outlet. Often resorting to pen names (or the even less distinctive "a lady" moniker), newspapers such as Philadelphia's *National Enquirer* in its "Literary Port-Folio" and *The Liberator*'s "Ladies Department" printed essays, letters, and poems attributed to Azza, Magawisca, Melpomene, and Zillah. Some offerings called for women to contemplate the plight of the slave; others asked women to take action and to speak out. For example, "Invocation to Woman" suggested:

> Send forth thine Angel voice
>   Throughout our guilty land;
> Its sweetly plaintive tone,
>   What tyrant can withstand?[97]

This poem, attributed to Melpomene, the Muse of tragedy, asked women to speak out against slavery but allowed them to cloak that transgression with their "Angel voice" and "sweetly plaintive tone" because only women could. Female intervention within the slavery debate served to remove politics from the forefront and legitimized moral suasion as a strategy. Political discussions suggested the ability to "negotiate," while the "Angel voice" of woman justified immediate emancipation.

CHALLENGES FACING AFRICAN AMERICAN COMMUNITIES: EMPLOYMENT, VIOLENCE, AND RIOTS

As the nineteenth century progressed, free African Americans faced growing threats to their rights and livelihoods. Churches, schools, and societies organized for elevation in the early nineteenth century were both a response to the challenges of gaining economic and political status and a conduit for additional backlash by the white majority. Progress followed by setbacks became the norm. Much of the pushback by whites was gendered, first demeaning African American women, which in turn emasculated African American men. When Black men were denied the authority of patriarchy, African American women found it difficult to perform the ritualistic traits of true womanhood. This in turn discredited the middle-class household, suggesting that African American men were not worthy of a civic role as voters and policy makers. While purposeful womanhood demanded action, true womanhood provided a shield for those actions and preserved class status for women of color.

In the antebellum North, employment had become racially segregated, which further threatened the economic and social standing of the free Black community. Guilds and labor groups worked to limit employment opportunities to free men of color. If they were unable to finance their own businesses, Black men were largely left with low-paying and often temporary employment. A letter to *The Liberator* signed "A Colored Philadelphian" provided two examples of this discrimination. First, the author explained that it was next to impossible for a parent to find a trade for their child. He wrote that "journeymen and apprentices generally refuse to work with them even if the master is willing, which is seldom the case." The Philadelphian next demonstrated the difficulty of finding even temporary employment by describing a recent heavy snowstorm that required the work of "thousands of persons" to clean the gutters and clear streets: "There was not a[n employed] man of color to be seen, when hundreds of them were going about the streets with shovels in their hands, looking for work and finding none."[98]

The endemic employment discrimination against Black men forced African American women into waged labor. Dual-income families were often necessary to maintain households, and the waged work required of Black women excluded them from meeting white standards of true womanhood. They were either employed as laundresses and domestics in white households or forced to make their private homes public by taking in boarders.[99] The Massachusetts Abolition Society recognized that employment discrimination meant that free people of color were often excluded from opportunities for economic uplift. The society established a special department, "an intelligence office for the especial benefit of colored youth, who desire places in business, and in the establishment of schools and moral and literary societies among them."[100] Unemployment and low-status jobs were not the only problems plaguing free Blacks in the urban North.

The development of African American organizations provided targets for angry white mobs. The rising middle class of African Americans, with a frail economic base to sustain them, raised the ire of those whites who saw themselves in competition with African Americans for economic resources. Urban violence was not unusual during the Jacksonian era. Changing work patterns, immigration, rapid growth in cities, and economic volatility all contributed to urban instability. However, free Blacks were heavily targeted in Philadelphia and other urban areas, resulting in speculation that the net loss of population among Philadelphia Blacks between 1840 and 1850 was largely the result of riots.[101] Individual acts of violence were also used by whites to discipline the African American population. In 1838 a young southern medical student in Philadelphia observed, "I tell you, they make the free Negroes walk a straight line." He explained that "students knocked one down the other day and beat him like the notion and the police stood and never said a word."[102]

Three different Philadelphia race riots demonstrate the anxieties white mobs had toward employment, abolition, public parades, and claims of respectability by African Americans. The Flying Horses Riot (August 1834) began at a carousel that was patronized by both Black and white members of the working class but soon spilled over into the outlying neighborhood. Integrated public spaces, particularly those that were entertainment venues, created anxiety about race and gender mixing that often led to violence. The vandalism during the Flying Horses Riot was directed at Black-owned property. Over thirty houses were destroyed, and a significant number of people were left homeless. Blame for the riot was placed on hiring practices among Black employers, who were believed to only "hire their own."[103] The riot was significant enough to be picked up in the national press. The *Maryland Gazette*, published in Annapolis, dedicated two columns of editorial space to its coverage and stressed the loss of homes and a church and the defenselessness of the African American victims.[104]

Antiabolition riots were a particular brand of mob mentality in the antebellum North. In the 1830s and early 1840s antiabolitionists saw themselves as defending the status quo and protecting their communities from outside influences. In the eyes of the mob, street violence had become an act of patriots, an attitude that continues today. Both sides saw the rhetorical potential of violence. The 1837 murder of abolitionist publisher Elijah Lovejoy by an Alton, Illinois, mob provided the movement with its first white martyr. The 1838 report of the Boston Female Anti-Slavery society records: "Deeply were our hearts stirred within us, as we read the lines written in blood, that the Priests of slavery had lain upon their altar that champion of free discussion, the fearless Lovejoy."[105] The headline that appeared in *The Liberator*, the paper of record for the antislavery cause, was indicative of the tone expressed in sympathetic newspapers across the country: "HORRIBLE OUTRAGE!—MOB LAW AND BLOODSHED!!" The editorial below this headline stated: "The Rev Elijah P. Lovejoy, well known for his perseverance in the cause of the slave, has at last fallen a martyr to abolitionism."[106] Even smaller towns experienced violence toward abolitionists, with meeting halls often the target, a pattern seen in violence toward free Blacks as well. Harvey Kitchel, a white abolitionist, described such an event in 1839: "There was to be a county Anti-Slavery Meeting a few weeks since. The night before it was to convene the Mtg House was blown up & burned to ashes! The meeting however was held over the still burning ruins—and warmth was delivered from them not to the body only."[107] Violence and the destruction of property not only made it more difficult for abolitionists to find large meeting halls but also restricted the locations available for free Blacks to host cultural and political gatherings. The threat of violence made the public performances of citizenship and racial elevation, particularly by women, less visible as they took place in segregated spaces.

The cause of abolition, particularly when it involved the racially integrated activism of women, was often met with violence. The Pennsylvania Hall Riot of 1838 is a prime example. The riot occurred during the Second Anti-Slavery Convention of American Women in the newly opened Pennsylvania Hall.[108] A large crowd rioted outside the building, ultimately burning it to the ground. The magnitude of the riot, the destruction of a major building, and the presence of well-known abolitionists ensured that the national press would cover this story. However, what is most interesting about the press coverage of the convention is that it focused not on the content of the speeches made by the famous activists but on the conduct of the average participants: "For a day or two previous to the confrontation, the members of the convention, women paraded the city with ostentation exhibiting the spectacle of blacks and whites—men and women—perambulating arm and arm along the most public streets."[109] Another paper reported, "At the celebration of the opening of the Hall, young white females were seated between young coloured men, and an intermingling of colours and sexes apparently prearranged took place."[110] A particularly invective tone was taken toward Angelina Grimké Weld, whose speech preceded the most violent rioting: "Mrs. Angelina Grimké Weld, it appears, was one of the agitators. Where Theodore, her newly acquired husband was, does not clearly appear. This is rather a queer honeymoon for Angelina and Theodore, wedded on Monday, bedded on Tuesday, and setting Philadelphia on fire on Wednesday."[111] Fears of racial "amalgamation" fueled mobs that included not only those with proslavery sentiments but also proponents of colonization.

From the beginning of gradual emancipation through the 1830s and 1840s, free Blacks were often figuratively and literally charged with being disorderly. African American women were suspected of sexual transgressions, and African American men were believed to be prone to violence. These stereotypes played to the mob mentality of angry whites and served to excuse their mob violence. Although all activists could potentially be victims of an angry mob, African American women were particularly at risk. Erica Armstrong Dunbar explains: "Constantly degraded and discriminated against because of their race, African American women found their virtue was always open to the scrutiny of others." However, she argues that these same women in Philadelphia used the opportunity to redefine themselves as wives and mothers who should be considered "respectable people."[112] While respectability did not necessarily prevent violence, African American women were able to shape public reaction by a community performance of respectability and true womanhood.

Antislavery women were beginning to realize that the work of abolition was dangerous. A Massachusetts delegate at the convention reported to her home society that it had been recommended that "colored sisters not... attend the meeting to be held in the [Pennsylvania] Hall... because they would be more exposed than others, as the mob seemed to direct their malice particularly towards the colored people."[113] While their status as "true *white* women" offered protection, white men such as Lovejoy and Black men and women were at risk of retribution from a hostile crowd. Despite the violence and destruction of Pennsylvania Hall during the 1838 convention, the group defiantly returned to Philadelphia in 1839. Lucretia Mott, who served as a vice president of the 1839 convention, described a message from the Philadelphia mayor on the second day of meetings. The mayor offered a variety of ways the women could avoid violence, including meeting in Clarkson Hall (location of the African American school), not meeting at night, and excluding or separating Black women from the proceedings. Mott replied, "We had never made a parade, as charged upon us, of walking with colored people, and should do as we have done before—walk with them as occasion offered.... [I]t was a principle with us, which we could not yield, to make no distinction on account of color."[114] Litigation over the riot and destruction of Pennsylvania Hall carried on for years. The initial report by the city, released in August 1838, admitted to a slow response by the police but maintained that the interracial participation of the conventioneers had provoked the crowds.[115]

African American uses of public spaces for political or ceremonial commemorations were also met with white violence. The 1842 Lombard Street Riot began after a temperance parade. This riot was unusually violent because of the large number of people gathered. Approximately one thousand temperance marchers participated, with a "great crowd present, composed of men, women, boys and girls, of all colors and descriptions, gathered together to look on this procession."[116] The *New York Spectator* stated that "great numbers of colored people fled to the other side of the river for safety" and criticized firemen for not protecting a Black church and a large African American–owned building that was intended to be used for meetings.[117] Although the temperance gathering was composed of men, many similar public celebrations included African American women as participants instead of as observers, placing them at risk of racial violence. The Lombard Street Riot took place in the heart of a prominent African American neighborhood made up of Black-owned businesses, public buildings, and middle-class homes. This meant that African American women were at risk, even if they were not participants or observers of the temperance parade. While the respectability of the inhabitants did not prevent the riot, it did serve to shape a public response that eventually condemned the violence.

THE PROMOTION OF TRUE WOMANHOOD AS A RESPONSE TO DISCRIMINATION AND VIOLENCE

When Barbara Welter devised her schema of true womanhood, she had at her disposal a large collection of written materials to analyze, proof of the popularity of the emerging print culture for women. White middle-class women had many magazines dedicated to their daily lives, and publishing houses released dozens of how-to manuals, gift annuals, and domestic fiction that women could turn to for cues about proper middle-class behavior. Unfortunately, the written documents of African American womanhood are harder to come by. Yet we know that the execution of true womanhood was seen as central to the elevation of the race as a whole. Mary Still, in her "Appeal to the Females of the A.M.E. Church," explained that "the moral or degraded condition of Society depends solely upon the influence of woman, if she be virtuous, pious, and industrious, her feet abiding in her own house, ruleing [sic] her family well." Still argued that the virtuous woman influenced more than her own home, that "like a tree planted by the river side, whose leaves are ever-green; she extends in her neighborhood a healthy influence, and all men calleth her blessed."[118] Despite the growth of the Black press, there were not specialized journals or newspapers for African American women. Thus, when domestic issues were raised, it was through the masculine gaze of a male editorial staff. James Horton confirms that "gender ideals of black society were heavily influenced by middle-class black males through the pages of black newspapers."[119] *Freedom's Journal* actively worked to vindicate African American women because "their humiliations were exceptionally great."[120] Reclaiming womanhood required a public intervention that the press could uniquely provide.

This masculine mediation through the Black press made Black womanhood less organic than its white, more female-driven counterpart and thus more problematic. For example, gender construction by the press would almost always represent the power differential between men and women and a desire to preserve that hierarchy. The preservation of patriarchy within African American homes provided Black males with civic status and gave a counternarrative for the true woman who might also be the breadwinner in her home. Second, the construction of gender would likely serve to further the interests of the male press (or African Americans in general), whether issues of racial uplift, moral reform, or abolition, as opposed to promoting the rights of women in isolation. This is one of the key differences between Black and white womanhood.

Limited page space was another concern of the Black press. Journals that targeted the white middle-class female could dedicate literally dozens of pages to fashion, homemaking, and marital advice, but the limited space available in an African American newspaper required it to cover issues deemed of importance to both men and women. For example, articles about female behavior and the role of women in the community were prevalent; articles actually containing household advice were almost nonexistent. There were no fashion hints in the Black press; instead, women were urged to be modest and simple in dress. While it was important to physically demonstrate middle-class status, it was equally important to invoke an image of frugality and seriousness. A related problem was the unseen secondary readership. While women's magazines such as *Godey's* had no one to please besides their own readers, the Black press faced a responsibility not only to the subscribers but also to advertisers, sponsors, and the white activist audience. These newspapers would want to ensure a serious and purposeful tone in their publications to guarantee ongoing financial support. Another challenge was the available audience for advice targeted at African American women. Smaller disposable incomes would limit not only access to printed material but also the ability to act upon much of the offered advice. The materialism in white domesticity simply could not be universally replicated in the free Black community, even if it was considered "middle class." Thus, there would be less of a market for domestic manuals and women's magazines. African American women were likely to glean most of their tips for womanhood from reprinted articles in the Black press.

Literacy is a final issue to be considered when evaluating the influence of Black print culture. Given the limited educational opportunities in the first decades of the nineteenth century, even for middle-class Blacks, African American literacy rates were lower than those of their white counterparts. However, literary societies served as an additional educational outlet, particularly for adult free women of color who might not have attended school as children. Urban areas with strong Black educational systems boasted high literacy rates. For example, the 1850 census for Boston reported a literacy rate for free people of color as close to 90 percent.[121] African American women organized early and established benevolent societies concurrent with or predating the societies founded by white women. Some of these organizations date to the 1790s and were initially established for mutual benefit. Perhaps because they served a broad purpose, African American literary societies were formed in northeastern cities decades before white women created similar groups after the Civil War. The preamble to the Female Literary Association (Philadelphia) demonstrates a commitment to uplift: "It therefore becomes a duty incumbent upon us as women, as daughters of a despised race, to use our utmost endeavors to enlighten the understanding, to cultivate the talents entrusted to our keeping that by so doing, we may in a great measure, break down the strong barrier of prejudice, and raise ourselves to an equality with those of our fellow beings, who differ from us in complexion, but who are with ourselves, children of one eternal Parent."[122] While members of the Female Literary Association saw it as their duty to provide educational uplift because of their "despised" status, by 1857 the suspicion of whites had tempered the goals of uplift: "We should ever keep in mind that the scrutinizing eye of the world which is no friend to our progress is upon us still."[123] By this time racial elevation was often seen as its own reward and did not require the promise of political equity to make it a worthy goal.

Since domestic literature targeted toward African American women was limited, did Black women access white prescriptive literature? The answer is not completely clear. The African American press reprinted some white domestic literature. However, the articles chosen did not include specific advice as to household management; instead, they offered more general codes of conduct for women. This suggests that behavior as opposed to basic household practices was paramount for the African American audience. For example, an 1837 article on "domestic habits" in the *Colored American* was clearly written for an African American audience, as the opening paragraph states, "Our colored population, as a people, have, and do suffer much both in character and condition, from early-formed inveterate domestic habits," but it also quotes Child's *American Frugal Housewife* when promoting domestic economy.[124] An article that appeared the next year, "Rules for Wives," was reprinted from Matthew Carey's *Practical Rules for the Promotion of Domestic Happiness* and called for women to be submissive and frugal and to cultivate their minds.[125]

Economic discrimination ensured that middle-class Black women would experience womanhood differently from whites. For example, prior to the Civil War, more than half of the middle-class Black women of Philadelphia were employed outside their homes. Their employment would seemingly fall outside the realm of white middle-class domesticity because it would take them out of the private sphere or require difficult physical labor. When describing the racial "typing" of employment in northern antebellum cities, historian Jacqueline Jones writes that it was a "division of labor calculated to demean the African-American community by the collective humiliation of its women."[126] Not content to accept this humiliation, the African American middle class publicly worked to include their community within the ideology of true womanhood. Newspapers strategically preached domesticity and the unique qualification of women to make a house a home.

As also seen in the white press at this time, prescriptions for feminine behavior often took the form of cautionary tales proclaiming disastrous outcomes for women who did not follow the norms of true womanhood. These stories not only policed the physical movements of women but also reinforced the "virtues" of true womanhood. For example, the *Colored American* warned women of the dangers of drink and how it threatened not only the intemperate female but also her home. Another article cautioned that a lack of domestic training could result in abandonment and "intemperance, suicide, homicide, and ... all the prevailing evils of the day."[127] Women who wanted to take a more activist role in antislavery and other reform movements had to push back against traditional domestic norms.

Traditional views of domesticity pervaded the articles on household advice. Hearth and home were sanctified. A happy result of "making and keeping that house really a home" was that a husband was less likely to stray: "Any well-disposed female can render the domestic fireside of a godly man more magnetic in its attractions than any other social circle whatever."[128] Household labor was portrayed as "entirely a woman's province" and as her duty, regardless of economic status, as the essay concludes: "It ought to engage much of the time and attention of every mistress of a family; nor can they be excused from this by any extent of fortune."[129] Household management was, however, also linked to racial uplift, as the *Colored American* editorialized: "Domestic Economy demands much more of our serious attention than it has ever received at our hands. For reasons which are obvious, it should be thoroughly taught the rising generation—its importance is great, as it will have such an immense influence upon our future prosperity."[130] By the 1860s there was a nostalgic longing for the woman who embraced the domestic aspects of the home. In many ways the fear that education would spoil the true woman was similar in both the Black and white presses.

Purity and piety were key aspects of the doctrine of true womanhood for both Black and white women. However, for the African American community, purity and piety were not just methods of social control over women but also a means for racial uplift. In a reprint from the *Boston Evening Gazette*, the *Colored American* endorsed the importance of piety: "Religion is every where lovely, but in a woman peculiarly so. It makes her but little lower than the angels. It purifies her heart, elevates her feelings and sentiments, hallows her affections, sheds light on her understanding and imparts dignity to her whole character."[131] Throughout these articles the importance of devotion and morality was stressed not only for the sake of the individual woman but also for her family and the entire community. Henry H. Garnet described his encounter with an ideal woman in a letter to a friend: "What a lovely thing she is! Modest, susceptible and chaste. She seems to have everything which beautifies a female, a good Christian and a scholar."[132] Mary Still warned her audience: "We should be careful also to have our conduct modest and our conversation chaste."[133] Purity and piety were particularly important traits for Black women to perform. Purity was important because whites assumed Black women were sexually promiscuous unless they demonstrated otherwise. Piety was important because Black women often practiced their religion in segregated churches, beyond the gaze of whites. Submissiveness was also suggested in much of the advice literature published by African American newspapers. Interestingly, it most often appeared in reprints from white sources. However, submissiveness of Black women was important because it proved the masculinity of Black men, who were often forced to be submissive to white men (and white women as well).

Given the similarities between the domestic literature of white and Black women, what is the value of a racialized interpretation? When examining true womanhood for African American women, form followed function. The dictates of the doctrine were in large part defined by their race-based utility. White women could use the constraints of true womanhood to empower themselves by elevating the importance of the private sphere. African American women used these same constraints to empower their communities to participate in the public sphere.

CONCLUSION

True womanhood served as an entrée into the middle class and a wider respectability. The very whiteness of its assumptions made true womanhood a viable strategy for the African American community to combat racism and claim an American identity.[134] For centuries, societies have looked to women and gender as markers of "civilization," particularly when encountering new cultures. It is not surprising that the African American community embraced this same trope while creating a civic identity in antebellum America. The racially mixed Female Anti-Slavery Society of Philadelphia proclaimed, "Yes, although we are *women* we still are citizens."[135] The reality of that claim depended upon the race of the woman reading it.

Was the use of domesticity and womanhood a successful strategy for African American women? Although free women of color often practiced political (or purposeful) womanhood and civic domesticity on a broader spectrum than their white counterparts, this was largely because Black women were forced to demonstrate their respectability, while for white women it was assumed until proven otherwise. When Lucretia Mott told the mayor of Philadelphia that the Anti-Slavery Convention of American Women would not need police protection, that she (Mott) had walked in the company of Black women several times in the last month without "incident," that was no doubt a true statement. However, would African American activists Sarah Mapps Douglass and Harriet Forten Purvis have made the same statement to Philadelphia's mayor? Purvis had been a primary target of verbal assault in the Pennsylvania Hall Riot the previous year because the mob thought her biracial husband was white. Her status of being a Forten by birth and a Purvis by marriage was not enough to shield her from an agitated crowd. Her education, wealth, and social status were not sufficient to protect her as an individual; instead, she needed the collective respectability of African American women to protect her and others from a mob. Because African Americans were so often targeted in mob violence, domesticity and respectability were important strategies to deploy. By demonstrating their own respect for order versus the lawlessness of the masses, African Americans enacted their own argument for equality.

CHAPTER 4

Creating an Empowered Private Sphere
Female Citizenship and Print Culture

Sarah Hale, Catharine Beecher, and Lydia Maria Child were three of the most prominent women in antebellum America. Through their domestic and political writing, these three contemporaries established a significant presence within the public sphere and contributed to the ideology of true womanhood. This idealized woman served her husband, home, and country through economic consumption and the cultural construction of the nation. Even though they enacted traditional performances of femininity, Hale, Beecher, and Child used the rhetoric of domesticity to become public advocates for the nation, although Hale and Beecher became more conservative with age. Despite their divergent partisan interests, the three authors were, on the surface, quite similar and made names for themselves independently of their husbands. Each published widely, was active in antislavery politics (although from very different perspectives), and seemingly embraced the feminine ideal of true womanhood, which they helped foster. They had broad social interests and public personas. Although each practiced the domestic arts differently, they all viewed domesticity as central to female power and as the key to feminine political capital however it might be deployed. Through their success in publishing, they manipulated the ideology of the true woman for their own political, economic, and social ends. All three challenged the male-dominated public sphere and through the printed word united women in the construction of new feminine identities. Hale and Beecher embraced the cultural code of true womanhood and broadened its significance to include a civic position for women as cultural nation builders. Child accepted the ideology of true womanhood (and personally practiced it much more closely than Hale or Beecher) but radically transformed its meaning by justifying the political participation of women based upon the confines and moral construction of true womanhood.

Successful with stand-alone books and political tracts, as well as articles in newspapers, magazines, and gift annuals, Hale, Beecher, and Child were among a growing number of professional female writers to emerge at this time. Authorship offered the nineteenth-century woman opportunities for public expression despite the fact that female writers were still something of an oddity during the early antebellum era. Hale, Beecher, and Child, like many professional and amateur female writers, participated in print culture both publicly and anonymously. Anonymity was important to women who were beginning to write for an audience. Professional writers who might have begun their careers anonymously soon learned that providing their name generated a readership that could be carried from one work to the next.

Hale, Beecher, and Child eventually attached their names to political writings because of the authority they had established in a female public sphere. An author's name could influence how readers understood and judged a particular work. For example, Catharine Beecher's family name provided her with the respectability owed a minister's daughter. Sarah Hale's use of her husband's name reinforced her authorship as the bereaved widow who faced raising five children alone. Even Lydia Maria Child, who gained little specifically from her husband's name, used the title "Mrs." when she published, demonstrating her respectability despite her progressive ideas. Hale, Beecher, and Child, who were among the first economically successful American female authors, helped create a women's print culture composed of both readers and writers. Through the promotion of new standards of education, new forms of printed materials, and, most importantly, new civic roles for women, American female print culture simultaneously created, perpetuated, and even subverted the notion of the true woman. This was true despite the many financial barriers women encountered when they attempted to enter the male-dominated world of publishing.[1]

The nineteenth-century woman often turned to publishing to supplement her household finances, particularly writing for magazines because they incurred less of an upfront cost. Social influence was not necessarily the first consideration when becoming an author. For example, Catharine Beecher authored textbooks not only to provide better materials for her students but also to stretch her limited pay as the principal of the Hartford Female Seminary. Harriet Beecher Stowe, writing to her husband, explained, "On the whole, my dear, if I choose to be a literary lady, I have, I think, as good a chance of making a profit by it as any one else I know of."[2] Sarah Hale believed that writing was the only financial option open to her. In a short autobiographical introduction to her poetry collection, Hale wrote, "The very few employments in which females can engage with any hope of profit, and my own constitution and pursuits, made literature appear my best resource."³ In a "Word with the Reader," in a reissue of her 1827 *Northwood*, Hale assured her gentle readers that she did not publish to "win fame." Instead, the book "was written literally with my baby in my arms . . . whose eyes did not open on the world til his father's were closed in death!"⁴ The true woman might achieve fame, but she did not seek it. Domestic advice was a steady financial supplement for other, less lucrative writing pursuits. Domestic literature was perhaps the most significant way that nineteenth-century female writers were able to expand their presence in the market without putting their social status at risk. A substantial number of women chose to do this, including women who published in a variety of genres. *Godey's* noted that "it is in keeping with the nature of our institutions that our literary women—those who cater for our intellectual wants and provide the wherewithal of our ideal life—should also furnish textbooks upon the practical art of housekeeping."⁵

Women's print culture, largely grounded in domesticity during the antebellum era, was the gateway for women to enter the public sphere. This chapter investigates the works of fiction, letters, essays, and political tracts of Sarah Hale, Catharine Beecher, and Lydia Maria Child and how they placed women into the public sphere. As these women became increasingly well known, they entered into public debates about social and political change. Hale and Beecher helped to promote the idea of true womanhood and labored to legitimize the cultural significance of women. The philosophies of Hale and Beecher suggested that following the dictates of true womanhood, particularly when it was read as white and middle class, would help women to exert their civic status. Despite personally practicing the ideology of true womanhood more closely than her counterparts, Child was more radical in her beliefs, and she engaged in activism beyond the traditional realm of women. Nevertheless, the radicalness stemmed from her understanding of true womanhood, the moral superiority of women, and their calling to enact the change necessary to bolster national greatness. All three of these authors used civic domesticity to justify the political engagement of women.

Race played an important yet understudied role in how women conceptualized womanhood. A true woman came from a place of privilege, but could privilege be obtained, and could it overcome race and class differences? Hale, Beecher, and Child were all opposed to slavery; however, they did not view African Americans in the same way. Hale and Beecher were colonizationists. Until at least the 1840s, women's efforts on behalf of colonization were seen to be benevolent rather than political, since there were few calls to change policies concerning the status of slavery. Beecher and Hale tended to view racial issues based on how they affected whites; thus, colonization was one way to alleviate the problems created by gradual emancipation. Free women of color were almost always considered as servants in white women's writings on domesticity; thus, the imagined audience for instruction on domestic management was the white middle-class woman. Unlike Hale and Beecher, Child was an abolitionist. The question of the status of slaves and free African Americans was considered to be political, making the defense of abolition a more transgressive belief than colonization. Child did not shy away from the issue and sought ways to influence people about antislavery politics; she even expressed a desire to vote in order to shape the national debate. By the end of the 1830s, Child had quit writing domestic advice and focused more exclusively on the issue of slavery. She believed that the respectability of womanhood was potentially available to any woman, regardless of race, and could assist in white acceptance in African American equality.

Hale's, Beecher's, and Child's influence was substantial and broad based. Hale's editorship of *Godey's* and Beecher's influence over female education were central not only to entrenching the ideology of true womanhood but also to providing it with political meaning. Child, who also wrote household advice, did not directly link domesticity to women's citizenship obligations to the state. Instead, she assumed a woman's natural right to political thought and pursued a lifetime of activism through her writing while also embracing the gender norms of the day that made women more persuasive. Even if individual women did not physically enter the public sphere, the surge in female print culture provided a platform for women to create a counterpublic to challenge women's lack of political influence. The architects of true womanhood reinforced the cultural code that defined women's lives, placed them within the context of race and class, and then magnified the significance of those norms.

THE EDITOR:
SARAH HALE (1788–1879)

Sarah Hale defined herself as a true daughter of New England, and it was a voice she often used in both her fiction and nonfiction. Sarah Josepha Buell was born in Newport, located in western New Hampshire. Hale was mostly educated at home with assistance from first her mother and later her college-educated brother. Hale believed that this lack of formal education had no negative consequences: "I owe my early predilection for literary pursuits to the teaching and example of my mother. We did not need the 'Infant School' to make us love learning."[6] Hale and Catharine Beecher both wrote about their intellectual mothers, whom they credited with influencing their own lifelong love of learning. This persuasive tactic not only legitimized their own academic pursuits but also served to illustrate the potential long arm of motherhood by linking women to the education of children.

The choice of a marriage partner or even the choice to remain single was one of the most significant influences on the nineteenth-century woman's future status. Sarah Buell, like fellow author Lydia Maria Child (née Francis), married an attorney. These two matches seemingly would protect both women's status as middle class. However, marriage did not financially protect either, and economic insecurity played a central role in launching their literary careers. Sarah Buell married David Hale in 1813, the day before her twenty-fifth birthday. Hale's marriage was apparently rewarding; she described it as a time of "unbroken happiness." Hale continued her intellectual development under her husband's tutelage: "We commenced immediately after our marriage a system of study which we pursued together."[7] Sarah Hale's emphasis on education in her autobiographical writing is no accident. She tied her intellectual development to her Dartmouth-educated brother and her legally trained husband. Because erudite men had sanctioned her mental improvement, Hale had the authority to promote education and the higher mental abilities of women.

David Hale's death in 1822 left Sarah in a lifelong state of mourning and with little money to ensure that she would be able to raise her five children without an additional source of income. Hale's first book was published under the name "a Lady of New Hampshire" and appeared after her husband's death with the assistance of his Masonic lodge for publication. *The Genius of Oblivion and Other Original Poems* (1823) might have been anonymously published, but Hale's authorship was no secret. The book was intended to raise money for the struggling widow and mother.[8] The collection was standard fare for the era. She opened with a dedication, followed by a lengthy epic poem and then a smattering of shorter poems dedicated to specific individuals, expressing various sentiments, or celebrating patriotic themes. Soon after the publication of *Genius*, Hale had a number of items published in the *Atlantic Monthly* and the *Literary Gazette*, as well as other smaller venues.[9] Her success with magazines set up the sale of her first novel, *Northwood*, published in 1827 to generally good reviews. A revised edition of the novel was released in 1852 that served as a response to *Uncle Tom's Cabin* and allowed Hale a chance to reintroduce her argument about regionalism and slavery during a more contentious time than its original publication.

Although today's popular tributes to Hale focus on her promotion of Thanksgiving as a national holiday and the nursery rhyme *Mary Had a Little Lamb*, the nineteenth-century woman would have known her for her editorship of *Godey's Lady's Book*. With the cultural cachet of longtime *Vogue* editor Anna Wintour, magnified by ten, Hale was the arbiter of femininity and fashion. Hale first began work as an editor for the *Ladies' Magazine* in 1827, the same year she published *Northwood*. In 1836 the *Ladies' Magazine and Literary Gazette* merged with *Godey's*, where Hale served as editor for an additional forty years.

It is difficult to overestimate the importance of *Godey's* to antebellum American culture.[10] Although paying subscribers were likely limited to white middle- and upper-class women with access to published materials, the readership of *Godey's* went far beyond its subscription base. Neighbors shared issues, and they were placed in public spaces. English professor Nicole Tonkovich explains that "as the magazine pioneered the use of illustrations, a reader need not even be literate to imagine herself addressed by its needlework patterns, engravings of domestic scenes, and fashion plates."[11] *Godey's* has remained in the collective memory long after it stopped publishing. For example, Laura Ingalls Wilder captured its importance in transferring eastern fashions to the western prairies in her popular *Little House* books. Caroline Ingalls pondered how much fabric she needed when making a skirt, since she had no idea if hoop skirts were still in fashion: "'I declare, I don't know,' Ma said, worrying about hoop skirts. 'Mrs. Boast had had a *Godey's Lady's Book* last year. If she had one now, it would decide the question.'"[12] The wide swath of readership for *Godey's* makes it easy to imagine a diverse audience, including free women of color, factory workers, domestic workers, seamstresses, rural women, and others, all seeking a change in status based on the pages of a women's magazine.

As editor of *Godey's*, Hale influenced how the ideology of true womanhood developed and what sort of authority it gave women. This authority was intended to be independent of politics and religion because publisher Louis Antoine Godey had declared those subjects off-limits in his magazine.[13] Each issue typically included a couple of articles signed by Hale, as well as the "Editor's Table" and "Editor's Book Table," which were unsigned but largely authored by Hale. Sarah Hale also influenced the selection of articles, poetry, and fiction that appeared in the pages of the magazine. In the January 1840 issue, Hale began a three-part series on domestic economy that was a mix of specific advice and recipes, as well as a justification of the importance of domesticity. This series predated the appearance of Catharine Beecher's *Treatise on Domestic Economy* by a little more than a year. The amount of print space devoted to the subject suggests its importance at this time. Commenting on Catharine Maria Sedgwick's novel *Means & Ends*, Hale touted the importance of cooking as an essential skill of the American wife and mother.[14]

Despite *Godey's* emphasis on the ornamental aspects of femininity, Hale was clearly beginning to reposition the ideas of American womanhood with the necessity of basic skills in running a household. As female education became more common, the doyens of domesticity sought to strike a balance between hearth, health, and head in the school curriculum. Hale undoubtedly supported female education; however, like many others during the antebellum era, she worried that women were putting refinement and education ahead of the domestic arts. This approach did not reflect an egalitarian turn in Hale's appreciation of class distinctions; instead, it affirmed them. A woman of means should not only make small talk in her parlor but also manage her staff in the kitchen. Writing in *Godey's*, Hale again embraced the sentiments expressed in Sedgwick's novel: "Italian and music are worthless accomplishments compared with the knowledge of bread-making."[15] As a mother of daughters, Hale's interest in female education was also personal. She sent her daughters to Catherine Fiske's Seminary for Young Ladies in Keene, New Hampshire, a boarding school with a national reputation. Fiske's school taught a mixture of traditional coursework, needlework, and at least some of the basics of the domestic arts. It is said that Fiske's "bread making was done on the scientific principles of chemistry," perhaps inspiring Hale's interest in women learning this art.[16] Hale did not expect women to bake their own bread on a regular basis; instead, she thought that knowledge allowed women to serve in a managerial role. Baking bread became a metaphor for all the skills a middle-class woman should have to remain in charge of her kitchen.

Sarah Hale thought women played the key role in determining the success of households and, by extension, the middle-class nation. In *Godey's* she explained: "It is usually in the failure of her part alone that the prospects of her family can be utterly blighted, and the whole happiness of domestic life marred and destroyed."[17] Given the importance of print culture to the antebellum public sphere, magazines like *Godey's* provided women with their own point of entry. Hale, Beecher, and similar authors seldom strayed from the cultural imaginings of the true woman, and within those constraints they argued that women were doing the work of nation building just like men. Yet even with the breadth of readership for domestic advice, authors did not necessarily challenge cultural norms. Instead, most reinforced those norms while cloaking them with civic significance. Women could and did claim citizenship from a less political perspective.

Sarah Hale believed that women could be political as long as they primarily served as helpmeets and labored on behalf of symbols and ideals as opposed to public policy. Before abolitionists became the most prolific organizers of ladies' fairs, Hale resoundingly endorsed these projects as the appropriate type of civic engagement for a young lady. In her 1835 book, *Traits of American Life*, Hale devoted a chapter to ladies' fairs. The types of fairs discussed were of a general charitable purpose, for example, to feed and clothe the poor, and were primarily local. Hale first addressed the objections people had to the public work of women and then proceeded to provide reasons why female participation was beneficial beyond mere fundraising. For example, she argued that the young ladies who produced the needlework for fairs typically had no need to perform such labor for themselves, "yet on such habits mainly depends the physical health of woman, and much of that cheerfulness of mind which makes her useful and agreeable at home."[18] Hale explained that the educated young woman should be conversant in "every department of womanly knowledge" so "she may truly exhibit sense, and taste, and elegance of fancy in her needle-work, as in reciting philosophy, quoting poetry, or playing the harp." Although Hale supported female education on the pages of *Godey's*, she feared that "in female education there is now danger from excess of mental culture. The mind is dragged and driven to make exertions beyond its abilities, and the constitution fails in the effort." Needlework provided a perfect antidote for the educational rigors experienced by girls. She concluded the essay with her unequivocal endorsement of fairs: "So far as Ladies' Fairs have relieved the rich from *ennui*, and the poor from suffering, they have done good, much good—and we hope they will be continued."[19] Hale's affiliation with middle- and upper-class concerns is evidenced by touting the benefits of the relief of women from boredom on an equal footing with feeding the poor.

Fine sewing and a concern for the afflicted seems to have been the extent of direct political action endorsed by Hale. In the chapter "Political Parties," Hale's story of Thankful Pope, who "lived and died an old maid, in consequence of a difference in political sentiment between herself and lover," was a cautionary tale for the politically aware young woman. Thankful tells the story of her failed romance to her two nieces. She describes her fiancé as being suitable in every way, until he changed his political affiliation. Aunt Thankful explains that "I made the sentiments of my party the standard of rectitude, and had George committed a murder, I should hardly have been more shocked than if he declared himself a republican."[20] Since he would not change his politics, Thankful sent her fiancé away; however, she always hoped that he would return. She told her nieces that she thought he might "throw himself at my feet and retract his political errors. But months and years passed on, and the next election still found him a republican."[21] Aunt Thankful expressed her contrition to her nieces about stubbornness, saying she could not bring herself to write him in case her advances were rejected. While one could read this short story as suggesting that strict adherence to party politics was wrong whether one was a man or a woman, Hale reveals that fiancé George happily resettled in Savannah and married after a few years. It is a cautionary tale because Thankful is punished for her beliefs by becoming an "old maid." Hale, via the voice of Thankful Pope, explains: "I do not say that ladies should abstain from all political reading or conversation, that they should take no interest in the character or condition of their country." Instead, the sin is female partisanship as Hale concludes that women's "influence should be expected to allay, not excite animosities: their concern should be for their whole country—not for a party."[22] For Hale, the true woman exercised her citizenship within the home. Instead of engaging in partisan politics, she soothed and calmed a divided nation from the comfort of her own hearth.

Like Catharine Beecher, Hale was both culturally outspoken and curiously apolitical, or at least against outright activism. In contrast, the more publicly timid Lydia Maria Child proclaimed big ideas. Hale's tendency was always moderation. She was against women's public speaking. A woman might recite Shakespeare, but "to mount the rostrum, and give utterance to her own views or opinions, was presumptuous, not to say indecent."[23] Female education was good if it did not overemphasize mental pursuits. Her household advice chided those who were overly frugal while also stressing that people should not live beyond their means. Hale's position on slavery is perhaps the most powerful example of this approach. She might have been antislavery, but Hale was not an abolitionist. She endorsed gradual emancipation, and her support for colonization revealed a hope that the biggest problem of the nineteenth century would literally go away. Hale wedded her views on race to her assertions about proper womanhood in a way that implicitly and explicitly raced the idealized woman. A true woman could engage in political influence but not explicit activism. Because Hale believed that the problem of race was solved by colonization, she never included women of color under the umbrella of true womanhood. For Hale, Black women never had the moral authority necessary to engage in political influence or claim civic status.

Sarah Hale's negative response to abolitionists grew over time as the movement became more active and, in her view, radical. Hale felt it important to put union before equality. Her book *Northwood*, originally published in 1827, was indicative of this view. Sometimes cited as the first American novel about slavery, the book is actually a novel that juxtaposes the imagined values of New England with those attributed to the South. For example, Hale included in the second chapter a portrait of the early days of a newly married couple. The vapid New Hampshire girl of nineteen who has jilted her solid New England farmer fiancé for a southern dandy from Charleston clashes with her new husband over slavery.[24] Sadly, this clash has nothing to do with the morality of slavery; instead, the young wife is frightened by the slaves and wants them to disappear, exclaiming, "I don't care where the creatures go, nor much what becomes of them, if they can only be out of my sight." Her new husband defends the practice of slavery as a cultural kindness because "they are contented and happy, and have no other home or country where they could be received."[25] The 1827 version of the novel offered several critiques of slavery delivered by different characters. Yet the emphasis was not on the suffering of those held in bondage; instead, it centered on the impact of slavery on the character of white Americans.

Northwood was reissued in 1852 in part as a response to *Uncle Tom's Cabin*.[26] The reissue was very similar to the original, although Hale added "a word to the reader." Hale placed the original publication within a historical context: "Northwood was written when what is now known as 'Abolitionism' first began seriously to disturb the harmony between the South and the North." Hale identified abolitionists as the source of sectional strife, not slavery itself: "No motives save the search for truth and obedience to duty prompted the sentiments expressed in this work."[27] The "truth" defended by Hale was the original compact of the Constitution, which recognized slavery and white supremacy. Because it was not in common use in 1827, the word "abolition" does not appear in the original version of the book. Despite the tone set in her introduction, it is surprising that the term is not more commonly used in the 1852 edition. Beyond the opening "word to the reader," the word "abolition" only occurs two other times in the book. Her novel ends with the protagonist, Sidney, born in Northwood but raised by his southern uncle and aunt, returning to Charleston with his New England bride: "They have resolved that every slave whose services are not needed to keep up the present income of the estate, shall be well fitted out and sent to Liberia. And thus, gradually, without disturbance to society, or danger of suffering to their servants, they hope to make them all eventually free, and prepared to do good by and with their freedom."[28] In the end, Sydney not only supports colonization but ensures the comfort of white society by "gradually, without disturbance," emancipating the family slaves.

Hale used her powers as the editor of *Godey's* to review books that shared her antiabolitionist/procolonization views. Given the publisher's prohibition of political topics in his magazine, the book review section was one place Hale could exert some influence. From 1852 to 1854 Hale did not include a single review of an antislavery book, including *Uncle Tom's Cabin*.[29] Her reissue of *Northwood* followed the serialization of *Uncle Tom's Cabin* in the *National Era* in 1851 and its appearance in book form in 1852. Hale's call for colonization at the end of *Northwood* is not altogether different from Harriet Beecher Stowe's decision to send many of her characters to Africa at the end of *Uncle Tom's Cabin*. However, the variance in how slavery is presented in the two books explains the different interpretations of the authors' intentions. Hale followed up the reissue of *Northwood* with *Liberia: or, Mr. Peyton's Experiments* in 1853. Despite the dwindling public support for colonization, Hale continued to promote the policy in her novels.

Hale as both an author and the editor of the most prominent American women's magazine of the nineteenth century was important in not only shaping the ideology of true womanhood but also giving that role an important social significance. Hale believed that women served the country by serving the home. Even though it was unstated, Hale's true woman was white and middle or upper class. Her commitment to colonization suggests she never envisioned women of color being integrated within the middle class. Thus, if domesticity and womanhood were understood by Hale as inherently attributes of white women, then African American women lacked the pathway for fulfilling their obligations of citizenship. Catharine Beecher shared many of Hale's views but was even more committed to presenting a nationalistic view of womanhood and was never shy about stating the importance of the white American woman.

THE EDUCATOR:
CATHARINE BEECHER (1800–1878)

An oft-repeated reflection of well-known nineteenth-century women was that their fathers either had longed for sons or had thought that their daughters were almost as good as sons. Margaret Fuller, Jessie Benton Frémont, and Elizabeth Cady Stanton were all raised and educated differently from the typical nineteenth-century girl. Louisa May Alcott and Laura Ingalls Wilder in their autobiographical writings of childhood served as a brother to their three sisters. Despite coming from a large family with many brothers, both Catharine Beecher and her sister Harriet Beecher Stowe also made these claims. First-born Catharine was close to her father and recalled that "my father never in his life praised me, although he used to say I was the best boy he had."[30] Harriet, who was separated by more than ten years in age from Catharine, remembered, "I, the sole little girl among so many boys, was sucked into the vortex of enthusiasm by father's well-pointed declaration that he wished 'Harriet was a boy, she would do more than any of them.'"[31] The exceptionalism suggested that by being the "best boy" or "like a boy," these nineteenth-century women gained permission to do more, but it did not give them license to be unfeminine.

For the Beecher children, managing the family's name and image was an important part of their mission and perhaps why Catharine and Harriet stressed their special relationship with their father. The rambunctious Beecher household described by Catharine, Harriet, and the other siblings seems inconsistent with the imagined family of the preeminent Calvinist intellectual and minister of the early nineteenth century. However, to fit within a more modern conception of family life, the Beecher home (whether accurate or constructed) was remembered as a relaxed and loving place. Harriet recalled the Beecher household as "inspired by a spirit of cheerfulness and hilarity," and her sister Catharine provided "a constant stream of mirthfulness."[32]

Catharine Beecher was driven to preserve her vision of a perfect gendered world. Her vision of femininity was complicated and often appeared contradictory. She viewed the domestic realm to be an exalted one for women, particularly if carried out in the proper way. She believed domesticity should be professionalized even if privately performed for one's own family. Whether a woman was engaged in domesticity for a husband, children, or extended family, she was also performing domesticity for the nation. Beecher also strongly believed in independence for single women. She hoped that their chosen profession, most appropriately teaching, would be compensated in such a way that single women could enjoy the comforts of a private home and the ability to practice domesticity even if only for themselves. Her goals for women often seemed conflicted; women should be subordinate to men, despite Beecher's own reluctance to subjugate herself. Beecher also advocated that female pursuits such as teaching and women's health should be overseen by women, suggesting that women were their own best experts. Some complain that Beecher was more engaged in self-promotion than she was in the promotion of women in general. Beecher likely saw the two as one and the same. Whether promoting herself as the principal of the Hartford Female Seminary, as an expert on domestic advice, or as the head of a national educational organization, Beecher established her own authority and then promoted women as central to making the United States exceptional, despite women's exclusion from political culture.

The death of her mother, Roxana Foote Beecher, when Catharine was sixteen led to Catharine's management of the family household. It was a position that gave her, a single woman without a home of her own, the authority to speak about domestic issues. Catharine Beecher, however, was not always a reliable narrator. Image management was her first priority. In various autobiographical essays, she kept her eye on maintaining credibility as an educational and domestic expert and preserving the exceptionalism of the Beecher family. Carefully chosen family stories were retold, and family members behaved in such a way as to serve as exemplars of true women and good citizens.

A few years after her father's second marriage, Catharine left the Beecher home in Litchfield, Connecticut, to found the Hartford Female Seminary. At age eighteen, younger sister Mary Beecher joined Catharine in Hartford, primarily as a teacher, but eventually she helped by keeping house. Projecting her own bias, Catharine wrote her brother, "Mary will try keeping house 5 or 6 weeks & if she can get along & likes it better than school I shall look for some one to take her place in school." Apparently certain of the choice Mary would make, Catharine finished the letter with the request "I hope that Mama & Aunt Home will look for a housekeeper for me in case Mary should conclude to go into school."[33] An antebellum home, even one for a few single women, could not run itself. Catharine recognized the need for help, but her priority was running the school. She had not yet internalized the civic importance of domesticity.

Teaching was fast becoming the preferred vocation for single women, and the promotion of education in the western United States became Beecher's primary cause. Teaching was a natural choice for Catharine. The family ran a school out of their East Hampton home to supplement Lyman Beecher's income. After moving to Litchfield, the family boarded students attending Miss Sarah Pierce's Litchfield Female Academy, a leading school for women at that time. With help from her brother Edward and sister Mary, Catharine founded the Hartford Female Seminary in 1824. The school started with seven students and expanded to several hundred before she left the seminary at the age of thirty-two. During that time the school grew from a hired room to a dedicated building with classrooms, lecture room, and study hall. Catharine saw the establishment of the school not only as a means for advancing women but also as a way of achieving some personal financial independence. She wrote her brother Edward, "Say to Papa and other friends that I am not going into partnership with any one. I shall be head & pay salaries & I mean to make money by it." She also requested that Edward place an advertisement, including a prospectus, for the school in the Boston papers, suggesting that she believed that the seminary would be more than a local "dame school."[34]

Prior to 1841, Beecher was best known as an educator, a daughter, and in some circles an opponent of women's public advocacy for abolition. With the publication of *A Treatise on Domestic Economy*, Beecher felt the need to boost her credibility as an expert in domesticity. Because she never had a home of her own, most of Beecher's post-*Treatise* writings mentioned her early training in housewifery. Perhaps such credentials were necessary, given a bemused letter written by her cousin Elizabeth Elliot Foote: "If it were not for these maiden ladies instructing the married ones how to keep house and take care of children I don't know what would become of us."[35] Even after the enormous success of both *A Treatise* and *The American Woman's Home*, published in 1869 and cowritten with her sister Harriet, Catharine continued to emphasize her credentials. In an 1874 work, Beecher wrote in the third person: "Much in those pages was offered, not only as a result of her own experience, but as what had obtained the approbation of some of the most judicious mothers and housekeepers in the nation."[36]

Catharine Beecher's *Treatise on Domestic Economy* sealed her renown as not only an educator but also a leading expert in household advice. She produced both the *Treatise* and a companion recipe book in Cincinnati while she was working with the Western Female Institute. The first book was designed "as a textbook for schools for young women, and other as a Receipt Book for all kinds of cooking and other family matters."³⁷ It would be shortsighted to think of this book as only a text, as it was one of the best-selling guides to domestic labor in the nineteenth century. In the first years after publication Beecher stressed that future profits would go to her plan to train teachers for the West. When soliciting support for her education project she also pushed sale of her book: "The 'Domestic Economy' was written in order to raise means to forward this enterprise. All the profits are devoted to it & therefore whatever your society can do to give the book currency will be a contribution to the object. I am anxious however that this fact should in no way be made public."³⁸

Like Sarah Hale, Beecher believed that domestic skills were a critical part of female education. For Beecher, this was a response to two very different approaches to female education, one that was purely academic and the other that was little more than a finishing school. She saw the importance of teaching girls chemistry and math within the context of domesticity as key to professionalizing domestic labor. The higher branches of learning were most valuable when they served the household. This approach was also rhetorically strategic. It served to answer opposition claims that girls did not need instruction in math and science or that young women were not capable of learning such subjects. Unlike the turn to female education based on republican motherhood, attaching education to true womanhood meant women learned for their own improvement and civic status as opposed to for their sons.

Catharine Beecher had a fairly narrow vision of what constituted suitable female employment. Teaching, domestic service, wife, mother, and author were all appropriate for women. The inclusion of the paid positions of teacher and domestic demonstrates a broader recognition of class differences than many of her contemporaries and highlights her concern that some women must support themselves. By 1838 Beecher was already a public figure, and she worked to see her sister Harriet become a recognized and successful author. Seeking outlets for her sister's work, Beecher turned to a former Hartford associate, author Lydia Sigourney: "Since I have been collecting Harriets [sic] pieces it has occurred to me that as every body who wants such sort of articles comes to you, that you might dispose of these pieces more profitably (for it is a money making effort) than she or I could do at this distance from the head quarters of literature."³⁹ Catharine managed Harriet's early career, providing help even when it had not been requested and even christening the new author Harriet Beecher Stowe so that the Beecher name would remain in the public spotlight.

Lyman Beecher's appointment to head the Lane Theological Seminary in Cincinnati ushered Catharine back to the family home and strengthened her ideas about domesticity. Beecher's years at her Hartford school were the only time that she did not live with family members or friends as a guest. Beecher left Connecticut to start a new school in Cincinnati and initiate her plan to educate women for teaching positions in the West. She also became more overtly concerned with the professionalization and financial stability of single women. Her Western Female Institute had the goal of training women for long-term careers in education, as opposed to catering to women who might teach a term or two.

Beecher's time in Cincinnati also strengthened her opinions on antislavery politics. Since at least her Hartford days, Catharine Beecher had been a supporter of colonization. As abolition became more prominent as a social movement, she became further removed from its goals and practices. Antislavery politics, particularly those of a student group led by Theodore Weld, challenged Lyman Beecher's tenure at Lane.[40] Cincinnati, a border town in a free state, kept antislavery politics at the forefront of controversy. Catharine Beecher, always willing to express her opinion, involved herself with antislavery politics beyond the Lane Seminary and the local scene in Cincinnati. She decided to take on abolition politics by criticizing women's participation in the movement; in particular, Beecher was opposed to the activism of Angelina Grimké. Born in South Carolina, Grimké (1805–79) was the daughter of a slaveholder. Angelina and her older sister, Sarah, left South Carolina and eventually settled in Philadelphia, where they joined the Quaker faith for a time. There, the sisters became involved in antislavery politics. Angelina eventually became an agent for the American Anti-Slavery Society. Grimké was not just any female activist. She was among the original female speakers for the society and had trained with former Lane Seminary student Theodore Weld. Grimké met Weld in 1836, and they were married in 1838, the day before the Second Anti-Slavery Convention of American Women began. Beecher lashed out against Grimké Weld on two separate levels. Beecher challenged the propriety of public female abolition advocacy and more generally challenged the work of abolition.

As the ideology of true womanhood became entrenched, literary women interpreted the implications of civic domesticity differently. Catharine Beecher argued that abolition activists were falsely flattering women as to their political power. Although she believed that women's work within the home was a key component of nation building, she did not believe that women should partake in partisan politics. The popular claim that women were morally superior to men because of their piety and purity did not legitimate more overt political activities, according to Beecher; instead, women should use their influence within the home. Despite her single and independent status, Beecher embraced the traits of submission and domesticity for women at home. Female antislavery activists would likely counter that they were not involved in partisan politics. Petitioning, fairs, and even public speaking and writing were all forms of moral suasion and apolitical, even if these efforts were directed at politicians. Beecher believed that women's civic status was best exerted when they sought to influence rather than act. She was particularly concerned with female participation within the abolition movement as women became intimately engaged in the most partisan issue of the day: "The moment woman begins to feel the promptings of ambition, or the thirst for power, her aegis of defense is gone." Beecher argued that involvement in partisan politics stripped women of social protection and cultural influence because these were based on a woman "retaining her place as dependent and defenseless, and making no claims, and maintaining no right but what are the gifts of honour, rectitude and love."[41] The modern reader might interpret Beecher as being opposed to women's political influence. Instead, for Beecher it was a question about how that influence was deployed.

Beecher's debate with Angelina Grimké over the appropriate role of women in the antislavery movement cemented her status as a public figure. In one of several contradictory positions taken by Beecher, she publicly engaged Grimké in a debate by claiming that women should remain in their appropriate sphere. In *An Essay on Slavery and Abolitionism with Reference to the Duty of American Females*, Beecher addressed Grimké: "Our acquaintance and friendship give me a claim to your private ear; but there are reasons why it seems more desirable to address you, who now stands before the public as an advocate of Abolition measures, in a more public manner."[42] Beecher made the rhetorically strategic argument that most people would agree with the principles espoused by Grimké, but they would not agree with her method. This moved the debate away from the morality of slavery to female propriety and gave Beecher the opportunity to analyze the public role of women. During the 1830s, Beecher also held a more moderate position on slavery by advocating gradual emancipation. This allowed her the sympathetic position of denouncing slavery while simultaneously defending the status quo. Beecher made arguments against both abolition and women's involvement in political issues. She urged "against joining the Abolition Society" because its "character and measures are not either peaceful or Christian in tendency but they are those which tend to generate party spirit, denunciation, recrimination, and angry passions."[43] Beecher's description of the abolitionists was the antithesis of accepted white female benevolence. It was also the antithesis of the Garrisonian approach of moral suasion, which was in many ways an inherently feminine approach to politics. Instead, Beecher advocated that women should act quietly and privately; they should not publicly engage in policy change.

Catharine Beecher was not against all forms of female organizing. She herself belonged to a literary society made up of men and women, had allowed the formation of benevolent groups at her Hartford Female Academy, and eventually saw female clubs as the key to financing her western education plans. Antislavery societies, however, were clearly another matter. She explained that a woman could organize "among her own sex, to assist her in her appropriate offers of piety, charity, maternal and domestic duty." However, being involved with "party conflict—whatever obliges her in any way to exert coercive influences throws her out of her appropriate sphere. If these general principles are correct, they are entirely opposed to the plan of arraying females in any Abolition movement."[44] Despite persuasive tactics such as the motto "Am I not a woman and a sister?" that sought to frame abolition work as benevolence between women, Beecher remained convinced that abolition was too political for the fair sex and that women should remain in their prescribed sphere.

Beecher chose to single out petitioning as an action engaged in by abolitionist women that violated proper female decorum, despite the fact that petitions were the only direct political tool open to women and had been used since the American Revolution. There was also the potential of privacy with a petition, as it could be signed at home, in church, or within gender-segregated benevolence societies. Beecher argued that "if petitions from females will operate to exasperate; if they will be deemed to be obtrusive, indecorous, and unwise by those to whom they are addressed," then "it is neither appropriate nor wise, nor right, for a woman to petition for the relief of oppressed females."[45] Beecher explained that instead, women should work indirectly. She reasoned that if women "by arguments and persuasions, can induce them [men] to petition, all the good that can be done by such measures will be secured. But if females cannot influence their nearest friends, to urge forward a public measure in this way, they surely are out of their place, attempting to do it themselves."[46]

Although her belief seems illogical today, Beecher believed that women could best protect their civic standing (and influence) by limiting their public participation. On the one hand, this belief is not surprising. For the first time, many average women were engaged overtly in political petitioning for the end of the slave trade in Washington, D.C. The success of the movement had led to a gag order on reading the petitions in Congress, and newspapers across the country covered the debate over the slave trade and the gag rule. The antislavery press endorsed the propriety of petitioning by women, suggesting that there was some public discussion about this political expression. Beecher's negative reaction to petitions was surprising when one considers her personal history. She organized and participated in an earlier petition campaign to prevent the removal of the Cherokee from their land in 1828. While Beecher seems to have forgotten this in her 1837 essay, she proudly discussed her activism almost fifty years later in her autobiographical *Educational Reminiscences and Suggestions*. She described meeting a missionary who thought "American women might save these poor, oppressed natives" and wrote that he asked her to "devise some method of securing such intervention." Beecher explained that she sought the help and guidance of some influential women of Hartford after writing her circular *To Benevolent Women of the United States*: "The result exceeded our most sanguine expectations. A simultaneous movement occurred, public meetings were held in all the cities to which our circulars went, and many other towns and cities followed the example."[47] It is worth considering that Catharine Beecher's narrow view of women's rights was influenced by her dislike of abolitionist politics and thus, by extension, female activists. In an effort to remain philosophically consistent, Beecher decided to attack the method of politics rather than the message.

In order to win over influential women, Beecher played to their vanity. Almost like the doctrine of the elect, Catharine explained that smart women understood the wisdom of maintaining their place in society: "For the more intelligent a woman becomes, the more she can appreciate the wisdom of that ordinance that appointed her subordinate station, and the more her taste will conform to the graceful and dignified retirement and submission it involves."[48] Like a good Calvinist demonstrating their religious status, a woman would behave in the manner prescribed by Beecher to prove her intelligence. The coarse and ignorant woman did not understand this: "An ignorant, a narrow-minded, or a stupid woman, cannot feel nor understand the rationality, the propriety, or the beauty of this relation, and she it is, that will be most likely to carry her measures by tormenting, when she cannot please, or by petulant complaints or obtrusive interference in matters which are out of her sphere and which she cannot comprehend."[49] In other words, Beecher believed that a true woman would recognize that her power and influence were within the home and not in politics. The activist woman could be ignored, because her behavior demonstrated her ignorance.

Beecher advocated using women as the solution to education problems in the United States. She believed that education was the patriotic duty of women, whether they served as teachers or helped finance the mission. Beecher worked hard to promote her plan for western schools, utilizing former students and the contacts that the Beecher name could snare. Writing to a former Hartford student and close friend of sister Harriet, Catharine explained her plan: "I am going to try to present this emergency to the ladies of intelligence & benevolence.... If I can [raise] enough to establish one or two High Schools to serve at the same time as *Teachers Homes*—I am sure I can interest ladies in the plan [if] I could meet them."[50] Beecher eventually moved beyond letter writing to, paradoxically, public lectures to promote her western education plan. Before she was a published author, Susan Warner described seeing Catharine Beecher speak about her plan to send teachers to the West: "Whatever anticipations might have been formed of somewhat bold, unbecoming, unwomanly in the exhibition, they were not fulfilled." She explained that "Miss Beecher made a most agreeable impression on me."[51]

Catharine Beecher argued that the young teachers going west would spread not only literacy and morality but also her domestic ideal, bringing civic domesticity and women's nation building full circle. She had teachers take copies of her *Treatise* to frontier towns to train both mothers and daughters. In her *Educational Reminiscences* Beecher reprinted several testimonials for her book in the form of letters to her about the writers' teaching experiences in the West. Books of all types were scarce, and books of domestic advice seemed to be particularly valued: "I would say that books might be loaned here to some extent with advantage. I have lent your *Domestic Economy* around, and have received applications for six copies from those who will pay."[52] Another teacher reported, "I have read your *Domestic Economy* through to the family, one chapter a day. They like it, and have adopted some of your suggestions to regard both *order* and to *health*."[53] Beecher's educational legacy is a mixed one. She was never able to achieve her goal of an endowed school for women. However, for better or for worse, she tied home economics to female education and made teaching the professional work of women.

Like those of many white members of the antebellum middle class, Catharine Beecher's views on race were conflicted and her actions often contradictory. The Beecher family engaged African American indentured servants from a young age (certainly too young to contract out their own labor). Beecher was involved with the colonization movement during the 1820s, although her work was less public at this time. Like many colonizationists, Beecher was against slavery but not comfortable with immediate emancipation, which might shift racial hierarchies in New England. A letter to her brother Edward revealed her interest in training a young man of color as a doctor and have him immigrate to Liberia. Beecher offered to board the young man in exchange for his household labor and asked Edward to find "a *black* boy or young man between 14 & 19—steady in his habits—who can read, write & cypher—who has a taste for knowledge & if possible to be found one who is pious. Can you help us in finding such a one—it is of great importance that the professional men of that colony should be Africans."[54] In a follow-up letter she wrote, "I have probably found a young man of colour who is pious to educate for a physician—a plan about which I wrote you some time ago. This arrangement will be a great comfort to Aunt E—as he is competent to do all the providing marketing & c."[55] Catharine equated African Americans with domestic service. Growing up in the early nineteenth century with young Black indentured servants might have been the extent of her experience with people of color. It is clear that while Beecher was interested in seeing the young man educated in medicine, she also was determined to derive labor for his board.

In the 1830s Catharine Beecher was opposed to many of the activities for racial uplift that white abolitionists were engaged in. Whether this aversion was based on her colonizationist beliefs (uplift should occur outside the United States), disagreements with abolitionists based on her father's experiences at the Lane Seminary, inherent racism, or some sort of combination of these factors, it is clear that her differences with abolitionists were not solely based on gender. In fact, gender decorum likely served as a way to cover more substantial feelings about racial difference and hierarchy.

In her *Essay on Slavery and Abolitionism*, Beecher criticized several specific projects to improve educational opportunities for free people of color in the North. In particular, she singled out the plans for an African American college in New Haven, as well as Prudence Crandall's school in Connecticut for African American girls. Beecher was quick to state that she was not opposed to education; instead, she had misgivings about how this benevolence should be carried out: "If a prudent and benevolent female had selected almost any village in New England, and commenced a school for coloured females, in a quiet, appropriate, and unostentatious way, the world would never have heard of the case, except to applaud her benevolence, and the kindness of the villagers, who aided her in the effort." Beecher focused on the curriculum, which included piano, drawing, and other lessons that she thought were unnecessary, stating that there were not "a dozen coloured families in New England in such pecuniary circumstances, that if they were whites it would not be thought ridiculous to attempt to give their daughters such a course of education."[56] Although much of New England took proud ownership of their antislavery work, many Connecticut residents wished to see postemancipation race work occur elsewhere. Racism in Cincinnati, where Beecher was living at the time, did not create sympathy in her; instead, it added to her distaste for the conflict surrounding abolition. Like Sarah Hale, Beecher placed the blame for racial unrest on activists and African Americans rather than on whites who opposed abolition.

Notwithstanding her opposition to women's work with abolition, Beecher did believe in the importance of female influence throughout her adult life, an acceptance of civic domesticity. From the introduction of her *Treatise*, in which she touted the unique influence of the American woman, to the dedication of her autobiographical *Educational Reminiscences*, she highlighted the domestic role of women. Beecher firmly believed that women had an important, although subordinate, role in the management of the house and building the nation. The woman does "much of the contriving, executing and governing in the family state, and in almost every department; while the husband or father listens to her results with the veto power which in most sensible families is seldom used."[57]

Catharine Beecher's views on female citizenship were more complicated than what she represented in her *Treatise on Domestic Economy*. Despite a busy life that often carried her beyond the traditional woman's sphere, Beecher did embrace the home as the place where typical women could exert their influence. Beecher's vision of the role of the female head of household was based on two critical assumptions: first, household management was difficult and could not be learned by just anyone, and second, the well-ordered middle-class home was what made the United States unique. The creation of that perfect middle-class home was the citizenship obligation that white women fulfilled for family and country. Cloaked in similar rhetoric that would eventually be labeled manifest destiny, the function of households and families was to tame the nation and propagate white middle-class values. Because white women "managed" their homes rather than performing all of the labor, like Sarah Hale, Beecher's vision further divided leaders and laborers, at least within the kitchen and parlor. Beecher's goal to professionalize housework by linking it to math and science meant that while any woman could engage in domestic service, including African Americans and immigrants, only an elite, educated, and presumably white woman could manage a home. As the separation between home and production grew, Beecher assigned middle-class white women with the job of cultural production, thus differentiating between civic domesticity and domestic labor. Her lifelong plan to educate the West had as much or more to do with giving white women the tools to practice civic domesticity, whether they were married or single, as it did with educating boys to be good citizens and public actors.

THE ACTIVIST:
LYDIA MARIA CHILD (1802–1880)

Lydia Maria Child was one of the most influential women of the nineteenth century due to her enormous publishing record, which addressed the significant antebellum era reform issues, including the status of Native Americans, slavery, and a variety of women's reform issues. Sometimes Child was warmly embraced by the public as the ideal woman, as demonstrated through her writings for children, wives, and mothers. More overtly political in her writing than Hale and Beecher, Child experienced periods of public vilification for her views.

Despite limited formal education, Child was a voracious reader and engaged in a correspondence with her older, college-educated brother about literature, beginning in her teen years and continuing throughout her life. It is not surprising that she felt called to be a writer. Like Sarah Hale, Child recognized that writing was one of the few options available to a woman of her class status that enabled her to support herself. Child worked as a teacher prior to her marriage and used her writing to supplement that income. Her first novel was not a money maker, but it did lead her to employment with the *Juvenile Miscellany*, a children's magazine that netted her approximately $300 per year in the 1820s.[58] After marriage, Child found herself often required to be the primary earner for both herself and her husband. Writing and editing allowed the couple to establish a modest and genteel household. Child, however, not only engaged in the bread-and-butter writing of short stories and domestic advice but also authored significant political works.

Given her relatively limited experience in keeping house, it is surprising that Child turned to domestic advice as the route to financial security. Although her first novel, *Hobomok, a Tale of Early Times* (1824), was a critical success, it did not net her much of a profit, given that at that time most new authors had to front the publishing expenses for a first novel, and publishers were often slow to reimburse them. *The American Frugal Housewife* was a departure for the author of a novel and the editor of a children's magazine. However, Child found a niche within household advice. The success of the *Juvenile Miscellany* acquainted enough mothers with her name that they willingly sought domestic advice from her. *The American Frugal Housewife* was much more than a mere collection of recipes and soon after publication was a success. One review asked, "Does anyone doubt her success? Let ten editions of the [American] Frugal Housewife answer such unbelievers. No book, so little like a novel, or a poem, ever had such a run."[59] *The American Frugal Housewife* provided the Child household with a good income in its first years of publication. Child earned approximately $2,000 in the first two years and even managed to publish the book in foreign markets.[60] In 1839, a decade after its original publication, Child was still able to use the yearly proceeds from the book to pay off debts and interest on notes incurred by a failed antislavery gift annual.[61]

Child followed her success with *The Mother's Book*. Although childless, as the editor of a children's magazine, the twenty-nine-year-old author had the credibility with her reading public to appear an authority on child-rearing. Child followed the trend of expanding the importance of motherhood beyond the individual family unit in her dedication: "To American mothers, of whose intelligence and discretion the safety and prosperity of our Republic much depend."[62] The republican mother of the federal era had the responsibility of ensuring that her sons were good citizens; the true woman, however, had her own civic obligation of ensuring the good standing of the nation. Child's early books provided a bridge between the two ideologies. Despite the publication date and unlike *The American Frugal Housewife*, in many ways the advice in this book is quite modern. It veers away from a harsh Calvinist approach to childhood and emphasizes the intellectual development of children. Child reinforced the need to raise children that are educated, confident, and healthy by providing advice on child-rearing from infancy to the teen years. The book was a popular success. Writing to her sister-in-law, Child exclaimed, "It is selling with astonishing rapidity. They cannot get another edition ready soon enough."[63] Both *The Mother's Book* and *The American Frugal Housewife* were written during the rise of domestic consumerism. What was once useful advice for a particular segment of the population by the mid-1830s had become less desired. Whether women were middle class or merely aspiring to that status, they began to seek advice that matched a more consumer-based model. Instead of updating her advice books, by the end of the 1830s Child's writing shifted away from the home and became more closely related to her political activism.

Unlike most authors of domestic advice who did not have to perform their own housework, Child was typically alone in her household chores. The Childs, who spent the bulk of the marriage in financial straits, often lived in boardinghouses. This meant that Lydia typically would only oversee a few rooms and no kitchen. But even within those constraints, Child herself performed the relatively limited domestic labor that was left to a woman not keeping her own home. On the occasions that the Childs rented a home she seldom had significant outside help. Her letters were full of examples of her housework, which she often portrayed as drudgery, while Hale and Beecher could exalt such labor because they seldom performed it themselves.

Despite the antebellum glorification of the domestic realm, housework clearly was not personally uplifting to Child. Because she and her husband lived on the financial edge of the middle class, housework was a chore that took her away from the writing that she and David Child needed to sustain their lifestyle. For Child, the rare opportunities for additional household help were a boon, as reflected in a gleeful letter written to her brother: "For the first time these six weeks, I have somebody in the kitchen to do my work; and there is a whole boys' school set loose in my brain, kicking up heels, throwing up caps, hurrahing."[64] Less expensive than owning or renting a home, boarding was still costly for a couple living on the brink of financial ruin, and letting a room or two would not lend itself to the type of entertaining expected for respectable activists: "David and I were both startled at the idea of $4 a week, not including dinner. Cannot a cheaper place be procured? He merely wants what is comfortable and respectable." Attempts to establish a self-sufficient rural household never ended well for the couple, as Child explained in the same letter: "We have considerable delay in selling the animals horse cow & c.... This perpetual breaking up makes me very sad. I do *so* long for a settled home, where we can both grow old together in peace!"[65] When work opportunities forced Lydia and David to live separately, like Catharine Beecher, Lydia became a perpetual houseguest.

From 1838 through 1841, Lydia and David lived in Northampton, Massachusetts, where they tried to farm sugar beets. The endeavor was purely based on their activism, as opposed to an interest or background in farming. The Childs hoped to replace sugar produced through slave labor as a way of applying economic pressure on the South, a clear indication of how food choice could have political meaning. Lydia Child was unhappy during her time in Northampton. They tried both renting rooms in town and living on their rented farmland. Both options left Lydia feeling isolated. She found the community to be politically and socially conservative, with some residents outwardly hostile to her abolitionist activism. The couple could afford only sporadic help with the work on the farm. Lydia found herself engaged in labor both indoors and out. Besides the physical toll the work took on her, the experiment was also a financial failure, driving the Childs further into debt. Without the budget for help on the farm or in the house, Lydia accepted a job editing a paper in New York City and left David to wrap up the sugar beet venture.

During the 1830s, Lydia became friends with Angelina Grimké Weld. This camaraderie was likely prompted by the shared experience of public women performing private tasks. Despite the gravity of the women's public work for abolition, the mundane labor of everyday life provided moments of shared levity: "I must stop to boast a little, and crow over you. I have cut and made a vest for Mr. C., cut and made a pair of pantaloons; cut and made a frock coat. There now! Do you presume to hold a candle to me?"[66] Child was often troubled by how women were viewed by society, something she shared in her letters to Grimké Weld: "Deeply, deeply do I feel the degradation of being a woman—not the degradation of being what *God* made woman, but what *man* made her."[67] Child's complex internalization of true womanhood created a desire for both a stable home and intellectual (and financial) opportunities.

Unlike Hale and Beecher, Child was an early supporter of women's suffrage. She was particularly interested in the 1856 presidential election and inspired by Jesse Benton Frémont, the wife of the Republican candidate, John Charles Frémont. "What a shame the women can't vote!" she wrote. "We'd carry our 'Jessie,' into the White House on our shoulders, wouldn't we? Never mind! Wait a while! Woman stock is rising in the market. I shall not live to see women vote, but I'll come and rap at the ballot box. Won't you?" Perhaps a bit disingenuously she continued, "I never was bitten by politics before, but such mighty issues are depending on this election that I cannot be indifferent."[68] Child made similar claims in other letters that year and peppered her correspondence with references to the election. In a letter to her husband, Child wrote: "I do long to have you back. Voting day will bring you, of course. If you don't come, I shall put on your old hat and coat, and vote for you."[69] She wrote another excited letter to two female friends: "For the first time in my life, I am a *little* infected with *political* excitement. For the sake of suffering Kansas, and future freedom in peril, I *do* long to have Frémont elected. Don't *you*? Let's *vote!*"[70] In an unusually gossipy letter to a friend, Child criticized a dandy who was uninvolved in politics but planning to cast his "virgin" vote for Frémont: "It was pleasant to learn that he had anything 'virgin' left to swear by. What a Rip! To lie sleeping fifty years, dreaming of kid gloves, embroidered vests, and perfumed handkerchiefs, taking it for granted that his country was all the while going forward in a righteous and glorious career." Despite the levity of the letter, her frustration came through when she complained that a disengaged man could vote "while earnest souls like you and me must await the results in agonizing inaction."[71] Child, like so many other northern women, was particularly invested in the 1856 presidential election. They expressed a concern for their own political rights in a way that female backers of William Henry Harrison did not sixteen years before. Child's lack of civic status coupled with paying taxes and being the family breadwinner troubled her throughout her adult life. To her attorney friend Ellis Gray Loring she explained, "I mean to petition the Legislature to exempt me from *taxes* or grant me the privilege of *voting*. Oh What a sex you are! It's time you were turned out of office. *High* time. You've been captains long enough. It's *our* turn now."[72] The link between women's rights and abolition was explosive in the late 1830s and the beginning of the next decade. Child often found the controversy difficult to negotiate and remained focused publicly on her antislavery work.

The importance of Child as a public advocate for antislavery politics is difficult to gauge. She certainly did not shy away from controversy. Her *Appeal in Favor of That Class of Americans Called Africans* (1833), a petition to allow interracial marriage, and correspondence with Virginia governor Henry Wise over the status of John Brown demonstrated a willingness to engage difficult public issues. However, despite her beliefs, Child managed to keep one foot in the parlor and another within the world of radical activism. Her gentle editorship of the *National Anti-Slavery Standard*, which targeted the reluctant abolitionist, satisfied few Garrisonians but perhaps served the purpose of providing a moderating voice pushing more people toward abolition. Whether she was being coy or truthful, Child was described as politically influential regardless of her personal intent: "The Democratic papers accused me of trying to influence the state election then pending. The fun of it is, that I did not know there was an election. . . . I know much better who leads the orchestras than who governs the State."[73] Although Child might have stayed out of partisan politics, she was committed to antislavery activism and organized several petition drives to the state legislature of Massachusetts, as well as to Congress.

Child physically avoided the public spotlight. She wrote, served as a delegate rather than a speaker at conventions, and worked as the editor of a newspaper. Child seldom stood before the public to express her opinions, refusing to engage in public lectures. However, she had no disagreement with other women speaking publicly, and she supported their forays into the public sphere. "I thought of you several times while Angelina was addressing the committee of the Legislature," she wrote a friend. "It was a spectacle of the greatest moral sublimity I ever witnessed. The house was full to overflowing." Child portrayed Grimké as being swept up in the moment of her public performance: "For a moment a sense of the immense responsibility resting on her seemed almost to overwhelm her. She trembled and grew pale. But this passed quickly, and she went on to speak gloriously, strong in utter forgetfulness of herself and in her own earnest faith in every word she uttered."[74] The claim of "moral sublimity" suggests that Child considered the public work of abolition an important and sacred duty. However, she remained reluctant to appear in public despite a willingness to attach her name to controversial written documents. Child never clearly articulated the reason for this reluctance; she might have merely faced a normal fear of public speaking. For most nineteenth-century women, this fear would never be noticed. But because of her fame and the spotlight put on female speakers, Child was constantly asked to speak and make public appearances, requests she refused.

Lydia was often engaged in petitioning, which served as one way to bridge the public/private sphere gap. She was involved in the first large female petition drive to end the slave trade in Washington, D.C., but she also petitioned to remove laws outlawing interracial marriage and to prevent the annexation of Texas. Yet the interactive aspects of petitioning were distasteful to Child, even when she was working with David: "My husband and I are busy in the most odious of all tasks, that of getting signatures to petitions. We are resolved that the business shall be done in this town [Northampton, Massachusetts] more thoroughly than it has been heretofore. But, 'Oh Lord, sir!'"[75] Perhaps her reluctance to be a public speaker was justified. Angelina Grimké Weld had faced not only ridicule and criticism but also the threat of physical endangerment. Child herself faced public criticism for her writings. When the press was not sympathetic to Child, they undercut her by attacking her husband. In 1841 the *Alexandria (Va.) Gazette* wrote under the title "The Gray Mare," "We have received an Abolition paper from New York City, called the 'National Anti-Slavery Standard,' of which Lydia Maria Child is 'editor,' and her husband, David Lee Child, 'assistant editor.'"[76] This was a topic of attack that troubled Child. When singled out as the only editor of the *Anti-Slavery Standard*, she bristled: "My peculiar situation is sufficiently disagreeable to me, without adding anything which seems like giving me the superiority over my gifted and beloved husband."[77]

Child participated in antislavery fairs, a form of activism that was considered appropriate for a woman of her class and status. In a letter to Louisa Loring, she wrote, "Since I came here [her father's home] I have been as busy as a bird building her nest. Writing, pasting, sewing, and knitting—sometimes for myself, sometimes for the Fair."[78] To her sister-in-law she explained, "You have doubtless learned the success of our Fair from the Liberator. My cradle-quilt sold for $5."[79] Despite her forays into petitioning and fairs, central to the ideas of civic domesticity, Child always returned to writing as her preferred means of political expression. It gave her a voice but also provided her with the shelter and shield of home and her femininity that public appearances would not. She believed that reform writing helped boost women's status and was particularly impressed with Harriet Beecher Stowe: "Mrs. Stowe's truly great work, 'Uncle Tom's Cabin,' has also done much to command respect for the faculties of women."[80] Because her writing was politically motivated, Child saw other reform literature in this light and as a respectable and useful means of persuasion.

Like many other women, by the 1830s, abolition had become Child's central cause. Women were encouraged to join the movement by William Lloyd Garrison, and he worried that women "undervalue[d] their own power, or through a misconception of duty" excused themselves from participation.[81] Some women felt more comfortable participating in women's antislavery organizations. Child was an early member of the Boston Female Anti-Slavery Society, although her dislike of single-sex organizations caused her to shy away from many of the group's activities.[82] In declining an invitation to the Third Anti-Slavery Convention of American Women, she wrote: "I will not disguise that I do not want to go to the convention.... I never have entered very earnestly into the plan of female conventions and societies. They always seemed to me like half a pair of scissors."[83] Lydia engaged in debates about slavery in her private letters and stories for children and by donating her writings to fundraising gift annuals, but she would not speak publicly for the cause. The *Appeal in Favor of That Class of Americans* was her boldest statement to date on slavery but was not followed with a more vigorous public performance of her political views. While Angelina Grimké tested the waters of activism by first publishing and then becoming a speaker, Child's often radical politics were limited to the written word. Case in point, on behalf of the Boston Female Anti-Slavery Society, Child agreed to author the "Address to Colored Americans," as well as a second document "prepared by her to Northern Legislators, both of which were accepted by the Convention and published by them for circulation."[84] Child, however, did not wish to attend the convention as an official delegate of the Boston group. She preferred to remain hidden behind her pen and never became the public face of the Boston society.

It wasn't a fear of controversy that stopped Child from speaking out. Her *Appeal in Favor of That Class of Americans* was a bold statement about emancipation, race, and race relations. The book, a departure from her domestic advice, created a new public persona for Child. She was already a public figure, so her new status as an activist put her safe persona as a purveyor of domesticity at risk. Not only did she seek to challenge slavery in this book, but, more significantly, she challenged her New England neighbors' views of race, integration, and the suitability of African Americans for citizenship.

Timing is important in understanding the significance of Child's *Appeal*. The promise of gradual emancipation was coming to fruition in the North, meaning northern whites were newly experiencing the consequences of emancipation, although their anxieties about this coming change had long been exposed in public culture. Free people of color began to seek educational and employment opportunities. Black institutions were established, especially churches, that challenged white assumptions about African American spiritual and intellectual capabilities. Within the span of a few short years, David Walker's *Appeal to the Colored Citizens of the World* was published, and although *Freedom's Journal* had folded, William Lloyd Garrison's *The Liberator* not only supported immediate emancipation but also reported the activities and achievements of free Blacks in the North. In her *Appeal*, Child openly challenged the motives and outcomes of colonization, called for social integration, and even suggested that interracial marriage should be a private choice rather than regulated by legislation.

It was not the act of writing or even the challenges she posed to white supremacy that stirred public controversy. Instead, the fact that Child was seemingly engaged in partisan politics as an advocate damaged her protected status as a "true woman." Although beginning to expand during the 1830s, women's means for political participation were still limited. Petitions shielded women through the anonymity of numbers. Antislavery fairs were tolerated by being the sheep's clothing covering a political argument. Child's book stood alone and was unapologetically engaged in political debate. Reviews often emphasized her gender. The *Quarterly Christian Spectator* noted: "The mind of the writer seems to be inspired with a most unlady-like political malignity, as if she were writing at the dictation of some sour and quarrelsome politician."[85] The *Colonizationist and Journal of Freedom* began with a much more positive assessment than the *Christian Spectator*. The review stated that the book deserved a "fair hearing" due to the "reputation previously acquired by the writer." Given the prolonged attack on colonization in Child's book, a tempered response was unexpected. The reviewer emphasized the commonalities between colonization goals and Child but mildly chastised Child for her lack of knowledge of the colonizationists.[86] Perhaps the most startling review appeared in Sarah Hale's *Ladies' Magazine and Literary Gazette*. The review was short, merely stating: "This is a most extraordinary work. We cannot now notice it, as it deserves, but we extract the preface, and entreat our readers—our sex ... *read the book*!" With this review, Hale provided her last endorsement of Child's work in both women's long careers.[87]

The impact of Child's *Appeal* took a toll on her professional career. Child was forced out of her affiliation with the *Juvenile Miscellany*, and the popularity of her household advice books declined. Sometimes the backlash was pure spite, as Child was denied her library privileges at the Boston Athenaeum.[88] The problems associated with her public stance on slavery followed her throughout the decade. In 1839, as she and David struggled to make a go of the sugar beet farm and to stay on top of old debts, Child realized she needed to find outside work. She wrote her good friend Louisa Loring that "I must earn something this summer. I am willing to do anything.... What to do I know not. I cannot take a school, while liable to be called away to follow Mr. Child's fortunes; and I am afraid my 'false position' toward the 'spirit of the age,' will cut off profit as an author."[89] No longer was Child viewed as the moral educator of children and champion of the middling household. She was now a public woman with dangerous views on race.

For Child, abolition eventually became both a cause and a career. Her decision to edit the *Anti-Slavery Standard* was driven primarily by financial need: "My task here is irksome to me.... [I]t was not zeal for the cause, but love for my husband, which brought me hither." She continued, "I am thankful that my work is for the anti-slavery cause. I have agreed to stay one year. I hope I shall then be able to return to my husband and rural home, which is humble enough, yet very satisfactory to me."[90] Despite the inroads women had made in publishing during the first decades of the nineteenth century, Child's presence at the helm of the *Anti-Slavery Standard* was unusual.[91] Given the controversy over the role of women in the abolitionist movement at this particular time, her presence was politically charged and a somewhat unexpected choice by the newspaper despite her fame.

The *Anti-Slavery Standard* under the editorship of Child was a departure from *The Liberator*. Her time away from Boston, largely spent in Northampton (a city with less of an abolitionist presence), allowed Child to view the movement from the outside, which suggested the need for a new direction for the cause.[92] Child recognized that there was an audience of potential supporters of abolition who lived outside of cities such as Boston and Philadelphia that were hotbeds for reform and political activism. While Child shared many of Garrison's ideas, she did not always share his preferred practices. She hoped to appeal to the more moderate abolitionist, someone who was antislavery but perhaps not yet involved in the related issue of women's rights, who might not shop exclusively free labor, or who wanted to attend conventions. As early as 1839, this vision began to develop: "I think there is now a large class of sincere abolitionists with narrow views of freedom, who require some other paper than the 'Liberator.' They are frightened, sincerely frightened, at new and bold views. They think the mere utterance of them is a danger of resolving all shapes back to chaos."[93] The *Anti-Slavery Standard* provided Child with a forum to be a strong abolitionist while presenting more moderate practices for her readership.

Although she had not compromised her views, this more moderate approach did not earn Child the support of her old allies. Child saw the purpose of the *Anti-Slavery Standard* as serving a strategic function of bringing new people into the movement. The Boston abolition old guard was leery of this new venture: "I am rather doubtful whether the gritty school quite approves of me now. I observe Garrison gives no indication, public or private, of interest in the Standard; the Westons commend nothing... and Mrs. Chapman, in her letters gives no opinion whether the paper is now advancing the good of the cause or not."[94] Disagreements between the various factions of the movement entrenched Child as an independent thinker and advocate. Due to the lack of assistance, minimal compensation, and barrage of criticism, Child eventually found her work on the *Anti-Slavery Standard* unbearable, and she resigned. She proclaimed that she was done with the movement: "Please take my name from the list, as I have retired from the anti-slavery cause altogether."[95] Lydia remained in New York after her resignation in hopes of rebuilding her literary reputation: "N. York affords advantages that no other place does. It has acknowledged me far more cordially than Boston ever did, and books published here have twice the sale."[96] New York was not only the center of publishing but also far more moderate in antislavery politics. By staying in New York, Lydia would not have to return to the hostile Boston abolitionists.

Although advocating a more moderate approach to abolition in the *National Anti-Slavery Standard*, Child's race politics had always been much more progressive than those of the typical activist. Child was an early supporter of legalizing interracial marriage. On March 29, 1839, at a time when the residents of northern states regarded the status and mobility of African Americans as an appropriate focus of public debate and resolutions, a petition was presented to the Massachusetts legislature with Lydia as the chief signatory. She in part staked her argument on the innate privacy of marriage, arguing that racial restrictions were "an unjustifiable interference with domicile institutions—inasmuch as it attempts to control by legislative action a connection which, above all others to be left to private conscience and individual choice."[97] Child also established her own authoritative voice. Speaking of herself as the author of the petition, she wrote that "she fully comprehends the origin of the law, its bearings past and present, the strong prejudice by which it is sustained, and the consequent unpopularity of her proceeding." She finally argued that this was her own opinion: "That she is not made the ignorant tool of evil designing persons, during the recent excitement, is evident from the fact that she six years ago published a book, in which she mentioned this very law, as a violation of the principles of justice and freedom." Child concluded the petition by addressing her own right to act, thus making a larger claim than the plea to legalize interracial marriage: "Lastly, your petitioner, as a freeborn woman sharing moral and intellectual advantages with all the sons and daughters of this intelligent Commonwealth, begs leave, dispassionately and respectfully, to protest against the contemptuous treatment effected to her sisters in Lynn."[98]

Despite her frustration with the movement during her stint as editor of the *National Anti-Slavery Standard*, Child's solid commitment to abolition was demonstrated in her support of John Brown after the raid on Harpers Ferry. Child was strategic in her public response. She distanced herself and other abolitionists from the violence of the raid, explaining that she did not "know of a single person who would have approved of it, had they been apprised of his [Brown's] intentions." Child, however, had sympathy for Brown. She wrote the governor of Virginia: "I, and thousands of others, feel a natural impulse of sympathy for the brave and suffering man."[99] Child engaged in the nurturing rhetoric of motherhood to justify her mission to John Brown's side. This approach excused her interest in the treasonous act and served to humanize Brown: "He needs mother or sister to dress his wounds and speak soothingly to him. Will you allow me to perform that mission of humanity? If you will, may God bless you for the generous deed."[100] Governor Wise also recognized the persuasive potential of this public exchange of letters. His response argued that it was dangerous to support abolitionists. After writing Child that she was welcome to visit Brown because constitutionally she was granted the freedom of movement, he implied the threat she might face while stating his intention to defend her: "Every arm which guards Brown from rescue on the one hand, and from Lynch law on the other, will be ready to guard your person in Virginia." Ever the gentleman, Wise next stated, "I could not permit an insult even to a woman in her walk of charity among us, though it be to one who whetted knives of butchery for our 'mothers, sisters, daughters, and babes.'"[101] Bleeding Kansas and the caning of Senator Charles Sumner changed Child's views on nonviolence and the Garrisonian use of moral suasion. She was now willing to recognize the potential need for violence as a response to slavery, although this shift was largely left to private letters. With her public support of Brown, even when shrouded in maternal instincts, Child was further differentiating her views from those of the typical female antislavery activist.[102]

Lydia Child had long believed that writing was her most powerful tool for political change. Despite her frustration with the abolition movement and her proclaimed retirement from the organizational aspects of the cause, she eventually returned to abolitionist projects. Bookending the Civil War were two important works: promoting Harriet Jacobs's *Incidents in the Life of a Slave Girl* and writing *The Freedmen's Book*. Child began planning *The Freedmen's Book* near the end of the war with an eye toward uplift and moral instruction. Ultimately published in 1865 by Ticknor and Fields, the book opened with her personal message to the freedmen and freedwomen: "I have prepared this book expressly for you with the hope that those of you who can read will read it aloud to others, and that all of you will derive fresh strength and courage from this true record of what colored men have accomplished under great disadvantages."[103] The preface explained the financial arrangements of the book (not for profit) and is signed "Your old friend, L. Maria Child." The book was primarily a collection of short biographies with some instruction included. Child listed the authors of each work (Child herself was the most often attributed author), marking African American authors with an asterisk.

Child, with significant foresight, recognized that emancipation alone would not solve bigotry. As early as 1839, Child worried that society would lag behind the law: "I have ceased to believe that public opinion will ever be sincerely reformed on the question till long after emancipation has taken place. I mean that for generations to come there will be a very large minority hostile to the claims of colored people; and the majority will be largely composed of individuals who are found on that side from any and every motive rather than hearty sympathy with the downtrodden race."[104] When the Thirteenth Amendment finally brought a constitutional end to slavery, Lydia remained worried that bigotry would thwart further legal advancements for African Americans. *The Freedmen's Book* demonstrated Child's continued belief in the power of the printed word. By providing a history of successful and "respectable" African Americans as models to ease the transition to freedom for former slaves, Child also hoped to provide a model for white Americans to ease their own transition to a postemancipation world.

CONCLUSION

True womanhood and civic domesticity prescribed the rhetorical strategies of women during the antebellum era. Some female opinion leaders, including Sarah Hale and Catharine Beecher, followed these cultural norms and redefined their significance, claiming citizenship and status for women. They did not challenge the role of women; instead, they reinterpreted the meaning of this role. Because true womanhood emerged from the shifting economy, class also shaped the significance assigned to this cultural role for women. As white middle-class women sought to fulfill a civic role within the nation, they needed to redefine their labor, thus creating a way to fulfill the obligations of citizenship. In order to keep the true woman sanctified, either the middle-class female became a supervisor of others, or her domestic labor became professionalized through science and math. For Hale, Beecher, and other similarly positioned women, it would not do for servants, immigrants, and people of color, those likely to perform domestic labor in other women's homes, to fulfill the obligations of citizenship. That role was exclusively for the *lady* of the house.

True womanhood could also be subverted for radical ends. Women like Lydia Maria Child and Angelina Grimké used the ideal of true womanhood to justify their political activism and moral authority. By defining women's activism as a moral necessity, the tropes of purity and piety—central to true womanhood—demanded action. For activist women, domesticity was less important because they saw themselves defined by their beliefs and actions rather than their labor. Under this activist model of womanhood, class was deemphasized because how the home was constructed and through whose labor were less important. Consumerism influenced even activist true women, and it was wielded as a weapon of reform. Boycotts, free labor stores, and even the Childs' sugar beet experiment were important ways that the market economy could be manipulated for social change. Lydia Child and other similarly engaged women viewed themselves as citizens with limited access to the public sphere and thus sought new ways to influence social and public policy. Hale's, Beecher's, and Child's views of race complicated their interpretation of true womanhood. As colonizationists, Hale and Beecher could not conceive of a womanhood that was not white. As an abolitionist, Child was open to the idea of nonwhite womanhood and believed that uplift and respectability in addition to legal protections were necessary for equality. For each of these women, the published word was necessary to influence the public sphere. Writing not only provided them with a level of financial security that contributed to their independence but also offered a level of fame that allowed them to influence others.

CHAPTER 5

Rewriting Race and Respectability
African American Women and Citizenship

> We spring upon the nation this little effort, hoping that many firesides will be made brighter, many a... daughter will catch the inspiration of womanly attainments, and bloom into beautiful and useful womanhood.
>
> —Monroe A. Majors, *Noted Negro Women: Their Triumphs and Activities*

Written in 1893 during the nadir of race relations, Monroe A. Majors's collection of short biographical sketches was meant to inspire a rising generation of young women. These stories about women from the past emphasized activism and uplift alongside femininity and decorum for a readership of African American girls who would eventually be labeled as both the new woman and the new Negro. That the tropes of womanhood past were still relevant at the end of the nineteenth century suggests that the race and gender work of antebellum women of color was still central to the politics of progress and uplift. We do not know if this theme was based on the perceived success of the deployment of white constructions of womanhood during the prewar years or if those tropes were so ingrained that it was difficult for authors like Monroe Majors to imagine another way. It is clear that the ideology of true womanhood, birthed by domestic manuals, sermons, and the magazines of white women, had permeated the consciousness of the Black middle class by the early 1830s. The rise of antebellum Black womanhood coincided with the rise of a Garrison style of antislavery activism that welcomed women and encouraged moral suasion. For women of color, true womanhood was political.

Womanhood for antebellum African American women was not an outgrowth of market sentimentality, as it was for white women. Middle-class African American women, despite the fact that their performance was not always embraced or even recognized by whites, practiced the four traits of true womanhood: piety, purity, submissiveness, and domesticity. Piety was practiced in racially segregated congregations, as Black churches became the norm. In churches that remained racially mixed, such as Quaker meetings, Black piety was performed from a separate pew. Whites presumptively challenged the purity of Black women. Women of color faced a near impossible binary: they were viewed by whites as either a sexually charged Jezebel or a sexually neutered mammy.[1] Sarah Forten and Sarah Douglass were relatively young when they entered the public sphere, and, given their social status, employment, and activism, it is difficult to imagine them as Jezebels. Purity for Black women, however, was judged by the stereotypes of the whole rather than the lived experience of the individual. By contrast, white women were assumed to be pure until their individual actions demonstrated otherwise.

Cultural standards of domesticity were also difficult for the middle-class African American woman to perform. The language of Catharine Beecher placed domesticity as central to democratic nation building, making the practice of true womanhood an end goal for white women. If, however, you and your family were denied representation within the nation, the outcome of domesticity served a different cultural end. The white doyens of domesticity did not imagine the Black home as civilizing or as a symbol of American progress, regardless of how closely it matched the white middle-class ideal. As the authors of domestic advice preached actions, race served as an impenetrable barrier to Black middle-class respectability. Many antebellum Black women worked outside the home. Their duty was not to raise the next generation of citizens but to provide the labor necessary to allow white women to deliver that education for their own young. Since Black children were largely denied access to a civil society—they would attend segregated schools and separate churches and were often excluded from the public displays of childhood's success, such as exhibitions and pageants—African American childhood served no larger civic purpose. Structural discrimination meant that the value-added significance of "keeping house" only went beyond domestic economy for white women. The final trait of true womanhood, submissiveness, was all too easy for women of color to fulfill. Unlike white women, who were only asked to submit to the power of their own husbands, Black women were asked to be submissive to almost all segments of society: Black and white men, white women, and sometimes even the white children that they tended. This very passivity that was so important for white women in Black women represented racial domination and the lack of status and power of their male kin. The fathers, brothers, husbands, and sons of Black women lacked the power to defend them from the injustices of society, further disempowering Black men within the public sphere.

The multiple jeopardy faced by women of color produced not only unique hardships when practicing true womanhood but also desired outcomes different from those of white women. In some ways, the experience of middle-class women in antebellum America was universal, as they all faced the restrictions of coverture. Single Black women lived at a precarious intersection of dependence and independence. Unmarried Black women faced fewer sanctions against earning their own wages and living outside the family home. However, independence was difficult to maintain. Higher-status employment opportunities for Black women were limited. There were not enough schools to employ the educated Black middle class, so women were forced into less profitable and lower-status employment. The number of Philadelphia's women of color identified as seamstresses, typically a low-paying, low-status, and less stable job, was staggering.[2] Most importantly, Black women frequently lacked a family safety net. Often there was not a home to return to, extra money to help out during times of illness, or even the shelter of respectability to guarantee that these women were considered one of the so-called deserving poor. This lack of a safety net is why so many African American women formed mutual aid societies.

In this chapter, I argue that African American women writers served as exemplars for womanhood and provided a means for creating civic space for themselves and civic status for Black men. Strong, visible, and believable examples of Black womanhood were necessary to challenge societal assumptions that the angel of the hearth must be white and that the middle-class home required a European American lord and master. Women of color used print culture as their entry into the public sphere of antislavery work. Their participation in the pages of the antislavery press or within the proceedings of abolition meetings allowed Black women to create a counterpublic that challenged the prejudice of the larger public sphere. White women enacted womanhood as their proof of a civic relationship to the state and a right to be heard. Black women sought the same things and in addition used the enactment of womanhood to promote the citizenship of their husbands, fathers, brothers, and eventually sons as patriarchs of their own homes. Although many members of the antebellum Black elite were involved in antislavery work, the project of uplift was meant to match monetary wealth with social practices and considered essential when claiming civil rights. Members of the Pennsylvania Black middle class of the 1830s were in large part the product of gradual emancipation or immigration, and their performance of middle-class virtues served not only as arguments on their own behalf but also as evidence for the potential virtue of those still enslaved.

For almost all published antebellum African American women, their first and only writing outlet was the antislavery press. However, rather than only wanting to speak on behalf of the slave, women of color published to prove the legitimacy of their claims to middle-class status and thus the concomitant claim of the patriarchal power of Black men. Citizenship for Black women was influenced by the multiple jeopardy of their race, sex, and class. If a woman's lack of political standing was based on coverture—that a woman's husband's citizenship served as her own—what did this mean for a woman of color? If her husband's civic status was in question, and in the 1830s urban North it was more precarious than ever, how could a woman advance her own citizenship?

To understand how Black female authors created civic status through writing, I examine the work of African American women's groups and specifically two antebellum women of color. These women had a more powerful political presence as unmarried women than they had as wives. Sarah Forten was the daughter of wealthy Black Philadelphian and antislavery activist James Forten. Sarah used the pages of *The Liberator* to express her political views, even when her words were penned anonymously. Sarah Douglass was also the daughter of antislavery activists. Although lacking the financial and social prestige of the Fortens, the Douglass family was solidly middle class and well known within the Philadelphia African American community. Douglass herself was active in antislavery and uplift work and published under both her own name and a pseudonym.[3] Women of color appropriated the tenets of white womanhood to create a political identity for both Black men and women.

AFRICAN AMERICAN WOMEN'S GROUPS: ABOLITION AND UPLIFT

Women of color have been organizing for at least as long as their white counterparts, forming mutual aid societies in the United States as early as the 1790s. During the 1830s, as Garrison-inspired abolitionist groups sprang up across the urban North, middle-class women of color actively participated in a variety of organizations. White abolitionist women believed that associations were one of the best ways for people of color to achieve racial uplift. While all antislavery groups were not racially integrated, white Garrisonian women believed that the abolition work of Black women was both legitimate and appropriate. The 1838 *Address to the Free Colored People of the United States*, prepared for the Anti-Slavery Convention of American Women, held in Philadelphia, called for women of color to expand their reform work beyond abolition: "Associations for Mental Improvement, Temperance Societies, Moral Reform Societies, and Peace Societies will naturally be suggested to your minds as among the most rapid and effectual means of raising your character as a people."[4] James Forten Jr., Sarah Forten's older brother, made similar claims for the need of women of color to focus on uplift in an address to the all-male American Moral Reform Society.[5]

The form and function of Black women's self-help organizations were different from those of their male counterparts. The membership was smaller, and meetings tended to be held in private homes. An educational rather than social purpose was demonstrated at meetings by opening and closing with prayer and including members' writings and oratory.[6] Since men met in lecture halls and women in parlors, formal exercises were necessary to inscribe an appropriate tone to women's meetings. For this rising class of African American women, it was important to provide opportunities for lifelong learning to match the reading rooms and debating societies created for Black men. Although younger society members likely received some formal education, older members might be working to improve their reading and writing skills. Literary societies established social networks that were unified by interests and class rather than by churches and geography. As Erica Armstrong Dunbar explains, "It was within the literary society that friendship and fraternization met with the political."[7] The advent of women's separate antislavery activism, in particular, provided Black women a unique opportunity to practice political and organizational skills free from the gaze of men. It also promoted activist networks within women's local communities that often spread outward in ways that could help with building other aspects of African American communities. Separate societies provided women the opportunity to gain a political footing while maintaining the propriety of a sex-segregated parlor. For women of color, organizations for uplift, such as literary societies, served a function not only for themselves but for their entire community. Black and white male activists accepted the image of the female on the pedestal and laid the responsibility of racial uplift at their feet.

The semipublic forum of women's literary societies paved the way for a female presence in political print culture. The *Genius of Universal Emancipation*, *The Emancipator*, and the Black-edited *Freedom's Journal* set the groundwork for the more influential *Liberator*, *National Anti-Slavery Standard*, and *North Star* in encouraging the participation of Black and white women in their pages. Newspapers promoted the organizational activities of African American women as proof of their respectability and middle-class status and the future potential for emancipated women of color. The newspaper editorialized: "The numerous societies which now exist among the people of color, in various places for their intellectual and moral improvements, are cheering evidence of their appreciation of virtue and knowledge and, if properly sustained cannot fail to remove many of the prejudices which prevail against them."[8]

African American women recognized the importance of *The Liberator* not only because it promoted their organizations but, more importantly, because it offered evidence of racial elevation and public engagement to a broader white audience. Organizational constitutions demonstrated women's ability to participate in civic engagement, highlighted their intellectual capacities, and shrouded their transgressive behaviors in piety and morality. The public recognition of club work provided by *The Liberator* was highly sought after. For example, Sarah Mapps Douglass, the secretary of the Female Literary Association, wrote Garrison because she was concerned about the fact that the group's constitution had not been published in his paper: "Did any person forbid the publication of the copy of the constitution of the F.L.A. forwarded to you.... [N]o one except myself had any right to forbid it.... Our design in whishing [sic] it published was that our sisters of other cities might be induced from our example to form *similar* associations."[9] James Forten, the father of Sarah Forten, wrote Garrison: "I am requested to state that the ladies of Providence are not the first to establish an Anti-Slavery Society—one was formed in this city in November last but from some inadvertence no notice of it was sent to the Liberator."[10]

African American women were often involved in riskier antislavery work than white women, who largely circulated petitions and volunteered in organizations such as the Philadelphia Female Anti-Slavery Society (PFAS). Even seemingly safe activities such as participating in conventions, fairs, and societies could become more dangerous for Black women due to their race. The *Pennsylvania Freeman* advertised the Fair for the Benefit of the Female Vigilant Association. The group of women, all likely African American, worked in tandem with the Vigilance Association, which was organized by African American men and provided supplies for fugitive slaves. Despite the precarious legal status of vigilance societies, the newspaper notice seemed to see nothing unusual about this behavior and described the fair in terms similar to those it would use for any other fundraising endeavor by white women: "We had the pleasure yesterday of looking at the tasteful arrangements and beautiful array of articles at this charitable sale which were certainly highly creditable to the skill industry, and refinement of a proscribed and calumniated portion of our community." Not only did the newspaper support the fair, it also chose to highlight the respectability and class status of the female members.[11]

Newspapers, pamphlets, broadsides, and books provided some of the few unfettered access points to the public sphere available to African Americans. Newspapers were particularly open to women. William Lloyd Garrison actively solicited their work in a personal letter to Sarah Douglass: "Remember that we have now have a Ladies' Department for the Liberator. Pray occupy it as often as possible with your productions, and get others of your society to do the same."[12] When women of color published in the paper, Garrison typically followed up with a request for more submissions, as evidenced by his introduction to a Boston woman's essay about segregation in churches: "There are few young white ladies who can prepare an essay for the press with more accuracy in regards to orthography and punctuation, or written in a more beautiful hand, than the following by a young colored lady. We beg for other favors."[13] Garrison was well aware of the persuasive power of these published works by women of color not only for the arguments themselves but as a demonstration of the intellectual capacity and refinement of these women. *The Liberator* often published letters anonymously attributed to "a colored female" that gave women a voice and an ability to demonstrate their respectability even as they challenged white racism. One such example was published in 1832. Addressed to a "brother in Christ," the letter argued, "They call us a free people, but we are not as free as we mean to be; for God has spoken, and shall he make it good?"[14] Other women followed suit, submitting poetry, letters, and essays, and even when writing anonymously they revealed their race and gender because their identity was central to their argument.

African American women were also involved in organizations centered on uplift rather than directly involved in abolition. One of the goals of racial elevation was to prove to whites who were neither proslavery nor supportive of Black equality that African Americans could lead "respectable lives" and be assets to their larger communities. Antebellum Philadelphia, with its large literate African American population, had at least three reading clubs for Black women, including "the Edgeworth Society, formed by admirers of the Irish novelist Maria Edgeworth; the Minerva Literary Association, organized for 'the encouragement and promotion of polite literature'; and the Female Literary Association, of which the Fortens and Sarah Mapps Douglass were members."[15] Black men at the outset did not universally accept the development of women's literary societies. However, James Forten's 1837 address suggested that despite the fact that his sex would "startle at the idea of women rising equal to them in the sphere of intellectual strength," there was a political value for all African Americans from this type of organization.[16]

Antislavery societies corresponded with one another and created alliances across regions. Although men and women both read the antislavery press, women remained the external "other" and were given special pages on which to publicize their activities regardless of race. There remained, however, some concerns with how women's organizations worked with men and an overall apprehension about mixed-sex societies. In a call for delegates to the Annual Council of Organizations for the Moral and Mental Improvement of the People of Color, it was requested that "female Societies, who have male directors ... send their directors as delegates."[17] Because of cultural restrictions such as these, some women engaged in political debates by camouflaging arguments as poetry that was published in the abolitionist press.

Likely due to the growth of female antislavery societies, more newspapers provided spaces for women to publish. David Ruggles's 1838 journal, the *Mirror of Liberty* (New York), included a "Ladies Department," where in the first issue he stated, "This department will always be open to the ladies, and we are sanguine that they will occupy it." What followed was a poem, "Woman's Rights." Although the title might suggest it was a call for political rights for women, in actuality it was an antislavery tract that argued that "women should not be made to toil and sweat, and bleed as slaves."[18] The importance of print outlets for women cannot be overestimated. In a world where women's right to vote was denied and their physical presence in public places was discouraged, women's published words provided a place for them in policy debates.

Abolition was the first significant and nationally organized political activism women had engaged in since the American Revolution. Just days after the founding of the American Anti-Slavery Society, a group of women, including Charlotte Vandine Forten and her daughters Margaretta, Harriet, and Sarah, future daughter-in-law Mary Woods, Grace Bustill Douglass and her daughter Sarah Mapps Douglass, and Sarah McCrummel, joined white women such as Lucretia Mott (who helped to call the meeting) to create the racially integrated Philadelphia Female Anti-Slavery Society.[19] White abolitionists not only worked to end chattel slavery but also saw as part of their mission the uplift of free people of color. For example, the *National Enquirer* reported on a meeting where "a very large and attentive audience was present." Lucretia Mott addressed the people of color, "urging improvement, education of their children, sympathy for the enslaved, abstinence from the products of slave-labor, a non-resistance of injuries, &c., &c." The *Enquirer* next reported to its readership that there was a positive reaction to the message: "The remarks were listened to with evident interest on the part of the colored people, and we doubt not left a salutary and happy effect upon their minds. Indeed as we passed some of them, on our way home, said one to another, 'Oh! She is a nice woman.'"[20] The condescension expressed in the article is reflective of the attitudes of some abolitionists. The people of color in the audience were portrayed as almost childlike in their interest in and acceptance of the "nice woman" and reinforced the need for African Americans to perform white ideals of respectability and intellect.

Antislavery societies granted Black women the opportunity to engage in direct political discourse through petitions sent to their state and federal governments.[21] However, despite the formation of integrated groups that at least on paper did not distinguish between the membership status of Black and white women, the fear of racial amalgamation plagued the impressions of these groups by the wider population. For people of color, this message was often mixed. Although interacting with whites could spur violence, abolition groups urged such integration: "Whenever facilities present themselves for uniting with associations of white people, it will undoubtedly be for the benefit of both parties, to improve the opportunity. Such efforts will often be attended with vexations and discouragements, but Christian forbearance and modest dignity under these trials, will be a rebuke none the less deeply felt because it is silent."[22] Even though the request suggested a desire for equality, African Americans took the greater risk of integration.

THE ABOLITIONIST POET:
SARAH FORTEN (1814–1883/84)

James Forten, often designated as a "gentleman of color" in the antislavery press, was an activist throughout his adult life. He wrote some of the first Black-authored political essays during the era of the early republic. Forten was an early opponent of colonization efforts and an early supporter of William Lloyd Garrison's brand of abolition.[23] His wealth and social standing brought prominent Blacks and whites to his Philadelphia home.[24] New England poet and abolitionist John Greenleaf Whittier was one such visitor. Not much older than the Forten daughters, he was taken with their refinement and inspired to write a poem celebrating their "excellence of mind," "chaste demeanor[,] and the[ir] taste refined."[25] The Forten children were all well educated. The Forten sons were only nominally employed in their father's sail loft; they were instead left to pursue their own interests in public activism, literature, and science. Sarah, his youngest surviving daughter, used the leisure time her family's wealth provided to be active in abolition and uplift, and she was engaged in writing that was published in the antislavery press. Over a relatively short time span, Sarah Forten published at least a dozen items, including poems and essays. She often wrote under a pseudonym, as was typical at that time. Initially, her identity was unknown even to her family, as James Forten revealed in a letter to Garrison after learning of her authorship: "As you are not acquainted with the author of 'Ada' and 'A,' I have discovered by accident that these pieces were written by one of my Daughters."[26] Although Garrison did not reveal her full identity, the next month he explained in *The Liberator* that "our correspondent 'Ada' and 'Magawisca,' we are proud to learn is a young colored lady of Philadelphia."[27] Garrison recognized the rhetorical power of attaching a racial identity to the poet. He highlighted her class status by remarking that she was a "*lady* of Philadelphia," and her writing served as proof to a white readership of the intellectual capacity and true womanhood of an African American woman.

Raised in a family of activists, Sarah Forten was exposed to the power of print culture from a young age. Early newspapers that supported the rights of people of color—such as Benjamin Lundy's *Genius of Universal Emancipation* and *Freedom's Journal*—were available to her at home.[28] This kept her current on political affairs and guaranteed her appreciation of the power of the press, particularly for those who were often powerless in the public sphere. In a letter to poet John Greenleaf Whittier's sister Elizabeth, Sarah captured the excitement of the growing abolition movement, which brought well-known activists not only to her city but also to her home: "You will scarcely be able to read this hasty scrawl. I am now writing with four or five gentlemen (all abolitionists) talking about [George] Thompson. Of course I can't help giving my ears to them, while my eyes only rest upon the paper." Sarah concluded by noting her good fortune: "Do you perceive that we are indeed highly favoured in having three such highly valued friends with us?"[29] Intersecting wealth and Blackness, the Forten home was an important stop for white abolitionists. Sarah Forten included in her letter to Elizabeth Whittier a description of Thompson's lectures, and she can hardly contain her pride over the famous lecturer's visits to her family home: "He has paid us two visits, and four admirable lectures from him have quite captivated our good citizens, never before have we listened to such surprising power of orator—never before has there been such an awakening of consciences—his eloquence surpasses any thing ever before heard."[30] An examination of the membership lists of organizations that included the Forten women, the leadership positions held by the Forten men, and the advertisements for public meetings, lectures, and conventions held in Philadelphia reveals that the Forten home on Lombard Street must have been a highly social place, particularly in the 1830s as the abolition movement was gaining steam.[31] Sarah Forten would witness much of the private workings of the early abolition movement, a privilege almost unheard of for someone of her age, race, and gender.

Despite her wealth and status, Sarah Forten experienced discrimination based on her color. Writing to Angelina Grimké, Forten explained: "We are not disturbed in our social relations: we never travel far from home and seldom go to public places unless quite sure that admission is free to all: therefore, we meet with none of these mortifications which might otherwise ensure. I would recommend to my colored friends to follow our example and they would be spared some very painful realities."[32] Even with the opportunities her family's wealth provided and a conscious effort to avoid public ridicule, she still felt the pain of rejection. As a member of the African Episcopal Church of St. Thomas, a participant in various organizations of African American women, and seldom part of the public life of Philadelphia, her exposure to whites was likely limited to abolitionists, adding to the hurt caused by their rejection: "I must also own that it has often engendered feelings of discontent and mortification in my breast when I saw that many were preferred before me, who by education, birth, or worldly circumstances were no better than myself. THEIR sole claim to notice depending on the superior advantage of being WHITE."[33]

In January 1838 Sarah Forten married Joseph Purvis, the younger brother of Robert Purvis, her sister's husband.[34] Robert, Joseph, and brother William Purvis (who died from tuberculosis in 1828) came to Philadelphia in 1819 with their white father and their Black mother, who had been born into slavery. Their wealthy father had hoped to move his family to England or Scotland but died in Philadelphia from typhus in 1826, leaving his three sons a shared estate valued at $250,000.[35] In 1835 Joseph Purvis purchased a 205-acre farm in Bensalem, Pennsylvania, named Eddington Farm, for $13,500 and two smaller farms that he rented out with the desire to be a farmer rather than remaining in the city like his brother.[36] Thus, Joseph had removed himself from the social circles of Philadelphia for almost two years before his marriage and provided Sarah with few opportunities to maintain ties to the city beyond family. Her sister Harriet continued as an activist after marriage, with her home serving as a salon of sorts for abolitionists, much as her father's home had in the 1830s. Sarah's marriage ended her antislavery work, as well as her writing.[37] Julie Winch somewhat dramatically captures the abrupt change in Sarah Forten's life: "Within weeks of her marriage, Sarah resigned from the Female Anti-Slavery Society, while her sister remained a lifelong member. She ceased writing poetry. She attended no more abolitionist meetings, helped organize no more anti-slavery fairs. She exchanged the life of an abolitionist for that of a farmer's wife."[38] Newspaper reports and PFAS document this change. The annual report of PFAS for January 1838 lists Sarah Forten as a manager for the society, and she does not appear in the 1839 report. How quickly she resigned her position is unknown.[39]

Even before moving to his farm in Bensalem, Pennsylvania, Joseph Purvis was not active in the antislavery movement or even within the Philadelphia elite African American community, despite having lived in the city as a boy and young adult. His name is absent from the newspapers, and he isn't even listed as a participant in different conventions, meetings, and organizations. Granted, he moved out of the city after the purchase of his farm in 1835, but his absence from organizational work before and after his move suggests that political activism was not his priority. Sarah Forten Purvis's absence from the pages of *The Liberator* and the rosters of women's organizations could be explained by her husband's lack of interest, by the fact that she started a family soon after marriage, by the isolation of the Bensalem farm, or merely by the fact that she found, like Virginia Woolf, that she needed a room of her own in which to write. Her lack of publishing at this time makes it difficult to track her life after marriage. While Sarah's formal work with abolition seemingly ended with her marriage, there would be exposure through family ties (the Bensalem farm was only twelve miles from Philadelphia—not close by antebellum standards, but certainly not too far away for visits), and in 1851 Joseph Purvis and his brother, Robert, subscribed to Frederick Douglass's *North Star*.[40] Jasmine Nichole Cobb summarizes Sarah Forten's life after marriage and, by extension, that of other middle-class women: "The end of Forten's activist career suggests that Black men were especially vigilant about free women's womanhood. A pregnancy and family might have produced demands that made it necessary for Forten to terminate her work outside the home. Marriage helped to shroud her sexuality and sexual desire, but at the expense of her political career."[41]

Details about Forten's daily life after marriage are limited. No longer a member of various women's organizations in Philadelphia, Forten's name did not appear in minutes, on rosters, or on the pages of *The Liberator*. The 1840 federal census provides a few clues. It was the first census conducted after Sarah and Joseph Purvis's marriage. Unfortunately, this census only includes the names of the heads of household, so Sarah Purvis does not appear by name. A John Powers (corrected on the census as Jos. Purvos) is listed for Bensalem, Pennsylvania, and in all probability represents the Purvis family. The household included ten members. Besides Sarah, Joseph, and a male child under the age of ten (Joseph Jr.), the remaining seven individuals are likely employees. Three of the presumed employees are women (none are old enough to be Joseph Purvis's mother, Harriet Judah), so Sarah likely had help with domestic chores and might have been spared early in the marriage from the more physically demanding household labor.[42] The four male laborers suggest that the farm was productive, and the family's finances were still sound. By contrast, Sarah's sister Harriet Purvis was in Philadelphia in 1840. The Robert Purvis household, located on the same street as Harriet and Sarah's childhood home, included eight free people of color. Besides the couple and their four children there were two women listed who likely provided domestic labor for the household, giving Harriet the time to continue her antislavery work.[43]

The intervening decade reveals that Sarah's life remained far removed from the activist circle she occupied in the 1830s. The 1850 census lists Sarah's husband, Joseph Purvis, as a farmer worth $30,000.[44] Although still a sizable number, personal wealth of $30,000 reflects a significant decline in the family's prosperity. Sarah and eight children are included (Joseph, James, William, Sarah, Emily, Alfred, Harriet, Alexander), revealing that Sarah gave birth to seven children in the span of ten years. Other people are listed as household members and are presumably live-in help. The entire Purvis family, including Sarah, is designated as mulatto, and all of the employees are designated as Black. There are two additional women listed as living on the property, Isabella Growden (age forty-two) and Sally Ann King (age nineteen). No profession is listed for either woman, but it is likely that Growden provided domestic labor and that King, who was probably married to George King (age twenty-five), a farmer on the property, might have also helped with domestic chores.[45]

The financial status of Sarah and Joseph Purvis was declining throughout the decade, and Joseph Purvis's death on January 17, 1857, placed the family's finances in free fall. Joseph had sold his original farm in Bensalem in 1853 and bought a new farm known as Fair View. The last decade of his life had been plagued by poor financial decisions. He had tried to follow the lead of his brother and the Forten men in dealing in the Philadelphia real estate market but was heavily in debt at the time of his death.[46] The 1860 census reflects this change in status. It lists Sarah as a widow with a personal wealth of $600, a substantial decline from the $30,000 listed in the 1850 census. All eight of the children remained at home except Harriet, who would have been twelve or thirteen at the time. Immediately after Joseph Purvis's death it is believed that several of the children stayed with Sarah's mother and sister Margaretta on Lombard Street, and perhaps Harriet remained with extended family for a longer period of time.[47] All of the children are listed as having attended school in the previous two years except for the two eldest sons. All of the family members are listed as mulatto, and there are no additional laborers listed as part of the household. Their neighbors at Fair View are listed as white and have substantially more wealth in land and personal property.[48] There is no record of how the Purvis family fit into the community dynamics of Bensalem. It is unknown whether or not the children attended (or tried to attend) the local school or if they attended an area church. Given that almost all the landowners were white, the Purvis family was likely isolated within the community, and their decline in wealth probably magnified this isolation. The 1863 tax record for Bensalem on the page lists "Negro Taxable," and Sarah Purvis is listed as a mulatto laborer rather than given a title more reflective of her former class status.[49]

Sarah Forten's declining fortunes were not only revealed in the public record. Friends and family members recognized that her home life was in disarray. For example, Sarah Forten's niece, diarist Charlotte Forten Grimké, wrote a year after Joseph Purvis's death: "Went to Aunt Sarah's this morning, as usual a scene of confusion and disorder greeted me. What a contrast to the elegance and order of

Byberry [Robert and Harriet Purvis's home]. Everything, everybody is very, very different. It grieves me to think about it."[50] Clearly, the Purvis household was a matter of concern among the family; however, beyond providing care and housing for some of Sarah's eight children, it does not appear that anyone stepped in to keep things financially afloat. It is likely that in the twenty years after James Forten Sr.'s death, the wealth of the extended family had dissipated. The Forten family was large, the sail loft had ceased to bring large profits by the end of James Forten's life, and his widow, Charlotte, and unmarried daughter, Margaretta, lived long lives and needed to be maintained. Perhaps the Forten and Purvis families had been subsidizing Sarah and Joseph for some time and were no longer able to contribute.

Regardless of the reason, during the 1860s Sarah Forten Purvis looked outside her family for assistance. At some point she took a loan from Theodore Weld, suggesting that she must at the minimum have maintained personal ties within the abolition community even if she was no longer active. Writing Weld in 1869, Sarah told him that she was unable to repay the loan. With a degree of formality, she began: "Dear Sir—Your letter is before me and in reply I must say that I cannot meet your demand now. I assure you it has not been forgotten, tho I have never been able to liquidate the debt. I well recollect the promise I made a long time ago to pay you—and I will do so—as soon as our Farm is sold."[51]

While the 1870 census suggests that the Purvis family finances were more secure, that does not seem to be the case. Without the shelter of her biracial husband or her family's wealth, Sarah Forten is designated as Black for the first time in the census. She is described as "keeping house," the designation given a female head of household who does not work for wages. Her personal worth is listed as $2,000 plus an additional $18,000 for real estate. Whether the amount was mistakenly entered or misreported, the numbers are much higher than they should be. The household included sons Joseph and William employed as farmers (James and Alfred had both died since the previous census), while daughters Sarah, Emily, and Harriet and the youngest child, Alexander, are all listed as "at home," suggesting that only the two eldest sons were employed.[52] In her letter to Theodore Weld, Sarah Forten Purvis reported that her oldest daughter was "Teaching School at Washington" and that her son "William is well—and a young man of good repute.... [H]e thinks of going south." She did not make note of Joseph's reputation but stated that he "is now in the City."[53] Winch's research suggests that these demographics shifted dramatically in just five years. She states that on April 24, 1875, Sarah and the two children who remained at home, William and Annie (Harriet), declared bankruptcy and sold their remaining property to pay off creditors. At that time, Sarah, William, and Annie moved to the Forten family home on Lombard Street, where Sarah kept house for her mother and brother.[54] Son Joseph Purvis was the last of the Purvis children to sell his claim to the family farm to his mother and two siblings. By 1873 his claim amounted to $100, a clear indication that much of the land had been sold off or borrowed against (and how inaccurate the $18,000 evaluation of the farm in the 1870 census was). Lacking steady employment, Joseph Purvis filed for a Civil War soldier's pension in 1879, classifying himself as an invalid.

Sarah Forten's role as an activist and her race and class status were largely shaped by her marriage. Prior to marriage, Sarah had the leisure time to engage in antislavery work and racial uplift and even the luxury to participate in a robust community of letters. Her marriage to Joseph Purvis, despite his wealth and biracial status, led to a slow change in her claim to true womanhood. As the family's financial security declined, Sarah Forten had fewer opportunities for activism and civic engagement. Widowhood further shaped her civic and social status. Because she had less wealth and no husband, official public documents classified her as Black as opposed to mulatto and as a farm laborer instead of a lady. The fate of Sarah Forten demonstrates how gender, class, and race molded how women of color experienced citizenship.

THE POETRY OF SARAH FORTEN

Involvement in the antislavery movement awakened Sarah Forten to activism. As she noted, "I confess that I am wholly indebted to the Abolition cause for arousing me from apathy and indifference, shedding light into a mind which has been too long wrapt in selfish darkness."[55] Her claims of indifference were likely an overstatement, given her father's work on behalf of people of color throughout her life. However, the advent of Garrison's *Liberator* provided women like Sarah Forten an outlet for personal artistic and political expression. A brief biography of Sarah Forten Purvis appeared in Monroe Majors's book *Noted Negro Women* (1893). She is listed as Miss Sarah Forten, her troubled marriage to Joseph Purvis forgotten in this tribute. The entry refers to her as "another one of our brainy women" and includes part of her poem written for the Anti-Slavery Convention of American Women, which Majors describes as a call for interracial cooperation. He optimistically concluded that with this poem, the racial strife of the abolition movement was resolved: "After this, the whites and the free Negroes met in the same conventions, and mutually exchanged their opinions, and together ever afterward dealt their terrific blows at the foundation of America's disgrace, and as we all gladly realize, drove the dreaded monster from this virgin land."[56] Whether it was the strength of her family name (although her married name was equally prominent within the movement) or the actual power of her poetry, over fifty years after resigning from the Pennsylvania Female Anti-Slavery Society, Sarah Forten Purvis was remembered as a significant literary figure of the movement.

Forten's first poem, "The Grave of the Slave," was published in *The Liberator* on January 22, 1831. In four short stanzas the poem mourns the lonely plight of the slave and concludes that death was a relief for one so downtrodden:

> Poor Slave! Shall we sorrow that death was thy friend.
> The last, and the kindest, that heaven could send?
> The grave to the weary is welcomed and blest.
> And death, to the captive, is freedom and rest.[57]

The poem was reprinted in other papers during the decade and eventually set to music. *The Philanthropist* attributed the work to Sarah Louisa as opposed to Ada, how Forten originally signed the poem, suggesting that despite her original attempt to mask her identity, before long the poem was directly associated with her. *The Philanthropist* emphasized Forten's decorum and class standing in its introduction to the poem: "The following lines were written by a colored female residing in Philadelphia. I ought to have said *young lady* even at the risk of exciting a sneer in certain doughfaces for her whole deportment bears testimony to the fact that she is truly such."[58] The editorial comments reveal the strategic use of Black women's poetry and prose beyond the stated political content. Sarah Forten's sweet and sentimental words served as proof of her capability to embody the traits of true womanhood.

When the poem was originally published, William Lloyd Garrison publicly thanked the author and invited more contributions. Her second poem appeared in the very next issue. "The Slave Girl's Address to Her Mother" engages the importance of home, both the current home created in slavery and the ancestral one:

> Torn from our home, our kindred and our friends,
> and in a stranger's land our days to end.
> No heart feels for the poor, the bleeding slave;
> no arm is stretched to rescue, and to save.[59]

Although there is nothing within the lines of the poem to suggest that this needs to be an address to "mother," Forten's choice of this title emphasizes the family ties of slaves and reflects one of the rhetorical strategies popular in the 1830s, an emphasis on shared gender roles and family structures between the enslaved and free.

"Past Joys" was published on March 19, 1831. By now Forten had enjoyed the pleasure of seeing her work in print as she wrote new poems. Still using the pen name Ada, Forten again played upon the theme of home and family and how they were denied to slaves:

> The mother, wife, or child beloved,
> he ne'er shall see again.
> His home—ah! That lov'd name recalls
> all that was dear to him.[60]

The theme of home was both a powerful and a safe trope used by female abolitionists. This approach removed the debate over slavery from politics and allowed female activists to maintain their status as true women. A concern with hearth and home made the abolitionist work of women acceptable and less overtly political, although they are clearly civically engaged in the issue. Also, abolitionist work served to promote the work of home building, a natural right that should not be denied to anyone, regardless of race, class, and status as enslaved.

Forten's poem "The Prayer" utilized two rhetorical strategies that were sensitive to her status as a lady. First, the poem shows that slaves (and, by extension, all people of color) embraced the power of prayer and Christianity. Next, Forten argues that if prayer makes people of color "children of God," then white Christians have an obligation to protect their spiritual siblings.[61] Sarah Forten's next published poem, "The Farewell," points to the hypocrisy of interracial abolition work. She writes that the relations are fleeting because "thou will soon forget the stranger thou has seen, / and in the gay and busy world, forget that I have been."[62] She never names activists as those who have forgotten the bonds of friendship, and other interpretations of the poem are possible. However, a few years later in a letter to one of the Grimké sisters, Forten clearly points out discrimination by abolitionists. Forten tells the story of "one of the best and least prejudiced men in the Abolition ranks." She states that the man said, "I can recall the time when in walking with a colored brother, the darker the night, the better Abolitionist was I." She hastened to add that although this unnamed activist no longer behaved in this way, "many, very many are anxious to take up the cross, but how few are strong enough to bear it."[63] A more positive view of the cross-racial ties among abolitionists is expressed in "The Separation," written after an antislavery convention was held in Philadelphia. The Forten men attended this convention and brought a stream of delegates into the Forten home. The introduction to this poem, again signed Ada, provides the context: "The following effusion is from a young lady of color, and has reference to the late Anti-Slavery Convention in Philadelphia."

> Friend after friend departs.
> And they are gone—that little band

Of friends—the firm and true!
We feel the void which absence makes
With joy, and sorrow too.

Their works shall live when other deeds,
Which ask a nation's fame,
Have sunk beneath Time's whelming wave,
Unhonored and unarmed.
Philadelphia, Dec 9th 1833 —ADA[64]

The camaraderie established with this 1833 convention seems very different from what Forten described eighteen months earlier in her poem "The Farewell." Whether she felt slighted within the PFAS as a member and was swept up in the optimism created by the convention of 1833 as an observer, the tone of the two poems is very different. At the very least, we know that despite her elite status, Sarah Forten often felt socially slighted by whites and was even more troubled when that community was comprised of women who allegedly shared the same political goals.

On February 1, 1834, William Lloyd Garrison published Sarah Forten's "An Appeal to Woman." He introduced the poem with the claim that Sarah and her family enacted the proof of the capabilities of people of color: "The following lines were written by a young and intelligent lady of color, who, with the other members of the family to which she belongs, has by her perseverance in study, &c. forced the respect even of those who would wish to crush the people of color on the earth. May her appeal not be in vain!" Forten's appeal could be interpreted as adhering to the PFAS motto that the southern slave was "a woman and a sister" but could also be seen as a challenge to white abolitionist women to recognize the work and equality of their sister abolitionists of color: although "our 'skins may differ,' but from thee we claim, / A sister's privilege, in a sister's name."[65]

This poem clearly hit a nerve for some and resulted in two published responses in verse. James Scott offered "A Reply to Ada," which endorsed Sarah Forten's poetic works as a way to combat discrimination. In part, he endorsed her writing as a form of activism, urging her to "use thy tongue and pen and mental power, to aid thy country in the trying hour."[66] An anonymous woman offered another "Reply to Ada" in the literary column of *The Liberator* validating Forten's standing as a Christian: "Daughter of Eve! My sister, and my friend, / to thee the hand of friendship I extend" and concluded that men should "grant the rights which they so boldly claim."[67] Sarah Forten's "Appeal to Woman" reached an even larger audience when it was recirculated in conjunction with the first Anti-Slavery Convention of American Women, held in New York in 1837. Included within the conference proceedings and published in antislavery newspapers and eventually as a stand-alone work, Angelina Grimké's *An Appeal to the Women of the Nominally Free States* argued for women to become active on behalf of the abolitionist cause. In the separately printed version of Grimké's work, a stanza of Forten's "Appeal to Women" appeared on the cover page.

> We are thy sisters—God has truly said,
> That of one blood the nations he has made
> Oh Christian Woman! In a Christian land,
> Canst thou unblushing read this great command?
> Suffer the wrongs which wring our inmost heart,
> To draw one throb of pity on thy part!
> Our skins may differ, but from thee we claim
> A sister's privilege and a sister's name.[68]

Remarkably, this is the only time that Sarah Forten's full name is attached to one of her works of poetry.[69]

During the first burst of poetry published in *The Liberator*, Sarah shifted genre from sentimental poetry to political essay. Interestingly, she changed her pen name to reflect the new form of her writing. She signed the essay Magawisca, a name taken from Catharine Maria Sedgwick's *Hope Leslie; or, Early Times in Massachusetts* (1827). A more recognizable pseudonym than Ada, Magawisca was surely selected for political impact. Magawisca was the daughter of Chief Monomotto and enslaved as a result of the Pequot War. The tone of "The Abuse of Liberty" is angry, atypical for an early nineteenth-century female writer. Much of the characteristic sentimentality that cloaked women's early antislavery writing is absent. In one paragraph, Forten mentions the "monstrous vice" of white men who "tear the unconscious husband from his tender wife, and the helpless babe from its mother's breast," but beyond that short line the claims of home and kinship ties are absent from her essay. She speaks of the rights denied Black men by their white counterparts and the remorseless actions of those who prop up the institution of slavery. In a particularly timely statement, she speaks of the anxiety felt by white men who are "in constant dread lest they [slaves], whom he unjustly condemns to bondage, will burst their fetters, and become oppressors in their turn."[70] Forten warned that God will not always allow slavery to continue: "He is just, and his anger will not always slumber. He will wipe the tear from Ethiopia's eye; He will shake the tree of liberty, and its blossoms shall spread over the earth."[71]

The date of Sarah Forten Purvis's death is disputed.[72] It does seem to be agreed that she was living in the Forten family home at 336 Lombard Street at the time of her death. The official city record states that she was buried at the St. Thomas cemetery; the document lists her race as Black and her occupation as "Lady."[73]

THE ACTIVIST EDUCATOR:
SARAH MAPPS DOUGLASS (1806–1882)

Sarah Douglass was the daughter of Robert Douglass, a hairdresser born in the British West Indies, and Grace Bustill, a milliner in the store next to Robert's shop.[74] Sarah Douglass had three brothers, Robert Jr., James, and William Penn.[75] Robert Douglass was a trained artist and portrait painter and was well known enough to have a short review of his paintings published in both *The Liberator* and the *Genius of Universal Emancipation*. In the same way white editors used Sarah Forten's poetry as proof of African American literary ability, these reviews stressed that Robert Douglass's talent proved that African Americans could have artistic skills.[76] The Douglass family was particularly involved in antislavery work, but they were also concerned with educational opportunities for people of color, as well as more general goals of racial elevation, including temperance. Robert Douglass Sr. subscribed to *The Liberator* and was a member of various African American organizations. He served as vice president, alongside James Forten and Robert Purvis, of a Philadelphia association to support the building of the Manual Labor School for Colored Youth proposed for New Haven, Connecticut.[77] Sarah's brother Robert Jr. was the most politically active of her siblings. Robert traveled to Haiti in 1838 with two other antislavery activists, Charles C. Burleigh and Lewis Gunn. Douglass provided commentary to the press and sketched the people and landscape on the island.[78]

Along with many of their Bustill relatives, Sarah and her mother, Grace, attended Quaker meetings, although they did not formally become members of the faith. They appear to be the only members of their immediate family who regularly attended meetings, suggesting that this was an enactment of their piety. Despite her devotion to the faith and appreciation for the Quaker commitment to antislavery politics, Douglass recognized the racism of many Philadelphia Quakers and was on several occasions the target of discrimination. In a letter to William Basset, an active abolitionist, she frankly stated, "*I believe they despise us for our color*. I have not been in Arch Street meeting for four years, but my mother goes once a week and frequently she has a *whole long bench* to herself."[79] Both Sarah and her mother were active in antislavery work. Grace Douglass was a founding member of PFAS. Throughout her life, Sarah Douglass typically served in the role of corresponding secretary of the various organizations in which she was a member.[80] Like the

Fortens and other prominent African American Philadelphia families, the Douglasses were firmly committed to doing their part for racial elevation and the abolition of slavery.

SARAH DOUGLASS'S TEACHING CAREER

Sarah Douglass was a fixture in Philadelphia as the preeminent African American educator at midcentury.[81] She began teaching at the school established by her mother and James Forten and spent a few years in New York City teaching at the Free African School for Girls.[82] After her return to Philadelphia, instead of teaching in someone else's school, she established her own, which at times received sponsorship from the Philadelphia Female Anti-Slavery Society.[83] As both teacher and administrator, she finally had control over curriculum and to some degree whom and how many students she taught. Initially, Douglass found it difficult to provide an effective educational environment for her students. In 1836 members of the Pennsylvania Abolition Society wrote that "the undersigned having seriously felt the want of a suitable room for the female coloured school under the care of Sarah Douglass and appreciating the general wish of the society to accommodate on this behalf."[84] Apparently, that wish was granted, as several months later Angelina Grimké observed in a letter, "We are glad to find thou hast a pleasanter situation for thy School & that Sister Smith gave thou a map of Palestine for it."[85]

Douglass's school was highly respected because of its emphasis on the higher branches of learning, and it was often held out as a model of African American potential to those visiting Philadelphia. Despite Douglass's attention to academic rigor, many reports instead emphasized the respectability of the students, who were "selected from our best families where their morals and manners are equally subjects of care, and of deep interest."[86] Douglass's school fulfilled an important service to the African American community. Her advanced studies provided girls the means to teach their own children someday. Many schools appeared on the pages of African American–edited or antislavery newspapers; Sarah Douglass, however, was one of the few instructors consistently identified by name. Notably, praise for her academic success was always mingled with equal praise for her ability to train moral, refined, and pure young women.

The school retained its status through the years. The 1849 census of people of color lists Sarah Douglass as a teacher at a private school and includes a description: "Sarah M. Douglass's is an excellent school of many years standing; she has a good cabinet and philosophical apparatus and teaches the higher branches."[87] The study of objects had become a teaching practice in the United States by the 1830s. Douglass's science cabinet demonstrated her modern teaching techniques.[88] The

1856 census of people of color again lists Sarah Douglass as an instructor at a private school that was established in 1835 with an enrollment of thirty: "S. M. Douglass teaches higher branches than are taught in Public Grammar Schools. The Managers of the Institute [ICY] in whose building her school is kept, have made an arrangement with her by which she will at all times have 25 girls preparing for admission into their school."[89]

The fact that she is listed in the 1856 census of Philadelphia's African American population, the year after her marriage, suggests that she did continue teaching after marrying William Douglass. The decision to remain employed was remarkable for the time and place, suggesting both a commitment to her profession on Sarah's part and the acceptance of the community of her skill as a teacher. Apparently, the administrators at ICY and the parents of her students did not want to lose an excellent teacher to marriage. In a letter written to a friend the summer she married, Sarah Douglass revealed that quitting her job was never a serious consideration, explaining that after "rest and country air" she hoped to return to her "school duties with new interest."[90] In December 1858 Douglass reflected on her career in teaching: "The employment chosen for me by my dearest mother has been a great blessing to me. May I be thankful."[91] Clearly, the decision to marry was not based upon the desire to leave her professional life and engage in full-time domesticity.

Unlike Forten, Sarah Douglass maintained a professional life alongside of activism and, eventually, marriage. The 1850 federal census lists Sarah as living with her brothers Robert Jr. and James (William Penn had died) and eighteen-year-old Emily Robinson, who likely provided domestic labor, since all three siblings worked outside the home. All four individuals are listed as mulatto, with each of the Douglass siblings listed as being worth $1,000 in real estate holdings.[92] Households enumerated as being neighbors of the Douglass family on the census are not given a racial designation and are presumably white.[93] Although financially comfortable, established in her career, and sharing her childhood home with her two brothers, in 1855 Sarah Douglass married William Douglass, the rector at the African Episcopal Church of St. Thomas.[94] William Douglass served as St. Thomas's second permanent rector from 1834 until his death in 1862. He was also active in the antislavery movement, although St. Thomas remained his primary mission. Early in his ministry, Douglass served as chair of a committee established to promote the *Colored American* in Philadelphia because of the "necessity of sustaining A PRESS amongst ourselves which shall be our own mouth-piece."[95] Later he became involved in a public debate with Frederick Douglass over his refusal to open the St. Thomas building for antislavery lectures and meetings. Despite this unpopular stance among activists, William Douglass was an important member of the African American Philadelphia elite, given the prominence of St. Thomas within the community. The wealthiest Black Philadelphians largely attended St. Thomas, while more working-class individuals attended Mother Bethel AME and other Black congregations. Unlike many of Philadelphia's African American ministers, William Douglass led a relatively comfortable life. St. Thomas provided a rectory and an adequate salary. Perhaps in part due to his large family, William Douglass supplemented his income by running a small private school.[96]

The decision to marry William Douglass was not an easy one for Sarah. In a letter to her friend Rebecca White, Sarah announced her impending marriage. She appears more resigned than joyful: "In the Seventh month, if nothing providential occur to [forestall,] I am to be married. After a long season of darkness, of deep searching and proving (in which I was enabled to say in sincerity thy will be done) light has dawned upon me and I go forward humbly and reverently in the fear of God." There was no proclamation of love or excitement in this letter, and she followed the announcement with the more practical claim that she "very much need[ed] some sheeting."[97] Douglass sent some of the letters she had received from William to her friend Sarah Grimké, who chided Douglass for her negative reaction to them: "So far as I can judge from the letters I think Mr. D must be a good man, a pleasant companion, an affectionate friend. I greatly admire too the sprightly mirthful tone of some of his letters, such as that about your age, and sadly was I surprised to find that you were displeased at his innocent raillery."[98] In a later letter to Grimké that has not survived, Sarah Douglass relented in some areas but expressed hesitation about intimate relations, as indicated by Grimké's reply: "I am glad you can reciprocate Mr. D's affection, and that you have told him so. Oh Sarah, how earnestly I hope you may find in him a husband in spirit and in truth. I do not wonder you shrink from sexual intercourse, yet I suppose in married life, it is as much the natural expression of affection as the warm embrace and ardent kiss. Time will familiarize you with the idea, and the more intimate your union with Mr. D the less you will turn from it."[99]

It is perplexing why Sarah chose to marry, given she was clearly conflicted about the union. One possible explanation could be the responsibilities of kinship, that Sarah felt an obligation to step in and help raise the children of the recently widowed William. While historians are typically quick to note that Sarah and William were not related, despite their shared last name, one researcher suggests that the two were related through their mothers and not through the Douglass name.[100] If Sarah chose marriage because of a sense of duty, it didn't change her daily life. She continued to teach for ICY and maintained her memberships in various organizations. If William Douglass sought a wife to help mother his large family or to serve as his partner in church duties, he found an intellectual match rather than a drudge to carry out the daily work of managing a large household.

The 1860 federal census was the only one that reflected Sarah Douglass's short marriage to William, and the details enumerated provide no further rationale for her marriage. His profession as an Episcopal divinity was noted, as well as his personal worth of $300; thus, Sarah Douglass did not marry him to improve her financial standing.[101] The entire family was designated as mulatto by the census taker and included William (age fifty), Sarah (age forty-five), and the Douglass children from his first marriage. Elizabeth (twenty-three), Sarah (nineteen), Mary (seventeen), and Caroline (fifteen) were all listed as being employed as dressmakers. The next three children (Francis, thirteen; Lacontena, nine, referenced as Lucretia in the 1850 census; and Anna, eight) are listed as attending school. Finally, Joseph (six) did not attend school. Interestingly, Mary and Caroline did not attend school and were already employed. Despite the status of William Douglass's position, this suggests an economic standing different from that of the Robert Douglass family (or less of a priority placed on female education). Although Sarah Douglass was both teaching and lecturing, she is not listed as having a profession. The households listed on the same page of the census and thus presumably neighbors of the Douglass family are all designated as either Black or mulatto and appear to be working class. For example, there is a woman with three children under the age of seven who is listed as a washerwoman and another nearby home that included eight seemingly unrelated women ranging in age from thirty-five to sixty who worked as washerwomen, cooks, a domestic, and a house cleaner. There was also a seventy-year-old man who worked as a porter and his two sons in their mid- to late twenties listed as a waterman and a fisherman.[102] Despite its mostly middle-class congregants, the St. Thomas rectory was in a working-class neighborhood, as opposed to the more prosperous neighborhoods of the Arch Street home of the Douglass family or the Lombard Street home of the Fortens.

It is difficult to reconstruct Sarah Douglass's married life. In her surviving letters from this time, she only mentioned William Douglass occasionally and her stepchildren even less often. In a letter to Rebecca White early in her marriage, Douglass reflected on her new home rather than her life as a wife and stepmother: "I am in my husband's study, a small three story backroom over looking what seems to *me* almost a paradise of a yard. It is so sweet and pleasant, so still and quiet, (for the youngsters are not yet astir)."[103] Sarah continued working as a teacher and added lecturing to her professional duties. She wrote to Rebecca White, "I have been invited by my New York sisters to lecture to them. Our managers [at ICY] have kindly consented to my going." She concluded the letter with a rare reference to William: "My husband was quite ill last week with neuralgia in his left eye, he is now able to go out though not well."[104] William Douglass died in 1862. As head of an important church within the Black community, his death was noted by other denominations. The *Christian Recorder*, the newspaper of the AME Church, noted that "Mr. Douglass was a man who was highly respected by all classes.... He leaves behind to mourn his loss a dear and affectionate wife and nine children, one of whom is married."[105] Eight years after William Douglass's death, the 1870 census reveals that Sarah was again living with her brothers James and Robert, but, oddly, her youngest stepchildren did not live with her.[106] Why the youngest children from her husband's first marriage were not with her is unclear. Perhaps it can be explained in part by the fact that her husband left no family home; the Douglass family had lived in the St. Thomas rectory since the 1830s. The youngest two children, Anna and Joseph, were under twelve at the time of their father's death. However, when and why Sarah separated from her stepchildren are unknown. The 1870 census reveals that Martha (thirty-eight) was the head of household and keeping house for Sarah (twenty-six), Mary (twenty-two), and Lucretia (eighteen), who are listed as teachers, and Anna (sixteen) and Joseph (fourteen), listed as attending school.

In 1880 Sarah was still living with her brothers James and Robert. The census taker recorded her occupation as a housekeeper (instead of keeping house), James as a barber, and Robert as an artist. They are listed as boarders. Given her age and health, I suspect that Douglass was not actually employed as a housekeeper but instead intended to be classified as the more class-appropriate designation of keeping house. The census taker, however, thought otherwise, listing her as a boarder. Did the Douglass siblings sell the family home because of financial need, or did they find boarding to be more convenient? Sarah faced financial difficulties at the end of her life. She retired from teaching in 1877 due to rheumatism. Despite working full-time throughout her life as a teacher, Douglass also maintained leadership positions in various antislavery and intellectual uplift organizations.

SARAH DOUGLASS'S ANTISLAVERY AND RACIAL ELEVATION WORK

Sarah Forten left her mark on society through her poetry and essays. Sarah Douglass, however, was even better known as an activist through her role as secretary of various organizations. Douglass's name was often found in various newspapers during the antebellum era as the author of calls to fairs, minutes for organizations, and various position papers offered by societies. While Sarah Forten typically used a pseudonym, Sarah Douglass readily added her name to letters and essays, particularly by the mid-1830s. Douglass and her mother signed their full names to a letter to the editor without the protective shield of Sarah's office of secretary, suggesting that by 1839 her name held status in the antislavery press. Douglass and her mother, Grace, proclaimed that they "do not believe that the cause of the slave will be injured by the dissensions in the anti-slavery ranks; it is the cause of God, and he can get the victory by the few as well as by the many."[107] It is significant that the two women rather than the entire Douglass family signed the letter. While the entire family likely shared this opinion, Grace and Sarah Douglass's standing as important female abolitionists gave weight to their signatures. Their support would serve to shame those who were causing the dissension in the ranks based on the involvement of women. Sarah Douglass demonstrated faith in the value of her own words, which was shared by Garrison in his decision to publish the letter.

Although it would be easy to consider Douglass's antislavery work as her most significant organizational activism, contemporaries also recognized the importance of the Female Literary Association, which promoted both racial uplift and a focus on abolition. William Lloyd Garrison, in a lengthy letter to Douglass, outlined the reasons "the formation of this Society" was a "source of unspeakable satisfaction to [his] mind." In a visit to Philadelphia in the summer of 1832, Garrison attended a meeting of the Female Literary Association and addressed the membership. Speaking in the third person, he offered his impressions of the group on the pages of *The Liberator*: "It was one of the most interesting spectacles he had ever witnessed. If the traducers of the colored race could be acquainted with the moral worth, just refinement, and large intelligence of this association, their mouths would hereafter be dumb." He included in this description some of the arguments he had expressed privately in a letter to Douglass, in particular the call for other women to form similar organizations: "Having been permitted to bring with him several of these pieces [which were read and critiqued at the meeting] he ventures to commence their publication, not only for their own merit, but in order to induce the colored ladies other places to go and do likewise."[108] Publications stemming from Garrison's visit included Sarah Forten's poem "The Farewell" and an essay by Douglass (atypically using the pseudonym Zillah) that addressed a bill before the Pennsylvania legislature "calling to prohibit the migration of negroes and mulattoes into the Commonwealth."[109] When asked if the bill had caused her despair for the rights of African Americans, she responded that she was "cast down, but not in despair," and then drew a parallel to the persecution faced by a Quaker woman during the colonial era.[110] By equating the right to migrate with more universally accepted ideas of freedom of worship and assembly, Douglass demonstrated the wrongness of the potential law and the willingness of people of color to continue their struggle.

A different commentary on the Female Literary Association appeared in *The Liberator* after the visit of another white abolitionist, Simeon Jocelyn of Connecticut. Jocelyn suggested to the women that they should meet in their own homes for meditation, "sympathizing over the fate of the unhappy slaves," and improving their own intellects. Because he believed that a somber tone should be maintained, he urged that "visitors should receive the simplest fare." He concluded that similar meetings should be "attempted by the colored females" of other cities.[111] The meeting description continued with mentions of psalm reading and hymn singing, emphasizing the piety and purity of this gathering of women of color. An essay by Sarah Douglass was included after the description provided by Simeon Jocelyn. Douglass began by addressing "My Friends—My Sisters, How important is the occasion for which we have assembled ourselves together this evening, to hold a feast, to feed our never dying minds, to excite each other to deeds of mercy, words of peace; to stir up in the bosom of each, gratitude to God for his increasing goodness."[112] In this brief introduction, Douglass captured the essence of the association in stated and unstated ways. She interspersed the goal of uplift with piety and service to God. Although there was political purpose to the group, it was wrapped in propriety and a claim to a shared Christian religion. Douglass concluded by stating that meetings should begin with a reading of the Holy Scriptures and that "the reading and conversation should be altogether directed to the subject of slavery." To challenge the assumptions of some whites that middle-class Black women put on airs and were ostentatious, Douglass confirmed the recommendation of Jocelyn that "the refreshment which may be offered to you for the body, will be of the most simple kind, that you may feel for those who have nothing to refresh body and mind."[113] Not only did this provide a meaningful purpose to their meetings, it also served to level the social costs of membership in consideration of the widely divergent economic standing of Philadelphia's African American middle class.

The very next issue of *The Liberator* included another essay by Douglass (again credited to Zillah). This essay, "A Mother's Love," tells the story of a liberated slave Douglass met and her story of the cruelty she faced as a slave for breast feeding her young child in the middle of the workday. Douglass called out free women: "American Mothers! Can you doubt that the slave feels as tenderly for her offspring as you do for yours? Do your hearts feel no throb of pity for her woes? Will you not raise your voices and plead for her emancipation—her immediate emancipation?"[114] Although Douglass did not originate this claim, this was a fairly early iteration of it. By linking women based on their sex and shared maternal instincts rather than making claims across racial differences, calls for the sanctity of motherhood were not only persuasive but, more importantly, justified women's entrance into this political debate. Douglass concluded her essay, "Calumniators of my despised race, read this and blush," implying that white women lost some of their status as true women when they refused to work on behalf of the slave.[115]

Douglass was active in other organizations as well, although the peak of her political and creative writing occurred during the early years of her membership in the Female Literary Association. Her higher productivity in the 1830s can be explained by her youth and energy, the excitement of new organizations and outlets for writing, and the reality that she was not yet running her own school. Although publishing less by the end of the decade, Douglass was engaged in correspondence with other antislavery activists and busy serving in leadership roles in various organizations. For example, African Americans founded the Philadelphia Woman's Association in 1849, and Sarah became a member and assumed her traditional role as corresponding secretary.

By 1859 Sarah Douglass's name was so synonymous with uplift and education that a group of Philadelphia African Americans founded the Sarah M. Douglass Literary Circle to honor her name and continue her efforts. The *Weekly Anglo-African* published a description of a meeting that included the presentation of a paper by Douglass herself titled "Florence Nightingale's Notes on Nursing" and reading in turn by the members. The newspaper reported that the meetings invariably adjourned with singing and were held semimonthly. A list of officers of the group reveals that the organization included men and women and that it wielded "a powerful influence over the literature and morals of our people here."[116]

Although teaching was the core of her identity, Douglass remained active in uplift efforts and antislavery work. Her membership in multiple organizations suggests she had her finger in many different pies. Douglass recognized a duty to be involved in the community, and her activities mirrored the work of her father and brother in terms of both uplift and politics. Black men in Philadelphia joined debating societies, held conventions, and engaged legislative bodies with memorials and essays. This is not to suggest that women such as Douglass blindly mimicked the actions of Black men but instead that there was recognition of the different proofs and modes of persuasion women brought to the table. Most importantly, women acknowledged that the work to be done was too critical to be left to just half the population.

Her attendance at antislavery conventions provided Sarah with a wider network of acquaintances than just her circle of Philadelphia associates. Sarah and her mother attended the first convention held in New York, as well as the two that followed in Philadelphia. Angelina Grimké wrote to Sarah that their presence served an important role in mitigating bigotry within the antislavery movement: "You *must* be *willing* to come in among us tho it *may be* your feelings *may* be wounded by... the avoidance of a seat by you or the glaring of the eye." Because Grimké believed in the value of Sarah's presence, Grimké continued: "To suffer these things is the sacrifice which is called for at *your hands* & I earnestly desire that you may be willing to bear these mortifications with Christian meekness, gentleness and love."[117]

Angelina Grimké's suspicion of bigotry among white antislavery women was not unfounded. In 1838 Douglass wrote to Abby Kelley, whom she presumably met at the New York convention. On stationery that bore the iconic image of a female slave in chains, Douglass confirmed her appreciation for Kelley's broader claims for African American civil rights: "Altho our enemies call us ungrateful, believe me dear friend, it is *vile slander*. We fully appreciate your kindness. Do write to me sometimes, it rejoices my very soul to meet with an Abolitionist who has turned her back on prejudice."[118] Douglass and Forten experienced discrimination from white abolitionists, demonstrating again that support for emancipation did not necessarily include support for equality and the importance of enactments of Black womanhood even for their allies.

The Philadelphia Female Anti-Slavery Society reacted to the violence the 1838 national convention faced and the burning of Pennsylvania Hall in a set of resolutions signed solely by Douglass in her position as secretary. Published in the antislavery press, PFAS members proclaimed that they would "redouble efforts to awaken the public mind to a sense of the ruin in which the enslavement of a part of our countrymen threatens to involve the liberties of all."[119] It was critical to stress the symbolic importance of returning to the site of violence, as Philadelphia was slated to host the next convention. Sarah Douglass remained active in the Philadelphia Female Anti-Slavery Society throughout the prewar years. She was listed in an 1844 call for an antislavery fair (along with Harriet Forten Purvis and Margaretta Forten, but Sarah Forten Purvis is notably missing) as an organizer.[120]

After marriage, when her reputation was protected by her status as a prominent minister's wife, Douglass began a series of public lectures on the subjects of anatomy, physiology, and hygiene. She audited lectures at a Philadelphia female medical college in 1853 and again in 1858 to prepare for her public lectures. Writing to Rebecca White, she explained, "I work very hard just now, and recreate by attending Ann Preston's lectures. I cannot describe the pure intellectual enjoyment they give me. How marvelously has God fashioned these poor bodies!" She further revealed her reluctance in the face of her duty to provide this information to women: "I hope to begin my lectures next month. I see duty clearly, yet I shrink and shiver and feel so little."[121] Once the lectures began they were well received. The *Weekly Anglo-African* reported that "these lectures deserve the highest commendation" and further supported the propriety of Douglass delivering the material, because despite the "delicacy of woman's character," such information was critical to women's and children's well-being. Discussions of her lectures almost always reflected upon Douglass's modesty and linked the human body to God's work: "The lecture of Mrs. Douglass breathed throughout a recognition of the God whose glorious handiwork they presented to view. They were not mere details of scientific facts, but were enriched by numerous and beautiful illustrations, well calculated to elevate the mind, and so practical as to engage the attention of many of whom theories, however grand and inspiring, are lost."[122] These articles not only served to protect Douglass's reputation as a "lady" but also helped to make it acceptable for women to attend the lectures. The African American press stressed her renown and presented her lectures as an extension of her pedagogical responsibilities: "Mrs. Douglass has been long known both in New York and Philadelphia as a most successful and self-sacrificing teacher. Many of our honored wives and mothers owe their intelligence to her faithful instructions. It is, then, fitting that they who received their early lessons from her, should now come to acquire that important knowledge which may secure the physical, and consequently no small degree of the moral and intellectual well-being of our future men and women." In 1860 Douglass was asked to give her lectures to a group of women in New York. This group offered their thanks in the form of a resolution that included their recognition that the audience did "admire the chaste and refined language, and modest demeanor of the lecturer, as well as the perfect gravity, with which she inspired her audience."[123] Douglass continued to support broader interests in African American rights and intellectual pursuits throughout her life, donating to a fund established by the Banneker Institute in Philadelphia "for the purpose of circulating speeches and documents favorable to universal suffrage."[124]

Sarah Douglass died on September 8, 1882. Her brother Robert wrote Rebecca White the next day, "It is a mournful duty I have to fulfill! We are in the dark shadow of a great sorrow! My dear sister, Sarah M. Douglass, has left us, departed this life, gone we trust to a better world! Her death was peaceful, although she had previously suffered for a long season, the most agonizing pain!"[125] Alexander Crummell, an African American Episcopal priest and abolitionist, memorialized her in the following: "Mrs. Douglass has spent a lifetime in the intellectual training of two generations of Philadelphia's men and women. Her pupils may be found in scores, if not hundreds of the mature and settled men and women of her native city. The very first people thereof and their children in turn, have sat at the feet of this refined and cultivated woman and received from her the ripe instructions of her well-cultivated mind."[126] Douglass was an important figure because she managed to transgress traditional boundaries for women of color while maintaining the image of womanhood. As an instructor of girls, Douglass mixed the traditional curriculum of reading, writing, and simple math with the higher branches, including science, and instructed young women in both the domestic arts and the art of true womanhood. Finally, the lecture series Douglass performed in the 1850s and 1860s provided women with important medical knowledge in a way that protected the reputation of both speaker and audience.

CONCLUSION

Sarah Forten and Sarah Mapps Douglass found a public voice through print culture. Both women began their public lives through print culture, thus entertaining a wider and longer-lasting audience. Their writings demonstrate a private belief in idealized womanhood, whether for its own sake, as a means for legitimating their own words and deeds, or for promoting the civic standing of Black men and women in the United States. Their political arguments were shrouded in acceptable traits such as maternal instincts and shared biological destinies that would transgress the barriers of race. The opportunities for publishing that were readily available to white women such as Sarah Hale, Lydia Maria Child, and Catharine Beecher were limited for women of color to the antislavery press or private publishing. While Black and white women both wrote of womanhood, white women had the luxury of prescribing behaviors, while women of color described their own adherence to those cultural standards.

How both women experienced their daily lives impacted their presence in the public sphere. Sarah Forten Purvis found that living in a rural area with a large family not only eliminated her time to write but also cost her the inspiration that club work and antislavery activism provided her. Sarah Mapps Douglass maintained her busy life of antislavery work, but the burdens of running her own school limited her ability to publish. By 1840 any mention of her name in the papers was limited to her position as secretary of various organizations or her teaching. Surprisingly, marriage to a widower with nine children seemed to have had little impact on her professional life, as she continued to teach and began to lecture on women's health, expanding her service to girls through teaching their mothers and other adult women.

The experiences of Forten and Douglass reveal the difficulties faced by women, particularly women of color, in making their voices heard in the public sphere during the antebellum era. Their experiences demonstrate that true womanhood could be deployed to justify a female's political voice or to demonstrate that men, particularly men of color, functioned as white men—as patriarchs of their wives and children with the authority to justify a civic standing. While opportunities for women of color to exert political power were difficult, these women also demonstrated the strategic ways women circumvented the constraints placed upon them. Particularly in antislavery work, women of color enacted the virtues of womanhood and the potential for all Black women after emancipation.

CONCLUSION

Reconstructing Womanhood
Domesticity, Citizenship, and *Minor v. Happersett*

The antebellum era was a critical time for defining citizenship. States' and the federal government's interpretations of who was and was not a citizen evolved largely because the U.S. Constitution did not define the term until the Fourteenth Amendment was ratified in 1868. Before the Fourteenth Amendment, definitions of citizenship were fluid and reflected the needs and prejudices of white male policy makers. White women and African Americans did not passively accept their secondary civic status. Middle-class white women used the transition to a market economy and the shifting purpose of their domestic labor to attach civic meaning to their work as wives and mothers. During the first half of the nineteenth century, instead of focusing on birthright citizenship or natural rights, women reinterpreted the ideology of true womanhood and the gendered expectations of female behavior as evidence of their importance within the nation and their fulfillment of the obligations of citizenship. While many women did not question their status as citizens at this time, they did struggle to find ways to meet the gendered expectations of citizenship. Because the traditional ways men demonstrated their civic standing were off-limits, culturally if not legally, women reimagined the meaning of middle-class femininity to confirm their status as citizens and *ladies*.

During the era of the early republic, African American men typically claimed a natural right to citizenship and used the language of the Declaration of Independence as evidence of the universality of basic rights. As state constitutions and eventually the U.S. Supreme Court explicitly curtailed the civic standing of African Americans, free people of color turned to the same strategies used by white women to demonstrate their fitness for citizenship. A well-ordered home run by a "true woman" provided proof of the middle-class respectability of African Americans and thereby their rightful claim of citizenship.

Print culture served as a central means for women and African American men to claim citizenship. Newspapers, books, journals, and political tracts provided an access point to the public sphere for those otherwise excluded. Marginalized groups formed organizations and established institutions to construct counterpublics that both allowed for mobilization and offered a critique of the status quo. Printed materials gave women and African American men the opportunity to publicize their arguments for civic status to a wider audience than culturally sanctioned practices would allow in public spaces. The written word also allowed marginalized groups to enact their arguments. Women could demonstrate their intellect, as well as the tenets of true womanhood, without transgressing the cultural norms that defined their femininity. This approach meant that despite conflicting views of women's suffrage and what female citizenship meant, both Catharine Beecher and Elizabeth Cady Stanton could agitate for women's civic standing.

Despite the growing antebellum activism of women, the volumes of published materials, and the formation of numerous political, benevolent, and intellectual organizations, women and African American men were not given the rights and privileges of citizenship on an equal basis with white men. Serious considerations of voting rights would not occur until after the Civil War. While denied the ballot, white women and African Americans nonetheless considered themselves to be citizens and worked to find ways to ensure that they received the benefits implied by that status. It is important to recognize that civic inclusion could be experienced in a variety of ways. For example, not all women who sought civic status also wished for the right to vote, as seen in the work of Sarah Hale and Catharine Beecher. Yet many women practiced the ideology of true womanhood in order to raise the cultural importance of their roles as wives and mothers. African American men, almost universally, sought equal status with white men. They deployed claims of middle-class respectability to claim economic and political rights for themselves and their families.

The decade after the Civil War produced legal answers to questions about who was a citizen and what that meant. The Fourteenth Amendment declared that "all persons born or naturalized in the United States and subject to the jurisdiction thereof, are citizens of the United States and of the State where in they reside." In other words, the amendment overturned the *Dred Scott* decision, which ruled that African Americans were not citizens. This decision marked a divergence in the strategies of Black and white women. African American women continued to search for civic standing for their entire household as opposed to pursuing voting rights expressly for themselves. With the widespread emancipation resulting from the Thirteenth Amendment and the end of the Civil War, issues of respectability and uplift remained important to African American claims for civic standing.

White women, during the second half of the nineteenth century, began to more actively seek the ballot (although they still had not formed a majority position), and calls for women's rights became synonymous with suffrage. Women of color also sought the ballot, but the racism of a large proportion of the suffrage movement made cooperation difficult. The rise of Jim Crow laws and increased racial violence also meant that Black women could not focus on their own voting rights in the same way white women could.

The debate over the Fourteenth Amendment, which introduced "male" to the Constitution, and the Fifteenth Amendment, which stated that the right to vote could not be denied "on account of race, color, or previous condition of servitude" but ignored sex, initiated a split within the women's movement that lasted more than twenty years. Elizabeth Cady Stanton even engaged in a rhetoric of women's virtue and moral superiority to justify women's enfranchisement. In reality, this was a scare tactic to persuade men that white women were needed to balance out the vote of Black men and immigrants.[1] The split in the antislavery movement in 1840 revolved around the question of female involvement. The split that became official in 1869 in the suffrage movement with the creation of the American Woman Suffrage Association, led by Lucy Stone, and the National Woman Suffrage Association, led by Stanton and Susan B. Anthony, was based on the status of Black men as voters. Ironically, movements for equality are often plagued with an unwillingness to endorse universal equality.

The long fight to prove women's citizenship was decided by the U.S. Supreme Court in *Minor v. Happersett* (1875). The court confirmed that "women born of citizen parents within the jurisdiction of the United States, have always been considered citizens of the United States, as much so before the adoption of the fourteenth amendment to the Constitution as since."[2] The court case involved Virginia Minor, a white citizen of both the United States and the state of Missouri whose attempt to register to vote was denied by the local registrar. Because the Missouri state constitution stipulated that "every male citizen of the United States shall be entitled to vote," the registrar determined that Minor was ineligible to vote. In its opinion, the court upheld female citizenship; it did not conclude that female citizenship conferred a right to vote. The court argued that "the right to suffrage was not necessarily one of the privileges or immunities of citizenship before the adoption of the fourteenth amendment, and that amendment does not add to these privileges and immunities." As a result, the court concluded that male-only provisions did not violate the federal Constitution: "In such a State women have no right to vote."[3] This ruling placed women in a similar situation to African American men during the antebellum era. Absent a federal constitutional amendment, the fight for Black male suffrage had to be fought in state courts or state constitutional conventions. For African American men, the passage of the Fourteenth and Fifteenth Amendments confirmed their right to vote, yet without police protections, Jim Crow attitudes made the exercise of their citizenship an uncertain proposition.

While the tenets of true womanhood remained important markers of race and class after the Civil War, white women increasingly understood domesticity as less central to their identities as Americans. In 1869 Catharine Beecher rereleased her *Treatise on Domestic Economy* as *The American Woman's Home*, coauthored with her sister Harriet. The new book replaced the lengthy introduction with its tribute to Tocqueville with a four-page promotion of the authors and a discussion of the need for women to be trained in their duties as wives and mothers. Despite the patriotic title, Beecher promoted woman's domestic duties as central to her own status, as opposed to building the nation at large: "It is the aim of this volume to elevate both the honor and the remuneration of all the employments that sustain the many difficult and sacred duties of the family state, and thus to render each department of woman's true profession as much desired and respected as are the most honored professions of men."[4] After decades of practicing the tenets of true womanhood, women continued to refine the meaning of their citizenship. While the performance of true womanhood did not ultimately translate into legal citizenship, its practice increased the breadth of the performance of citizenship to include the everyday practices of men and women. The strategies developed during the antebellum era created access to the public sphere and provided a template for civic claims by future generations.

NOTES

INTRODUCTION. Gendering Rights and Racializing Gender

1. Lydia Maria Child to Ellis Gray Loring, Wayland, 24 February 1856, in *Letters of Lydia Maria Child*, ed. Harriet Winslow Sewall, with a biographical introduction by John G. Whittier and an appendix by Wendell Phillips (Boston: Houghton, Mifflin and Company, 1883), 74. Child apparently had an interest in spiritualism and softened her belief with humor. Many of her letters reference agitated rapping after her death.

2. Michael Warner, *The Republic of Letters: Publication and the Public Sphere in Eighteenth-Century America* (Cambridge, Mass.: Harvard University Press, 1990), xi–xiii.

3. Barbara Welter, "The Cult of True Womanhood, 1820–1860," *American Quarterly* 18 (Summer 1966): 151–74.

4. Kathryn Kish Sklar, "AHR Roundtable: Reconsidering Domesticity through the Lens of Empire and Settler Society in North America," *American Historical Review* 4 (October 2019): 1250.

5. Jürgen Habermas describes the bourgeois public sphere as "the sphere of private people [who] come together as a public; they soon claimed the public sphere regulated from above against the public authority themselves to engage them in a debate over the general rules governing relations in the basically privatized but publicly relevant sphere of commodity exchange and social labor" (*The Structural Transformation of the Public Sphere*, trans. Thomas Burger [Cambridge, Mass.: MIT Press, 1991], 27). Habermas's description of the public sphere has been widely criticized because it lacks a discussion of marginalized groups (among other critiques), yet it remains a starting point for almost all discussion of the public sphere.

6. For an analysis of the performativity of citizenship, in this instance the role of blood donation by gay men, see Jeffrey Bennett, *Banning Queer Blood: Rhetorics of Citizenship, Contagion, and Resistance* (Tuscaloosa: University of Alabama Press, 2009), esp. 5–10.

7. Sharon Romeo, *Gender and the Jubilee: Black Freedom and the Reconstruction of Citizenship in Civil War Missouri* (Athens: University of Georgia Press, 2016), 11.

8. "Letter from Bishop Allen," *Freedom's Journal*, 2.

9. Rochelle Raineri Zuck, *Divided Sovereignties: Race, Nationhood, and Citizenship in Nineteenth-Century America* (Athens: University of Georgia Press, 2016), 99. David Walker called for the need for a freedom struggle in the South. Maria Stewart was well known afterward for making a public claim for African Americans to adopt similar beliefs in the North. She was the author of four substantial pieces in newspapers before leaving the public eye.

10. Derrick R. Spires, *The Practice of Citizenship: Black Politics and Print Culture in the Early United States* (Philadelphia: University of Pennsylvania Press, 2019), 3.

11. The Black Public Sphere Collective, *The Black Public Sphere: A Public Culture Book* (Chicago: University of Chicago Press, 1995).

12. As quoted in Spires, *The Practice of Citizenship*, 18.

13. Terri Diane Halperin, *The Alien and Sedition Acts of 1798* (Baltimore, Md.: Johns Hopkins University Press, 2016), 31–32.

14. Matthew Frye Jacobson, *Whiteness of a Different Color* (Cambridge, Mass.: Harvard University Press, 1998), 4.

15. Marian L. Smith, "'Any Woman Who is Now or may hereafter be Married . . .': Women and Naturalization ca. 1802–1940," *Prologue Magazine* 30 (Summer 1998), https://www.archives.gov/publications/prologue/1998/summer/women-and-naturalization-1.htmlro.

16. The Naturalization Act of 1798 increased the waiting period for residency from five years (established in 1795) to fourteen years to stall the process of immigrants being integrated within the nation. Halperin, *Alien and Sedition Acts*, 36–38.

17. Brook Thomas, *Civic Myths: A Law and Literature Approach to Citizenship* (Chapel Hill: University of North Carolina Press, 2007), 3–4.

18. Melissa Harris-Perry, *Sister Citizens: Shame, Stereotypes, and Black Women in America* (New Haven, Conn.: Yale University Press, 2011), 36–37.

19. Julie Roy Jeffries, *The Great Silent Army of Abolitionism: Ordinary Women in the Antislavery Movement* (Chapel Hill: University of North Carolina Press, 1998). While Jeffries uses this phrase in the title of her book, it is typical in its everywoman account of female activism.

20. Raia Prokhovnik, "Public and Private Citizenship: From Gender Invisibility to Feminist Inclusiveness," *Feminist Review* 60 (Autumn 1998): 85.

21. Joan Wallach Scott, *Gender and the Politics of History*, rev. ed. (New York: Columbia University Press, 1993), 2–4.

22. For a detailed discussion of this idea, see Barbara Welke, *Law and the Borders of Belonging in the Long Nineteenth Century United States* (Cambridge, Mass.: Harvard University Press, 2010). Corinne T. Field argues that equal adulthood is a useful way of understanding nineteenth-century claims for citizenship. Referencing women's rights activists, she explains that they sought "equal adulthood because paying attention to individual maturation allowed them to connect otherwise disparate demands for political rights, control of their own labor, sexual autonomy, cultural power, and familial authority—all of which were things adult white men claimed for themselves but regularly denied to children, men who were not white, and all women" (*The Struggle for Equal Adulthood: Gen-

der, Race, Age, and the Fight for Citizenship in Antebellum America [Chapel Hill: University of North Carolina Press, 2014], 5).

23. Melinda Chateauvert, "Framing Sexual Citizenship: Reconsidering the Discourse on African American Families," *Journal of African American History* 95 (2008): 215.

24. By the 1800s female literacy was on par with that of males in middle-class households. See Mary P. Ryan, *Womanhood in America: From Colonial Times to the Present*, 2nd ed. (New York: New Viewpoints, 1979), 92–93. The 1850 census reveals that less than 1 percent of the New England native-born women over the age of twenty were unable to read and write. See John E. Murray, "Generation(s) of Human Capital: Literacy in American Families, 1830–1875," *Journal of Interdisciplinary History* 27 (1997): 416. There is now speculation that literacy rates would be higher if writing skills were separated out when determining literacy.

25. Benedict Anderson, *Imagined Communities* (London: Verso, 2006), 35–36.

26. J. G. A. Pocock, "The Ideal of Citizenship Since Classical Times," in *Theorizing Citizenship*, ed. Ronald Beiner (Albany: State University of New York Press, 1995), 33. Another essay in this collection, by Michael Ignatieff ("The Myth of Citizenship," 53–77), discusses the Aristotelian model for citizenship, stressing the subservient role of *oeconomia*, the domestic realm, when assessing civic virtue.

27. Jeanne Boydston, *Home & Work: Housework, Wages, and the Ideology of Labor in the Early Republic* (New York: Oxford University Press, 1990).

28. Kathleen Canning, *Gender History in Practice: Historical Perspectives on Bodies, Class, and Citizenship* (Ithaca, N.Y.: Cornell University Press, 2006), 19.

29. Leonore Davidoff, "Gender and the 'Great Divide': Public and Private in British Gender History," *Journal of Women's History* 15 (2003): 11.

30. Davidoff, 12.

31. Leslie M. Harris, *In the Shadow of Slavery: African Americans in New York City, 1627–1863* (Chicago: University of Chicago Press, 2003), 112. Jane E. Dabel, in *A Respectable Woman: The Public Roles of African American Women in 19th-Century New York* (New York: New York University Press, 2008), 32–34, describes the difficulty African American women had in maintaining high standards of cleanliness given the absence of fresh air and potable water in often terribly overcrowded conditions. Despite the difficulty, women of color were provided advice (often not possible to follow given living conditions) by the Black press and worked to demonstrate the respectability of not only themselves but also their homes.

32. Chateauvert, "Framing Sexual Citizenship," 201–7.

33. Elsa Barkley Brown, "Negotiating and Transforming the Public Sphere: African American Political Life in the Transition from Slavery to Freedom," in Black Public Sphere Collective, *The Black Public Sphere*, 128.

34. Kimberlé Crenshaw, "Mapping the Margins: Intersectionality, Identity Politics, and Violence against Women of Color," *Stanford University Law Review* 43 (1991): 1241–99; Jennifer Nash, "Rethinking Intersectionality," *Feminist Review* 89 (2008): 1–15; and Brittney Cooper, "Intersectionality," in *The Oxford Handbook of Feminist Theory*, ed. Lisa Disch and Mary Hawkesworth (New York: Oxford University Press, 2016), 385–406.

35. Eileen Boris argues that "constructions of citizenship developed out of notions

of whiteness, blackness, Anglo-Saxonism, womanhood, and manhood, revealing the role of culture in the creation of civic status" ("Citizenship Embodied: Racialized Gender and the Construction of Nationhood in the United States," in *Identity and Intolerance: Nationalism, Racism, and Xenophobia in Germany and the United States*, ed. Norbert Finzsch and Dietmar Schirmer [Washington, D.C.: German Historical Institute and Cambridge University Press, 1998], 315).

36. Susan Zaeske, *Signatures of Citizenship: Petitioning, Antislavery and Women's Political Identity* (Chapel Hill: University of North Carolina Press, 2003). For an analysis of women's calls for political rights prior to Seneca Falls, see Lori D. Ginzberg, *Untidy Origins: A Story of Women's Rights in Antebellum New York* (Chapel Hill: University of North Carolina Press, 2005); and Nancy Isenberg, *Sex and Citizenship in Antebellum America* (Chapel Hill: University of North Carolina Press, 1998).

CHAPTER 1. The Expanding Female Sphere

1. Phillis Wheatley, *Poems on Various Subjects, Religious and Moral* (Denver, Colo.: W. H. Lawrence & Co., 1887), 14.

2. Abigail Adams, letters of 31 March 1776 and 7 May 1776, in *Early American Women: A Documentary History, 1600–1900*, ed. Nancy Woloch (Boston: McGraw Hill, 2002), 128–30.

3. Lori Ginzberg, *Untidy Origins* (Chapel Hill: University of North Carolina Press, 2005), 13.

4. State legislatures were particularly prolific in revising their own constitutions at this time. Political scientist Robinson Woodward-Burns writes that between 1792 and 1850 "states called fifty-six revision assemblies, empowering forty-nine to draft new documents, ratifying thirty-four constitutions, and proposing and ratifying dozens of amendments. In contrast, Congress passed only 2 of the 511 proposed amendments—the narrow Eleventh and Twelfth Amendments" (*Hidden Laws: How State Constitutions Stabilize American Politics* [New Haven, Conn.: Yale University Press, 2021], 47).

5. Eve Kornfield, *Creating an American Culture, 1775–1800* (Boston: Bedford / St. Martin's, 2001), 7.

6. The Federal Militia Act of 1792 specifically limited service to "free able-bodied white male citizens of the respective States" (Barbara Young Welke, *Law and the Borders of Belonging in the Long Nineteenth Century United States* [New York: Cambridge University Press, 2010], 35).

7. Thomas Janoski, *Citizenship and Civil Society: A Framework of Rights and Obligation in Liberal, Traditional, and Social Democratic Regimes* (Cambridge: Cambridge University Press, 1998), 182.

8. Linda Kerber, "The Meanings of Citizenship," *Journal of American History* 84 (1997): 835–36.

9. Pauline Schloesser describes a "gendered citizenship" based on her reading of Linda Kerber and Mary Beth Norton. This incomplete citizenship stemmed not from actual participation in government but instead from the protections coming from the state. See

The Fair Sex: White Women and Racial Patriarchy in the Early American Republic (New York: New York University Press, 2002), 2.

10. Jan Lewis, "'Of Every Age, Sex & Condition': The Representation of Women in the Constitution," *Journal of the Early Republic* 15 (1995): 372–73.

11. William Blackstone, *Commentaries on the Laws of England* (1765–1767), quoted in Schloesser, *The Fair Sex*, 30.

12. Linda Kerber, *No Constitutional Right to Be Ladies* (New York: Hill and Wang, 1998), 11.

13. Joan Hoff, *Law, Gender & Injustice: A Legal History of U.S. Women* (New York: NYU Press, 1991), 87–89.

14. Gretchen Ritter, *The Constitution as Social Design: Gender and Civic Membership in the American Constitutional Order* (Stanford, Calif.: Stanford University Press, 2006), 69. For a discussion of coverture, property, and the civic standing of women, see Linda K. Kerber, "Why Diamonds Really Are a Girl's Best Friend: Another American Narrative," *Daedalus* 141 (2012): 89–100.

15. Mackenzie v. Hare, 239 U.S. 299 (1915); Linda Kerber, *Toward an Intellectual History of Women* (Chapel Hill: University of North Carolina Press, 1997), 301; and Nancy F. Cott, "Marriage and Women's Citizenship in the United States, 1830–1934," *American Historical Review* 103, no. 5 (December 1998): 1440–74.

16. "A Republican Festival," *National Intelligencer and Washington Advertiser* (Washington, D.C.), 9 February 1803.

17. Shane White. "'It Was a Proud Day': African Americans, Festivals, and Parades in the North, 1741–1834," *Journal of American History* 81 (1994): 34. For a lengthier treatment of African American festivals and their role in the creation of collective identity and memory, see Mitch Kachun, *Festivals of Freedom: Memory and Meaning in African American Emancipation Celebrations, 1808–1915* (Amherst: University of Massachusetts Press, 2003).

18. David Waldstreicher, *In the Midst of Perpetual Fetes: The Making of American Nationalism, 1776–1820* (Chapel Hill: University of North Carolina Press, 1997), 235.

19. Mary P. Ryan, *Mysteries of Sex: Tracing Women and Men through American History* (Chapel Hill: University of North Carolina Press, 2006), 154. While Ryan would deny that women were completely absent from the public sphere, she argues that their presence was secondary and served primarily a symbolic function: "Women, largely absent from all the institutional sites of the public—from polling places, city councils, public offices . . . were an extreme case of the social exclusions of early American republicanism. . . . [H]owever, some women had a particularly honored place in the ceremonial representations of the public" ("Gender and Public Access: Women's Politics in Nineteenth-Century America," in *Habermas and the Public Sphere*, ed. Craig Calhoun [Cambridge, Mass.: MIT Press, 1992], 265–66).

20. Judith Sargent Stevens, *Some Deductions from the System Promulgated in the Page of Divine Revelations, Ranged in the Order and Form of a Catechism* (Norwich, Conn.: Trumball, 1782), iii–v, collected in *Judith Sargent Murray: A Brief Biography with Documents*, ed. Sheila L. Skemp (Boston: Bedford / St. Martin's, 1998), 129.

21. Linda K. Kerber, *Women of the Republic* (Chapel Hill: University of North Carolina Press, 1980), 11–12.

22. Skemp, *Judith Sargent Murray*, 82.

23. "The Gleaner Contemplates the Future Prospects of Women in This 'Enlightened Age'" (1798), in Skemp, 185.

24. Jeanne Boydston, "Making Gender in the Early Republic: Judith Sargent Murray and the Revolution of 1800," in *The Revolution of 1800: Democracy, Race, and the New Republic*, ed. James Horn, Jan Ellen Lewis, and Peter S. Onuf (Charlottesville: University of Virginia Press, 2002), 240–66.

25. Christy Clark-Pujara, *Dark Work: The Business of Slavery in Rhode Island* (New York: NYU Press, 2016), 76.

26. Edward Countryman, *Enjoy the Same Liberty: Black Americans and the Revolutionary Era* (Lanham, Md.: Rowman & Littlefield Publishers, 2012), 45–48. See also Benjamin Quarles, *The Negro in the American Revolution* (Chapel Hill: University of North Carolina Press, 1961).

27. Wheatley, *Poems on Various Subjects*, 9–10. Eighteen men affixed their names to this statement, including John Hancock and colonial governor Thomas Hutchinson.

28. Thomas Jefferson, *Notes on the State of Virginia* (1785, 1787), ed. David Waldstreicher (Boston: Bedford / St. Martin's, 2002), 178. Perhaps Jefferson decided not to question Wheatley's authorship because he did not want to challenge the authority of the white males who vouched for Wheatley in the book's foreword.

29. Hoff, *Law, Gender & Injustice*, 18.

30. Michael Grossberg, *Governing the Hearth: Law & Family in Nineteenth Century America* (Chapel Hill: University of North Carolina Press, 1985), 4–10.

31. Michael Kimmel, *Manhood in America: A Cultural History* (New York: Free Press, 1996), 29.

32. Jeanne Boydston, *Home and Work: Housework, Wages, and the Ideology of Labor in the Early Republic* (New York: Oxford University Press, 1990), 43.

33. Kerber, *Women of the Republic*, 11–12.

34. Mary Beth Norton, *Liberty's Daughters* (Ithaca, N.Y.: Cornell University Press, 1980), 297–99.

35. Mary P. Ryan, *The Empire of the Mother* (New York: Harrington Park Press, 1985), 145.

36. Joanne Pope Melish, *Disowning Slavery* (Ithaca, N.Y.: Cornell University Press, 1998), 134.

37. Barbara Welter, *Dimity Convictions: The American Woman in the Nineteenth Century* (Athens: Ohio University Press, 1976).

38. Kathleen Brown explains that "the tax levied on African women in 1643 was the earliest distinctive and clearly unfavorable treatment of African people to be enshrined by law in Virginia" (*Good Wives, Nasty Wenches, and Anxious Patriarchs* [Chapel Hill: University of North Carolina Press, 1996], 116). This tax on African women as laborers served to create a difference between the status of white and Black women despite the fact that women of both races were likely to labor in the fields. This 1643 tax provides a legal

marker of racial difference based on gender; however, cultural uses of gender to define racial difference can be found even earlier. See Jennifer Morgan, *Laboring Women* (Philadelphia: University of Pennsylvania Press, 2004), esp. chap. 1. For a more general overview, see Kirsten Fischer, "The Imperial Gaze: Native American, African American and Colonial Women in European Eyes," in *A Companion to American Women's History*, ed. Nancy A. Hewitt (Malden, Mass.: Blackwell, 2005).

39. Shirley J. Yee, *Black Women Abolitionists: A Study in Activism, 1828–1860* (Knoxville: University of Tennessee Press, 1992), 42.

40. Elizabeth White Nelson, *Market Sentiments: Middle-Class Market Culture in Nineteenth-Century America* (Washington, D.C.: Smithsonian Books, 2004), 81.

41. *Fifth Annual Report of the Boston Female Anti-Slavery Society* (Boston: Isaac Knapp, 1838), 9.

42. Susan Zaeske, *Signatures of Citizenship: Petitioning, Antislavery, and Women's Political Identity* (Chapel Hill: University of North Carolina Press, 2003), 19, 35.

43. "From the *Charter Oak*: Petitions! Petitions! Petitions!," *Pennsylvania Freeman*, 5 December 1839. For a discussion of the controversy in Congress over the petitions and the gag rule, see chapter 4 in Joanne B. Freeman, *The Field of Blood: Violence in Congress and the Road to Civil War* (New York: Farrar, Strauss and Giroux, 2018).

44. Kate Masur, *Until Justice Be Done: America's First Civil Rights Movement, from the Revolution to Reconstruction* (New York: W. W. Norton and Company, 2021), 98.

45. Manisha Sinha, "An Alternative Tradition of Radicalism: African American Abolitionists and the Metaphor of Revolution," in *Contested Democracy: Freedom, Race, and Power in American History*, ed. Manisha Sinha and Penny Von Eschen (New York: Columbia University Press, 2007), 11, 17–18.

46. Absalom Jones, "Petition of Absalom Jones and Seventy Three Others, 1799," in *Early Negro Writing, 1760–1837*, ed. Dorothy Porter (Baltimore, Md.: Black Classic Press, 1995), 330. Jones is discussed in more detail in chapter 4.

47. "Laws of the African Society, Instituted at Boston, Anno Domini 1796," in Porter, 9. I believe this is a direct claim of citizenship rather than a declaration of residency because of the separation of the phrases "true and faithful citizens" and "the Commonwealth in which we live."

48. "Constitution and By-Laws of the Brotherly Union Society, Instituted, April, 1823," in Porter, 51.

49. Access to print material increased across the board during the antebellum era, meaning publication was no longer the tool of the elite. According to the document collection *Pamphlets of Protest: An Anthology of Early African-American Protest Literature, 1790–1860*, ed. Richard Newman, Patrick Rael, and Phillip Lapsansky (New York: Routledge, 2001), "by 1850, nearly four times as many daily newspapers circulated throughout the country as there had been two decades earlier, and the costs of production had plummeted by 600 percent" (3).

50. Rowland Berthoff, "Conventional Mentality: Free Blacks, Women, and Business Corporations as Unequal Persons, 1820–1870," *Journal of American History* 76 (1989): 757.

51. Tapping Reeve as cited in *Antebellum Women: Private, Public, Partisan*, ed. Carol

Lasser and Stacey Robertson (Lanham, Md.: Rowman & Littlefield Publishers, 2010), 95. Judge Reeve was a close friend of the Lyman Beecher family.

52. Ginzberg, *Untidy Origins*, 66–67.

53. Carole Shammas, "Re-assessing the Married Women's Property Acts," *Journal of Women's History* 6 (1994): 9.

54. "Ought a Married Woman to Hold Property?," *American Ladies' Magazine* 8 (1837): 27.

55. For example, James Forten not only was a successful sail maker but also served as a landlord and money lender to both Blacks and whites and provided mortgages on land that he sold (Julie Winch, *A Gentleman of Color: The Life of James Forten* [New York: Oxford University Press, 2002], 102–6). Forten's son-in-law Robert Purvis engaged in "buying, selling, and renting real estate properties and lending money" (Margaret Hope Bacon, *But One Race: The Life of Robert Purvis* [Albany: State University of New York Press, 2007], 30).

56. "Constitution and Rules to Be Observed and Kept by the Friendly Society of St. Thomas's African Church, 1831, Philadelphia," in Porter, *Early Negro Writing*, 30.

57. "Letter from Patterson," *The Anglo-African* (New York), 10 March 1860.

58. For a useful historiography of African American voting rights, see Van Gosse, *The First Reconstruction: Black Politics in America from the Revolution to the Civil War* (Chapel Hill: University of North Carolina Press, 2021), 8–17.

59. "Passports for Colored People," *National Era*, 27 September 1849.

60. Christy Clark-Pujura, *Dark Work: The Business of Slavery in Rhode Island* (New York: NYU Press, 2016), chap. 3.

61. Ira Berlin, *Many Thousand Gone* (Cambridge, Mass.: Belknap Press, 1998), 22–24.

62. Bennett Liebman, "The Quest for Black Voting Rights in New York State," *Albany Government Law Review* 11 (2018): 389–90.

63. William Yates, *The Rights of Colored Men to Suffrage, Citizenship and Trial by Jury* (Philadelphia: Merrihew & Gunn, 1838), 19–20. It was ultimately decided to strike "white" from the qualifications by a vote of 63–59. For a detailed analysis of African American voting rights in New York State leading to the 1821 state constitutional convention, see Gosse, *First Reconstruction*, 315–76.

64. James Brewer Stewart, "Modernizing 'Difference': The Political Meanings of Color in the Free States, 1776–1840," *Journal of the Early Republic* 19 (1999): 701. Eric Ledell Smith explains that by 1838 states had taken one of four positions on African American suffrage: (1) no exclusion, (2) required significant taxable property holdings, (3) outright exclusion from voting, or (4) states originally allowed Black male suffrage and later amended state constitutions to prohibit it ("The End of Black Voting Rights in Pennsylvania: African Americans and the Pennsylvania Constitutional Convention of 1837–1838," *Pennsylvania History* 65 [1998]: 279). Leon Litwack explained in his classic work that by "1840, some 93 percent of the northern free negro population lived in states which completely or practically excluded them from the right to vote" (*North of Slavery: The Negro in the Free States, 1760–1860* [Chicago: University of Chicago Press, 1961], 75).

65. "One of the Possible Effects of Negro Suffrage," *United States' Telegraph* (Washington, D.C.), 15 August 1836.

66. For a detailed overview of the 1837–38 Pennsylvania Constitutional Convention, see Roy H. Akagi, "The Pennsylvania Constitution of 1838," *Pennsylvania Magazine of History and Biography* 48 (1924): 301–33. Between the process of the state house voting to amend the state constitution and the public voting on ratification, the state supreme court decided in *Hobbs v. Fogg* (1838) that "black men held a status inferior to that of freeman and, therefore, were ineligible to vote." This made the final vote on ratification unnecessary in formalizing the disfranchisement of adult Black males in the state. See Edward Price, "The Black Voting Rights Issue in Pennsylvania, 1780–1900," *Pennsylvania Magazine of History and Biography* 100 (1976): 359. There was not a singular vision of voting rights reflected in the 1838 constitution. For example, while the new constitution limited voting rights to white men, it also cut the residency requirement for voting in half.

67. Price, "Black Voting Rights," 357.

68. Sean Patrick Adams, "Hard Times, Loco-Focos, and Buckshot Wars: The Panic of 1837 in Pennsylvania," *Legacies* 11 (2010): 12–17.

69. *Journal of the Convention of the State of Pennsylvania to Propose Amendments to the Constitution* (Philadelphia: Thompson & Clark, 1838), 2:149.

70. *Journal of the Convention*, 2:149.

71. Nicholas Wood, "'A Sacrifice on the Altar of Slavery': Doughface Politics and Black Disenfranchisement in Pennsylvania, 1837–1838," *Journal of the Early Republic* 31 (2011): 83–84. It seems that abolitionists did not believe that the new constitution would be ratified. Angelina Grimké wrote to Sarah Mapps Douglass, "I am glad to find it is believed that amended Const'n will not be ratified by the people of Penn'a" (25 February 1838, in *Letters of Theodore Dwight Weld, Angelina Grimke Weld and Sarah Grimke 1822–1844*, ed. Gilbert H. Barnes and Dwight L. Dumond [Gloucester, Mass.: Peter Smith, 1965], 575).

72. *Present State and Condition of the Free People of Color in the City of Philadelphia* (Philadelphia: Pennsylvania Society for Promoting the Abolition of Slavery, 1838), 3–4.

73. Robert Purvis, "Appeal of Forty Thousand Citizens, Threatened with Disfranchisement, to the People of Pennsylvania," reprinted in Newman, Rael, and Lapsansky, *Pamphlets of Protest*, 140.

74. Paul Finkelman provides a useful table for the rights of free Blacks in the North in 1830. He finds that of the twelve northern states, African Americans could vote in Maine, New Hampshire, Vermont, and Massachusetts; they had some voting rights in New York and Pennsylvania; and they had no suffrage rights in Connecticut, Rhode Island, New Jersey, Ohio, Indiana, and Illinois. In 1860 full voting rights in the North were provided in Maine, New Hampshire, Vermont, Massachusetts, and Rhode Island. Limited voting rights were permitted in New York, Ohio, and Michigan. African Americans did not have voting rights in Connecticut, New Jersey, Pennsylvania, Indiana, Illinois, Iowa, Wisconsin, Minnesota, California, and Oregon. See "Prelude to the Fourteenth Amendment: Black Legal Rights in the Antebellum North," *Rutgers Law Review* 17 (1986): 424–25.

75. For an excellent comparative analysis of women's suffrage in the late nineteenth and early twentieth centuries, see Dawn Langan Teele, *Forging the Franchise: The Political Origins of the Women's Vote* (Princeton, N.J.: Princeton University Press, 2018).

76. Edward Raymond Turner, "Women's Suffrage in New Jersey: 1790–1807," *Smith College Studies in History* 1 (1916): 168. Apparently when the election laws were amended in 1796 there was no debate about female suffrage (169).

77. Alexander Keyssar argues that the decision did not seem to reflect any view that women lacked the innate ability to vote; instead, it was a desire to prevent corruption by clarifying election laws. See *The Right to Vote: The Contested History of Democracy in the United States*, rev. ed. (New York: Basic Books, 2009), 43–44.

78. *Official Report of the Debates and Proceedings in the State Convention Amended May 4th 1853 to Revise and Amend the Constitution of the Commonwealth of Massachusetts* (Boston: White & Potter, 1853), 2:726.

79. *Official Report of the Debates*, 2:734.

80. *Official Report of the Debates*, 2:734.

81. *Official Report of the Debates*, 2:750–51.

82. "Female Lecturers," *Boston Courier*, 26 October 1843.

83. Rev. Dr. Bishop, "A Good Wife," *American Ladies' Magazine* 8, no. 4 (1837): 229.

84. "Woman's Sphere," *American Ladies' Magazine* 8 (1837): 265–66.

85. Jennifer Harbour, *Organizing Freedom: Black Emancipation Activism in the Civil War Midwest* (Carbondale: Southern Illinois University Press, 2020), 26–27.

86. Linda Kerber, *Towards an Intellectual History of Women* (Chapel Hill: University of North Carolina Press, 1998), 301.

87. Bacon, *But One Race*, 43–44.

88. Sarah M. Grimké to Elizabeth Pease, 25 August 1839, in Barnes and Dumond, *Letters*, 792.

89. "Passports to People of Color," *North Star*, 13 April 1849.

90. "American Citizenship," *North Star*, 13 April 1849.

91. "Official Injustice—No Protection for Colored Men," *National Era*, 5 July 1849. Also see "Official Colorphobia," *North Star*, 31 August 1849.

92. Edlie L. Wong, *Neither Fugitive nor Free* (New York: NYU Press, 2009), 241–42.

93. Masur, *Until Justice Be Done*, 268.

94. Elizabeth Stordeur Pryor, *Colored Travelers: Mobility and the Fight for Citizenship before the Civil War* (Chapel Hill: University of North Carolina Press, 2016), 59.

95. Stephen Kantrowitz, *More Than Freedom: Fighting for Black Citizenship in a White Republic, 1829–1889* (New York: Penguin Press, 2012), 46.

96. Martha S. Jones, *Vanguard: How Black Women Broke Barriers, Won the Vote, and Insisted on Equality for All* (New York: Basic Books, 2020), 37–38.

97. William Saunders, "Mr. Editor," *Christian Freeman*, 20 July 1843.

98. Kantrowitz, *More Than Freedom*, 46.

99. "Legal Rights Vindicated," *Frederick Douglass' Paper* (Rochester, N.Y.), 2 March 1855.

100. Joanna Brooks, "The Early American Public Sphere and the Emergence of a Black Print Counterpublic," *William and Mary Quarterly* 62 (2005): 70. For a useful overview to counterpublics, see Robert Asen, "Seeking the 'Counter' in Counterpublics," *Communication Theory* 10 (2000): 224–46.

101. "Women Lecturers," *Pennsylvania Freeman*, 28 June 1838.

102. Maria Morfitt (Locey), first diary entry, Oregon City, 1859, MSS 2968, Locey Family Papers, Oregon Historical Society Research Library, Portland.

103. "Ladies Celebration of the Fourth of July," *Southern Times & State Gazette* (Columbia, S.C.), 18 August 1837.

104. Nancy Fraser describes counterpublics as "parallel discursive arenas where members of subordinated social groups invent and circulate counter discourses to formulate oppositional interpretations of their identities, interests or needs" (*Justice Interruptus: Critical Reflections on the "Postsocialist" Condition* [New York: Routledge, 1997], 81).

105. Louisa Adams Park, 20 December 1800, Women's History Sources, vol. 1, collection 7660, Park Family Papers, 1800–1890, American Antiquarian Society, Worcester, Mass.

106. James Armstrong to My Own Sweet Mary, 26 January 1841, John Armstrong Family Papers, Minnesota Historical Society, St. Paul. Mary, eighteen at the time of this letter, and James eventually married. Mary lived in Columbus, Ohio, while James practiced law elsewhere in the state. The Locofocos (1835 through the 1840s) were a more radical faction of the Democratic Party. During the 1840 presidential election Whigs used "Locofoco" as a more general derogatory term for all Democrats.

107. Adaline Lindsley, undated diary entry (between 7 April and 8 May 1841), D.310, Adaline Lindsley Papers, Rare Books, Special Collections, and Preservation, River Campus Libraries, University of Rochester, Rochester, New York.

108. Elizabeth Krynski and Kimberly Little, "Hannah's Letters: The Story of a Wisconsin Pioneer Family, 1856–1864, Part I," *Wisconsin Magazine of History* 74 (Spring 1991): 171.

109. Dred Scott v. John F. A. Sandford, 60 U.S. 393 (1857).

110. *Dred Scott*, 60 U.S. 393 (1857).

111. John Codman Hurd, *The Law of Freedom and Bondage in the United States* (1858; repr., New York: Negro Universities Press, 1968), 1:435.

112. Ethan Greenberg, *"Dred Scott" and the Dangers of a Political Court* (Lanham, Md.: Lexington Books, 2009), 221–23. Besides ruling on the citizenship of African Americans, the *Dred Scott* decision argued that Congress could not ban slavery in the territories; thus, the Missouri Compromise was deemed unconstitutional. The broad sweep of this opinion is one of the reasons why antislavery activists were so alarmed. See also Paul Finkelman, *Supreme Injustice: Slavery in the Nation's Highest Court* (Cambridge, Mass.: Harvard University Press, 2018).

113. James Oakes, *The Crooked Path to Abolition: Abraham Lincoln and the Antislavery Constitution* (New York: W. W. Norton and Company, 2021), 118.

114. Alexandria Ocasio-Cortez (@aoc), Twitter, 9:35 a.m., 29 June 2019.

CHAPTER 2. Constructing Home and Nation

The epigraph is from Mrs. L. H. (Lydia Huntley) Sigourney, "On Domestic Employment," *Ladies' Pearl* 1 (August 1841): 56.

1. Monika Swasti Winarnita, "Motherhood as Cultural Citizenship: Indonesian

Women in Transnational Families," *Asia Pacific Journal of Anthropology* 8 (December 2008): 306.

2. Joke Hermes, *Re-reading Popular Culture* (Malden, Mass.: Blackwell Publishing, 2005), 10.

3. The emergence of a distinctly feminine print culture encouraged women to create intellectual communities beyond their relatively limited geographic location. Benedict Anderson argues that print capitalism "made it possible for rapidly growing numbers of people to think about themselves, and to relate themselves to others, in profoundly new ways" (*Imagined Communities*, rev. ed. [London: Verso, 1991], 36). Newspapers, magazine articles, and books of all kinds helped women to identify not only as Americans but also as middle-class women who shared an American identity.

4. Nancy Fraser, *Justice Interruptus* (New York: Routledge, 1997), 81.

5. Although she does not focus on the United States, Carol Gold provides a long list of potential information to be gleaned from cookbooks in her first chapter, "First Course," in *Danish Cookbooks: Domesticity and National Identity, 1616–1901* (Seattle: University of Washington Press, 2007).

6. Sarah A. Leavitt, *From Catharine Beecher to Martha Stewart: A Cultural History of Domestic Advice* (Chapel Hill: University of North Carolina Press, 2002), 4.

7. Literacy rates had increased dramatically during the years of the early republic. It is projected that roughly 90 percent of native-born men and women could both read and write. Mary P. Ryan, *The Empire of the Mother: American Writing about Domesticity, 1830–1860* (New York: Harrington Park Press, 1985), 14. More particularly, at midcentury in New England, literacy was projected to be even higher, with 93 percent of Black adults and 98 percent of white adults literate. Ronald J. Zboray and Mary Saracino Zboray, "Home Libraries and the Institutionalization of Everyday Practices among Antebellum New Englanders," *American Studies* 42, no. 3 (Fall 2001): 66.

8. "Mothers and Daughters," *American Ladies' Magazine* 8, no. 5 (1837): 284.

9. Mary Kelley, *Private Woman, Public Stage: Literary Domesticity in Nineteenth-Century America* (New York: Oxford University Press, 1984), 12–13. The real commodity value of the $6,000 Sedgwick earned from 1835 through 1841 valued in 2019 (with a start year of 1841) would be $181,000. I used the purchasing power calculator at measuringworth.com to reach this number.

10. Catharine Sedgwick, *Live and Let Live; or Domestic Service Illustrated* (New York: Harper & Brother, 1837), 182.

11. Harriet E. Wilson, *Our Nig; or, Sketches from the Life of a Free Black* (1859). Although Wilson adheres to the tenets of domesticity in her novel, she also recognizes that the physical space of home is very different for an African American woman. For a lengthier analysis of Wilson and other nineteenth-century African American authors writing against a white vision of home, see Rafia Zafar, *We Wear the Mask: African Americans Write American Literature, 1760–1870* (New York: Columbia University Press, 1999), esp. chap. 5, "The Black Woman in the Attic." See also Linda M. Grasso, *The Artistry of Anger: Black and White Women's Literature in America, 1820–1860* (Chapel Hill: University of North Carolina Press, 2002); and Naomi Greyser, *On Sympathetic Grounds* (New York: Oxford University Press, 2018), chap. 5.

12. Melissa Ladd Teed, "A Passion for Distinction: Lydia Huntley Sigourney and the Creation of a Literary Reputation," *New England Quarterly* 77 (March 2004): 52.

13. William A. Alcott (1798–1859), a doctor, educator, and vegetarian, authored dozens of books, including *The Young Housekeeper* and *Lectures on Life and Health*. Sylvester Graham (1794–1851) was a health reformer and father of the graham cracker. He also authored *Lectures on the Science of Human Life* and *Lectures to Young Men on Chastity*.

14. "Comfort at Home," *Ladies' Repository* (Cincinnati) 12, no. 12 (1852): 474.

15. Catharine Beecher, *A Treatise on Domestic Economy* (1841; repr., New York: Schocken Books, 1977), 100–105; Catharine E. Beecher and Harriet Beecher Stowe, *The American Woman's Home* (1869; repr., Hartford, Conn.: Harriet Beecher Stowe Center, 1975), 150–57.

16. Catharine Beecher, *Letters to the People on Health and Happiness* (New York: Harper & Brothers Publishers, 1855), 196n10.

17. Suellen Hoy, *Chasing Dirt: The American Pursuit of Cleanliness* (New York: Oxford University Press, 1995), 87–88.

18. Linda K. Kerber, *Women of the Republic: Intellect & Ideology in Revolutionary America* (Chapel Hill: University of North Carolina Press, 1980), 11.

19. Mary Beth Norton, *Liberty's Daughters: The Revolutionary Experience of American Women, 1750–1800* (Ithaca, N.Y.: Cornell University Press, 1980), 298–99. For a historiographical examination of the use of "republican motherhood" and citizenship for women in early America, see Pauline Schloesser, *The Fair Sex: White Women and Racial Patriarchy in the Early American Republic* (New York: New York University Press, 2002), 1–11.

20. Bishop, "A Good Wife," *American Ladies' Magazine* 8 (1837): 228; and Mrs. H. J. W. Lewis, "Domestic Influence," *Ladies' Repository* 17 (August 1848): 48.

21. "Whisper to a Wife," *Colored American*, 18 March 1837.

22. "Trials of the Housewife," *Ladies' Wreath* 1 (1846): 162. Although this essay appeals to the image of the middle-class wife as the angel of the hearth, other articles emphasized more concrete financial contributions women made by running a well-ordered home.

23. Nancy F. Cott, *The Bonds of Womanhood: "Woman's Sphere" in New England, 1780–1835* (New Haven, Conn.: Yale University Press, 1977), 61. Also see Catherine E. Kelly, *New England Fashion: Reshaping Women's Lives in the Nineteenth Century* (Ithaca, N.Y.: Cornell University Press), 3–4.

24. Jeanne Boydston, *Home and Work: Housework, Wages, and the Ideology of Labor in the Early Republic* (New York: Oxford University Press, 1990), 142–63. It's important to note that Boydston recognizes the role women played in the transition to the new economy and vehemently denies that they were "absent." She states that "the material conditions of the transition may have given rise, not to the exclusion of women from the market, but to the expanded dependence on the market labor of women, performed both within and outside the household" (Jeanne Boydston, "The Woman Who Wasn't There: Women's Market Labor and the Transition to Capitalism in the United States," *Journal of the Early Republic* 16 [1996]: 184).

25. See Lawrence Martin, "The Genesis of *Godey's Lady's Book*," *New England Quarterly* 1, no. 1 (1928); Bertha-Monica Stearns, "Early New England Magazines for Ladies," *New England Quarterly* 2, no. 3 (1928); Bertha-Monica Stearns, "Early Western Maga-

zines for Ladies," *Mississippi Valley Historical Review* 18, no. 3 (1931). Not only were periodicals for women popular, domestic novels were also big sellers. According to an 1858 issue of *American Publishers' Circular*, seven of the seventeen best-selling publications in "recent years" were written by women. See Mary Kelley, *Private Woman, Public Stage: Literary Domesticity in Nineteenth-Century America* (New York: Oxford University Press, 1984), 26. Kelley's book traces the success of the "literary domestics."

26. Leslie J. Harris, "Motherhood, Race, and Gender: The Rhetoric of Women's Antislavery Activism in the *Liberty Bell* Giftbooks," *Women's Studies in Communication* 32 (Fall 2009); Isaac West, "Performing Resistance in/from the Kitchen: The Practice of Maternal Pacifist Politics and La WISP's Cookbooks," *Women's Studies in Communication* 30 (Fall 2007).

27. Barbara Welter, *Dimity Convictions: The American Woman in the Nineteenth Century* (Athens: Ohio University Press, 1976), 21.

28. Welter, 21.

29. "Woman's Lot," *Ladies' Repository* 17, no. 10 (1849): 332.

30. Laurel Thatcher Ulrich, *A Midwife's Tale: The Life of Martha Ballard, Based on Her Diary, 1785–1812* (New York: Alfred Knopf, 1990), 220–21.

31. Mary Lee to Hannah Lowell, 19 June 1811, Boston, in *Henry and Mary Lee: Letters and Journals with Other Family Letters, 1802–1860*, ed. Frances Rollins Morse (Boston: T. Todd, 1926), 105.

32. Mrs. Daniel W. Coxe, receipt book, Margaret Burd Coxe Collection, 1813–31, Historical Society of Pennsylvania, Philadelphia. Coxe's account book reveals that her longest work relationship was with her laundress, who did out-work (she worked with the Coxes in order to provide work outside the house instead of within it).

33. Kelly, *New England Fashion*, 25, 27.

34. Adaline Shaw to Affectionate Father, 28 May 1848, Miscellaneous Manuscript Collection, Sophia Smith Collection, Smith College, Northampton, Massachusetts.

35. Harriet Beecher Stowe [Christopher Crowfield], *House and Home Papers* (Boston: Ticknor and Fields, 1865), 63–64. Stowe later suggested that women learn to do their own domestic work, because if they did, then they would be able to better train their servants or do the work themselves and be happy with the outcome. Stowe reassured the young housewife that she could remain a "lady" and do her own work (126).

36. James Oliver Horton and Lois E. Horton, *In Hope of Liberty* (New York: Oxford University Press, 1997), 114. The authors also cite similar results in Buffalo and Cincinnati.

37. Catharine Beecher, *Miss Beecher's Domestic Receipt Book*, 269–70, 280–82.

38. Kristin Hoganson, "Garrisonian Abolitionists and the Rhetoric of Gender, 1850–1860," *American Quarterly* 45, no. 4 (1993): 559.

39. Joseph Richardson, *A Sermon, on the Duty and Dignity of Woman. Delivered April 22, 1832* (Hingham, Mass.: Jedidiah Farmer, Printer, 1833), 10–11. A Dartmouth graduate (1802), Richards was the minister of the First Parish Unitarian Church in Hingham, Massachusetts.

40. Amy Kaplan, *The Anarchy of Empire in the Making of U.S. Culture* (Cambridge, Mass.: Harvard University Press, 2002), 24–25.

41. *Columbian Lady's & Gentleman's Magazine,* October 1845, 190.

42. "Woman's Sphere," *Ladies' Repository* 1 (1841): 38.

43. Catharine Beecher and Harriet Beecher Stowe, *The American Woman's Home* (New York: J. B. Ford and Company, 1869), n.p.

44. Lydia Sigourney to My dear Friend & Sister, 13 December 1855, Lydia H. Sigourney Collection, Harriet Beecher Stowe Center, Hartford, Connecticut. Sigourney almost always asked to be remembered by name to the various servants. For example, in the postscript to this letter she wrote, "P.S. Ann will not be content without her respects to Mrs. Baldwin. Remember me to your good people, Sylvia, Susan, and Mary Ann."

45. Rebecca Allison, "I trust it will not be an intrusion," 17 January 1848, RG 5, series 2, Allen Family Papers, Swarthmore College Friends Historical Archive, Swarthmore, Pennsylvania.

46. James Armstrong to My Dear Mary, "Past Monday's mail," 11 December 1841, P1450, box 1, John Armstrong Family Papers, Minnesota Historical Society, St. Paul. James Armstrong is reporting the gossip he has heard about his fiancée, Mary Nelson, to her. This dialogue goes on in several letters as Armstrong initiates the subject by asking Nelson if she is friends with Dilworth.

47. Mary Ann Nelson to My Dear James, 21 December 1841, P1450, box 1, Armstrong Family Papers.

48. Catharine Maria Sedgwick, *The Power of Her Sympathy: The Autobiography and Journal of Catharine Maria Sedgwick,* ed. Mary Kelley (Boston: Massachusetts Historical Society, 1993), 82. For a general discussion of antebellum reading practices, particularly among women, see Ronald J. Zboray and Mary Saracino Zboray, "'Have You Read . . .': Real Readers and Their Responses in Antebellum Boston and Its Region," *Nineteenth-Century Literature* 52 (September 1997): 139–70; and Cathy N. Davidson, *Revolution of the Word: The Rise of the Novel in America,* expanded ed. (New York: Oxford University Press, 2004).

49. Zeloda Barrett, Diary, Zeloda and Samantha Barrett Diaries and Chap Books, 1804–31, Connecticut Historical Society, Hartford.

50. Blanche Brown Bryant and Gertrude Elaine Baker, eds., *The Diaries of Sally & Pamela Brown 1832–1838 and Hyde Leslie 1887: Plymouth Notch, Vermont* (Springfield: William Bryant Foundation, 1970), 30–32.

51. Coxe, receipt book.

52. Anne Sinkler Whaley LeClercq and Emily Wharton Sinkler, *An Antebellum Plantation Household* (Columbia: University of South Carolina Press, 1996), 18.

53. Adaline Lindsley, "Time works wonderful changes," 8 January 1841, Adaline Lindsley Papers, Rare Books, Special Collections, and Preservation, River Campus Libraries, University of Rochester, Rochester, New York. Lindsley was born in 1820 to a middle-class farmer and his third wife. In 1845 she married an itinerant preacher and died of tuberculosis on Christmas Day 1847.

54. Ely Burchard to My Dear Child, 29 January 1849, Miscellaneous Manuscript Collection, Sophia Smith Collection, Smith College, Northampton, Mass.

55. Ronald J. Zboray, *A Fictive People: Antebellum Economic Development and the*

American Reading Public (New York: Oxford University Press, 1993), xix. Mary Kelley quantified the growth of the publication market in dollar terms, stating that the gross income from the book trade rose from $2.5 million in 1820 to $12.5 million in 1850 (*Private Woman*, 10–11).

56. Keith Stavely and Kathleen Fitzgerald provide a detailed analysis of the book in *United Tastes: The Making of the First American Cookbook* (Amherst: University of Massachusetts Press, 2017).

57. Believed to be authored by Eliza Smith, *The Compleat Housewife* was originally published in England in 1727, and it had reached its eighteenth British edition by 1773. For a more complete genealogy of the American editions of this book, see Genevieve Yost, "*The Compleat Housewife or Accomplish'd Gentlewoman's Companion*: A Bibliographical Study," *William and Mary Quarterly*, 2nd ser., 18, no. 4 (October 1938): 419–35.

58. Janet Theophano, *Eat My Words: Reading Women's Lives through the Cookbooks They Wrote* (New York: Palgrave, 2002), 233.

59. Mary Tolford Wilson, introduction to *The First American Cookbook: A Facsimile of "American Cookery," 1796* (New York: Dover Publications, 1984), xi–xiv.

60. Amelia Simmons, *American Cookery* (Hartford, Conn.: Hudson & Goodwin, 1796; repr., New York: Oxford University Press, 1957), n.p. I have cited this edition because it has modernized the font and spelling for ease of reading.

61. Simmons, n.p.

62. Jane E. Hassler, manuscript cookbook, Philadelphia, 1857, Szathmary Family Culinary Archives Cookery Manuscripts, Special Collections Department, University of Iowa Libraries, Iowa City. Ellen Emlen also provided notations in her manuscript cookbook for where the recipe came from, changes she had made, and evaluations of recipes. For example, at the bottom of a recipe for oyster soup, Emlen noted, "A better recipe amongst loose recipes" (*The Historical Society of Pennsylvania Presents the Cookbook of Ellen M. Emlen, Written in Her Own Hand* [Philadelphia: Historical Society of Pennsylvania, 2011], 94).

63. Abigale Wellington Townsend, manuscript cookbook (ca. 1840); Mrs. Samuel Leeds, manuscript cookbook and travel diary (ca. 1856); anonymous manuscript cookbook (ca. 1850); and Mrs. Sparkman, manuscript cookbook (ca. 1850–70), all in Szathmary Family Culinary Archives Cookery Manuscripts.

64. Anne Sinkler Whaley Leclercq, *An Antebellum Plantation Household*, reprint ed. (Columbia: University of South Carolina Press, 2015).

65. Mary Ryan argues that the "family advisors of the 1830s did not assume that such important household activities were solely the responsibility of the wife." While Child clearly avoids a strictly feminine focus and, as Ryan points out, there were many training manuals written for men, the majority of cookbooks and household manuals of this period do appear to be focused on women, which further suggests that the cultural shift took hold between the publication of Child's book and Beecher's *Treatise*. See Ryan, *Empire of the Mother*, 25–26.

66. For a lengthier discussion of Child's household advice, see Carolyn L. Karcher, *The First Woman of the Republic: A Cultural Biography of Lydia Maria Child* (Durham, N.C.: Duke University Press); and Hildegard Hoeller, "A Quilt for Life: Lydia Maria Child's *The American Frugal Housewife*," *American Transcendental Quarterly* 13, no. 2 (1999).

67. Boydston, *Home and Work*, 123. Boydston explains how this works, as households required paid labor for the cash to purchase some goods and services. Equally, they depended on unpaid labor in the household to process those commodities into consumable form and to produce the goods and services directly, without recourse to the cash market.

68. In Carolyn Karcher's analysis of *The American Frugal Housewife* she discusses Hale's review of the book, "*The Frugal Housewife*, by the Author of *Hobomok*," *Ladies' Magazine* 3 (January 1830): 42–43. Karcher states that Hale's reviews of Child's previous writings "had hitherto been warmly supportive in every respect" (*First Woman*, 647).

69. Sara Josepha Hale, *Early American Cookery: The Good Housekeeper* (1841; repr., New York: Dover Publications, 1996), preface.

70. Frances Harriet Green, *The Housekeeper's Book* (Philadelphia: William Marsh and Co., 1837), 2.

71. Jeanne Boydston, Mary Kelley, and Anne Margolis, *The Limits of Sisterhood: The Beecher Sisters on Women's Rights and Woman's Sphere* (Chapel Hill: University of North Carolina Press, 1988), 13. For a discussion of Beecher's work and a more general biography, see Kathryn Kish Sklar, *Catharine Beecher: A Study in American Domesticity* (New York: W. W. Norton and Company, 1976).

72. Beecher, *Treatise on Domestic Economy*, 2.

73. Beecher, 18.

74. Beecher, 4.

75. Alexis de Tocqueville's *Democracy in America* would have been familiar to Beecher's readers and target audience. By 1839 the book was being prepared for its third American edition. *New York Spectator*, 19 September 1839.

76. Beecher, *Treatise on Domestic Economy*, 9.

77. Beecher, 9.

78. "The Social Position of Women," *Ladies' Wreath*, 1 May 1846, 28.

79. Valerie Gill offers a comparison of the writings of Beecher and Charlotte Perkins Gilman (Beecher's great-niece) and their manipulation of domestic space in an effort to improve the lives of women. Gilman advocated kitchenless houses, with the cooking done outside the home by professionals. See Valerie Gill, "Catharine Beecher and Charlotte Perkins Gilman: Architects of Female Power," *Journal of American Culture* 21, no. 2 (1998): 17–24.

80. Catharine Beecher, *A Treatise on Domestic Economy* (New York: Marsh, Capen, Lyon and Webb, 1841), 143.

81. "Notices of New Books," *United States Democratic Review* 9, no. 42 (1841): 605.

82. Carolyn Karcher explains the effect of Beecher's book on the success of Child's *American Frugal Housewife*: "It was the year after the publication of Beecher's volume that reprints of *The Frugal Housewife* began to slack off with the twenty-eighth edition of 1842. Hitherto reprinted almost every year, and as many as twelve times between 1829 and 1832, Child's manual was reissued only twice in the mid-1840s, one in 1855, and once each in 1860 and 1870" (*First Woman*, 131).

83. Catharine Beecher, *Miss Beecher's Domestic Receipt-Book* (Mineola: Dover Publications, 2001). Reprint of the 1850 publication.

84. William A. Alcott, *The Young Housekeeper; or, Thoughts on Food and Cookery* (Boston: Charles D. Strong, 1851), 18–19. Although nineteenth-century cookbooks were more likely to be written by women, domestic advice was often written by men (typically based on their occupations as either ministers or doctors). Alcott was one of the relatively few men who wrote more traditional cookbooks (although they were still couched within the genre of domestic advice).

85. Harry Haff, *The Founders of American Cuisine: Seven Cookbook Authors, with Historical Recipes* (Jefferson, N.C.: McFarland & Company, 2011), 52.

86. Bonnie Thornton Dill, "The Dialectics of Black Womanhood," *Signs* 4, no. 3 (1979): 553.

87. Patrick Rael, *Black Identity and Black Protest in the Antebellum North* (Chapel Hill: University of North Carolina Press, 2002), 150–52. Also see James Oliver Horton, *Free People of Color* (Washington, D.C.: Smithsonian Institution Press, 1993), 103.

88. Beth Maclay Doriani, "Black Womanhood in Nineteenth-Century America: Subversion and Self-Construction in Two Women's Autobiographies," *American Quarterly* 43, no. 2 (1991): 199–222; and Laurie Kaiser, "The Black Madonna: Notions of True Womanhood from Jacobs to Hurston," *South Atlantic Review* 60, no. 1 (1995): 97–109; Lydia Maria Child, *A Romance of the Republic* (Boston: Ticknor and Fields, 1867).

89. Ann Plato, *Essays: Including Biographies and Miscellaneous Pieces, in Prose and Poetry*, Schomburg Library of Nineteenth Century Black Women Writers (1841; repr., New York: Oxford University Press, 1988).

90. A survey of the antebellum African American press reveals almost no specific household advice and only one article of any length. The article, titled "Hints," provides guidance that promotes economy rather than guidelines for status and fine living. See the *Anglo-African*, 24 September 1859. African American women, however, were often targeted in news articles prescribing feminine behavior.

91. Robert Roberts, *The House Servant's Directory* (Boston: Munroe & Francis, 1827).

92. Tunis G. Campbell, *Hotel Keepers, Head Waiters, and Housekeepers' Guide* (Boston: Coolidge and Wiley, 1848), 5.

93. Campbell, 7–8. Beyond the scope of this discussion, Campbell provided some insight into the growing number of respectable women who traveled unaccompanied by a sheltering figure: "Ladies who may be traveling alone, should not be left to come to the table without being seen by the proprietor, and brought in and seated; or, if he is not able to attend to them himself, they should be seated before the gong is rung, in order to avoid the confusion that generally attends the rush when the doors are thrown open and everybody is trying to get their seats" (41–42). Although the inclusion is brief, it suggests that women took advantage of emerging modes of public transportation, and the woman traveling alone was not a complete anomaly.

94. For a general discussion of all four of these books, see Rafia Zafar, "Recipes for Respect: Black Hospitality Entrepreneurs before World War One," in *African American Foodways: Explorations of History and Culture*, ed. Anne L. Bower (Urbana: University of Illinois Press, 2007), 139–52, particularly 139–44; Jessica B. Harris, *High on the Hog: A Culinary Journey from Africa to America* (New York: Bloomsbury, 2011), 163–66. Michael W. Twitty describes the difficulty of tracing African American foodways and the impor-

tance of analyzing both traditional texts (cookbooks—even white-authored ones) and less accepted texts (such as family stories and recollections). See "The Unbearable Taste," *Common-Place* 11, no. 3 (April 2011).

95. Malinda Russell, *A Domestic Cook Book: A Facsimile of the First Known Cookbook by an African American* (Detroit: Inland Press, 2007), 3.

96. Russell, 3.

97. Russell, 3. While the tidbit about going by her maiden name is interesting, there is not enough information to speculate as to her reason.

98. Russell, 4. Her commercial success in Tennessee does help to position her as a professional rather than merely an employee in a private home.

99. Russell, 5.

100. Rafia Zafar, "The Signifying Dish: Autobiography and History in Two Black Women's Cookbooks," *Feminist Studies* 25, no. 2 (Summer 1999): 453.

101. Asel Clark to My Dear Girl, 9 June 1834, Clark-Warner Family Papers, 1834–1877, Sophia Smith Collection, Smith College, Northampton, Massachusetts.

102. Psyche Williams-Forson argues that there should be "a retheorizing of Black women's pursuits of freedom and citizenship by considering how they used African American domestic spaces to engage the market economy and enact social change" ("Where Did They Eat? Where Did They Stay? Interpreting the Material Culture of Black Women's Domesticity in the Context of Colored Conventions," in *The Colored Conventions Movement: Black Organizing in the Nineteenth Century*, ed. P. Gabrielle Foreman, Jim Casey, and Sarah Lynn Patterson [Chapel Hill: University of North Carolina Press, 2021], 88).

CHAPTER 3. The Infrastructure of Race

1. Jeremiah Burke Sanderson to Mr. Nell Sir, 23 June 1840, box 2, manuscript 542, Post Family Papers, Rare Books, Special Collections, and Preservation, River Campus Libraries, University of Rochester, Rochester, New York.

2. Mary Robbins Post, n.d., box 1, manuscript 256, Post Family Papers. Isaac (1798–1872) and Amy Kirby Post (1802–89) were activists from Rochester, New York, involved in abolition, women's rights, and other progressive causes of the nineteenth century.

3. Shelley Fisher Fishkin, "Interrogating 'Whiteness,' Complicating 'Blackness': Remapping American Culture," *American Quarterly* 47 (1995): 428–66. See also Toni Morrison, *Playing in the Dark: Whiteness and the Literary Imagination* (New York: Vintage Books, 1993).

4. *Address of the Female Anti-Slavery Society of Philadelphia to the Women of Pennsylvania, with the Form of a Petition* (Philadelphia: Merrihew and Gunn, Printers, 1836), 7, emphasis in the original.

5. For example, E. W. Clay's 1828–30 cartoon series, Life in Philadelphia, included caricatures of the city's free Black population in most of the drawings. These mocking cartoons were popular, widely reproduced, and copied in other urban areas.

6. Kabria Baumgartner, *In Pursuit of Knowledge: Black Women and Educational Activism in Antebellum America* (New York: NYU Press, 2019), 5.

7. Julie Winch, ed., *The Elite of Our People* (University Park: Pennsylvania State Uni-

versity Press, 2000), 87. It is projected that in 1820 one in nine African American heads of household owned real property. According to Gary B. Nash and Jean R. Soderlund, the rate was low when compared to whites and slightly lower than that of "recently arrived immigrants from impoverished backgrounds" (*Freedom by Degrees: Emancipation in Pennsylvania and Its Aftermath* [New York: Oxford University Press, 1991], 172).

8. Emma Lapsansky, "Friends, Wives, and Strivings: Networks and Community Values among Nineteenth Century Philadelphia Afroamerican Elites," *Pennsylvania Magazine of History and Biography* 108 (1984): 4.

9. Nazera Sadiq Wright, *Black Girlhood in the Nineteenth Century* (Urbana: University of Illinois Press, 2016), 33.

10. Patrick Rael, *Black Identity and Black Protest in the Antebellum North* (Chapel Hill: University of North Carolina Press, 2002), 150–52.

11. Lora Romero, *Home Fronts* (Durham, N.C.: Duke University Press, 1997), 63.

12. W. E. B. Du Bois, *The Souls of Black Folk* (New York: Pocket Books, 2005), 7.

13. Paul J. Polgar, "'To Raise Them to an Equal Participation': Early National Gradual Emancipation and the Promise of African American Citizenship," *Journal of the Early Republic* 31 (2011): 233.

14. Emma Jones Lapsansky, "'Since They Got Those Separate Churches': Afro-Americans and Racism in Jacksonian Philadelphia," in *African Americans in Pennsylvania: Shifting Historical Perspectives*, ed. Joe William Trotter Jr. and Eric Ledell Smith (University Park: Pennsylvania State University Press, 1997), 95–96.

15. *The Liberator*, 28 August 1846, 139.

16. St. Thomas Church Vestry, minutes of vestry meeting, 21 November 1821, 17 April 1822, 17 December 1828, Archive of the African Episcopal Church of St. Thomas, Philadelphia. The organization was incorporated in 1815 and was only open to middle-aged women who were unmarried and church members. A typed transcript from the Charter Book 2 of the church archive reveals that well over half of the original signatories to the charter document were only able to use a mark.

17. Constitution of the Benevolent Daughters of St. Thomas, February 1827, Documents, Archive of the African Episcopal Church of St. Thomas.

18. St. Thomas Church Vestry, minutes of vestry meeting, 15 July 1828, Archive of the African Episcopal Church of St. Thomas.

19. The Historical Society, *Absalom Jones: His Life and Legacy* (Philadelphia: African Episcopal Church of St. Thomas, 2006).

20. Richard S. Newman, *Freedom's Prophet: Bishop Richard Allen, the AME Church, and the Black Founding Fathers* (New York: New York University Press, 2008), 130.

21. Newman, 131.

22. James Horton and Lois Horton, *Black Bostonians,* rev. ed. (New York: Holmes and Meier, 1999), 42–46.

23. Martha Jones, *All Bound Up Together* (Chapel Hill: University of North Carolina Press, 2007), 37.

24. Carla L. Peterson, *Doers of the Word: African-American Women Speakers and Writers in the North (1830–1880)* (New Brunswick, N.J.: Rutgers University Press, 1995), 74.

25. Jualynne E. Dodson, *Engendering Church: Women, Power, and the AME Church* (Lanham, Md.: Rowman & Littlefield, 2002), 41–43.

26. Mary Still, "An Appeal to the Females of the A.M.E. Church," in *Pamphlets of Protest*, ed. Richard Newman, Patrick Rael, and Phillip Lapsansky (New York: Routledge, 2001), 256.

27. Karlyn Kohrs Campbell, *Man Cannot Speak for Her: A Critical Study of Early Feminist Rhetoric* (New York: Praeger, 1989), 17–19.

28. *North American and Daily Advertiser* (Philadelphia), 22 July 1842.

29. "A Question," *The Liberator*, 4 June 1831.

30. Richard Allen tells the story of why free Blacks left St. George's and began new congregations in his autobiography, *The Life, Experience, and Gospel Labors of the Rt. Rev. Richard Allen to Which Is Annexed the Rise and Progress of the African Methodist Episcopal Church of the United States of America* (Philadelphia: F. Ford and M. A. Riply, 1880), 14–19.

31. *The Liberator*, 4 October 1850, 159.

32. *Society of Friends in the United States: Their Views of the Anti-Slavery Question, and Treatment of the People of Colour* (Darlington, England: John Wilson, Market-Place, 1840), 23–24. The likely source of this quote is African American Quaker Sarah Mapps Douglass of Philadelphia. A letter written by Sarah Grimké to Sarah Douglass solicited this information: "I have received a few days ago a letter from England making some enquiries relative to the prejudice against color which exists in this country. I want thyself and thy dear mother to weigh the matter well." "Consider too whether you are prepared to have your own names published and the names of those who have manifested towards you this prejudice. State the circumstances that occurred in N.Y. both to thy mother and thyself" (Sarah M. Grimké to Sarah Douglass, 14 January 1839, in Barnes and Dumond, *Letters*, 744).

33. William J. Watkins, *The Liberator*, 9 January 1852, 7. Watkins was the uncle of Frances Ellen Watkins Harper, an author and activist. Orphaned at the age of three, Harper was raised by her aunt and uncle.

34. Julie A. Reuben, "Patriotic Purposes: Public Schools and the Education of Citizens," in *The Public Schools*, ed. Susan Fuhrman and Marvin Lazerson (New York: Oxford University Press, 2005), 1–10.

35. St. Thomas Church Vestry, minutes of vestry meeting, 20 July 1825, Archive of the African Episcopal Church of St. Thomas. Ann Flower's decision to endow the education of boys is most likely a reflection of the more limited opportunities for African American girls at the time of her death than any endorsement of the relative lack of importance of female education.

36. "African Free Schools in the United States," *Freedom's Journal* (New York), 28 May 1827.

37. Anti-Slavery Convention of American Women (Philadelphia), *Address to the Free Colored People of the United States* (Philadelphia: Merrihew and Gunn, 1838), 4.

38. Nancy Slocum Hornick, "Anthony Benezet and the Africans' School: Toward a Theory of Full Equality," *Pennsylvania Magazine of History and Biography* 99 (October 1975): 404.

39. Carter G. Woodson, *The Education of the Negro prior to 1861* (Washington, D.C.: Associated Publishers, 1919), 77–78.

40. Charles Andrew, *History of the New-York Free School* (1830; repr., New York: Negro University Press, 1969), 25.

41. Margaret Hope Bacon, "The Pennsylvania Abolition Society's Mission for Black Education," *Pennsylvania Legacies* 5 (November 2005): 21–26. The New York Manumission Society was founded in 1785. Like the PAS, the NYMS believed that education for free Blacks was key to garnering public support for abolition. A model school was established in 1787.

42. Stacey M. Robertson, *Hearts Beating for Liberty: Women Abolitionists in the Old Northwest* (Chapel Hill: University of North Carolina Press, 2010), 29.

43. Matthew Carey, "Correspondence on Internal Improvements: Account of Schools for Coloured Persons in the City of Philadelphia," March 1822, Record 36, Edward Carey Gardiner Collection, Historical Society of Pennsylvania, Philadelphia. The first public schools for African Americans in Philadelphia were established in 1822, the same year as Carey's survey.

44. Clarkson Institute of Pennsylvania, minute book, 1834–38, Pennsylvania Abolition Society Papers, Historical Society of Pennsylvania, Philadelphia.

45. Bacon, "Pennsylvania Abolition Society's Mission," 22.

46. William H. Robinson, ed., *The Proceedings of the Free African Union Society and the African Benevolent Society, Newport, Rhode Island, 1780–1824* (Providence, R.I.: Urban League of Rhode Island, 1976), 153.

47. *Proceedings of the Free African Union*, 160.

48. *Proceedings of the Free African Union*, 162, 172–73. The group eventually gave ten dollars toward the maintenance of the school.

49. "African Free School," *National Advocate* (New York), 13 May 1824.

50. Karen Fisher Younger, "Philadelphia's Ladies' Liberia School Association and the Rise and Decline of Northern Colonization Support," *Pennsylvania Magazine of History and Biography* 134 (2010): 235–61. Members of the Boston Female Anti-Slavery Society touted their economic patronage of the Samaritan Asylum for Indigent Colored Children in an annual report (*Fifth Annual Report*, 6).

51. Miss Crandall to *The Liberator*, 25 May 1833.

52. Mark S. Weiner, *Black Trials* (New York: Vintage Books, 2004), 100–101. Weiner's chapter devoted to the Crandall trial provides an excellent overview of the legal components of this controversy.

53. Prudence Crandall to Mr. Jocelyn Sir, 26 February 1833, Foster Rice Collection, Connecticut Historical Society, Hartford. Simeon Jocelyn was a white abolitionist who served as the founding pastor of the Dixwell Avenue Congregational Church.

54. Prudence Crandall to Mr. Jocelyn, Dear Friend, 9 April 1833, Foster Rice Collection.

55. "Miss Crandall Imprisoned!," *Observer and Telegraph* (Hudson, Ohio), 18 July 1833.

56. "Trial of Prudence Crandall," *New-York Spectator*, 29 August 1833. This argument preceded by twenty-five years the similar claim made by the U.S. Supreme Court in the *Dred Scott* case.

57. Prudence Crandall to Simeon Jocelyn, 17 April 1833, Foster Rice Collection.

58. Susan Stanfield, "Teaching across the Color Line: Antebellum Anxieties and the Prudence Crandall Controversy," *New England Journal of History*, Fall 2016, 57–81.

59. "The School for Colored Girls, Washington, D.C.," *Frederick Douglass' Paper*, 3 March 1854. A later newspaper article described the school during the winter 1852–53 session in the following manner: "The pupils present were of various ages from eight to sixteen years and were plainly but neatly and comfortably clad. They consisted of mulattoes, and quadroons for the most part, though some were obviously of pure African blood, and others could with difficulty be distinguished from whites" ("Miss Miner's School at Washington," *Frederick Douglass' Paper*, 12 January 1855).

60. For a detailed discussion of the problems faced by Miner, see Druscilla J. Null, "Myrtilla Miner's 'School for Colored Girls': A Mirror on Antebellum Washington," *Records of the Columbia Historical Society, Washington D.C.* 52 (1989): 254–68.

61. Harriet Beecher Stowe, "The Ladies Anti-Slavery Society of Glasgow," 18 November 1853, E. Bruce Kirkham Collection, Harriet Beecher Stowe Center, Hartford, Connecticut.

62. Margaret Hope Bacon, "'One Great Bundle of Humanity': Frances Ellen Watkins Harper (1825–1911)," *Pennsylvania Magazine of History and Biography* 113 (January 1989): 23.

63. Kay Ann Taylor, "Mary S. Peake and Charlotte L. Forten: Black Teachers during the Civil War and Reconstruction," *Journal of Negro Education* 74 (Spring 2005): 131–34.

64. Eliza Newell to the Board of Education, 28 September 1843, Pennsylvania Abolition Society Papers.

65. Martha Holcomb to Gentlemen, 18 February 1847, Pennsylvania Abolition Society Papers.

66. Martha B. Gordon, 18 February 1847, and Charlotte Van Dine, 18 February 1847, Pennsylvania Abolition Society Papers. Three letters of application on the same day suggest an active interest in an open position. Charlotte Van Dine's reference was the respected educator, Sarah Mapps Douglass, suggesting that she studied at her school.

67. Elizabeth Reynolds to the Board of Education of the Clarkson School, 1 March 1833, Pennsylvania Abolition Society Papers. It seems likely that the school came up with the money to pay Reynolds, as she is mentioned as the teacher who is let go with the closing of the female school in 1838.

68. Jane Stokley to the Board of Education, 11 March 1847, Pennsylvania Abolition Society Papers.

69. "Institute of Colored Youth," *National Era*, 7 October 1852. For other examples of ICY's curriculum, see "Institute of Colored Youth," *The Liberator*, 15 May 1857; and W. E. B. Du Bois, *The Philadelphia Negro* (1899; repr., Philadelphia: University of Pennsylvania Press, 1996), 87. In 1852 ICY tuition was ten dollars per term, including "books and stationery."

70. *Frederick Douglass' Paper*, 21 September 1855, emphasis in the original. An ad for the soon-to-be-opened high school in Philadelphia stated, "Satisfactory references as to moral character, literary acquirements and ability for the government of such a school, will be required. A colored man would be preferred qualifications being equal" (*National Era*, 27 May 1852).

71. "The Colored Race in Boston, a Colored Man," *Boston Courier*, 12 September 1842. For a more thorough analysis of the Boston and Black identity, see Scott Hancock, "The Elusive Boundaries of Blackness: Identity Formation in Antebellum Boston," *Journal of Negro History* 84 (1999): 115–29.

72. Hilary J. Moss, "The Tarring and Feathering of Thomas Paul Smith: Common Schools, Revolutionary Memory, and the Crisis of Black Citizenship in Antebellum Boston," *New England Quarterly* 80 (2006): 221–22, 224–25, 237–38.

73. William J. Watkins, *The Liberator*, 9 January 1852, 7.

74. "Sixty-First School Festival at Faneuil Hall," *The Liberator*, 4 August 1854, 123.

75. William Cooper Nell, letter, 3 July 1850, box 3, manuscript 847, emphasis in the original, Post Family Papers. Also see Baumgartner, *In Pursuit of Knowledge*, 164–65.

76. "Abolition of Caste Schools," *The Liberator*, 31 August 1855, 138.

77. Bacon, *But One Race*, 101, 108–10.

78. Robert Purvis, "Byberry, Nov. 4th 1853, Dear Sir," in *The Mind of the Negro as Reflected in Letters Written during the Crisis, 1800–1860*, ed. Carter G. Woodson (Washington, D.C.: Association for the Study of Negro Life and History, 1926), 178–79.

79. Elizabeth Wicks, "Address Delivered before the African Female Benevolent Society," in Newman, Rael, and Lapsansky, *Pamphlets of Protest*, 114–21.

80. *The Present State and Condition of the Free People of Color of the City of Philadelphia: Report of a Committee of the Pennsylvania Society for Promoting the Abolition of Slavery* (Philadelphia: Merrihew and Gunn, 1838), 26–27.

81. The 1856 census of Philadelphia's African American community found that of the 9,001 people surveyed, 1,710 could demonstrate basic reading, writing, and math skills, 1,482 could read and write, 1,680 could read, and 4,123 could not read. "The Colored Population of Philadelphia," *New York Herald*, 29 May 1856.

82. William Whipper, "An Address Delivered in Wesley Church on the Evening of June 12, before the Colored Reading Society of Philadelphia for Mental Improvement," in *Early Negro Writing, 1760–1837*, ed. Dorothy Porter (Baltimore, Md.: Black Classic Press, 1995), 107–8.

83. *The Present State and Condition*.

84. "Librarians Second Annual Report," *Frederick Douglass' Paper*, 27 April 1855. The report includes other interesting tidbits. For example, it tracked the gender of readers, noting that 233 were male and 217 were female. The previous year, 4,088 books had been loaned out, and 1,554 had been loaned for use in the reading room, for a total of 5,642. In his first annual address to the Philadelphia AME conference, Bishop Daniel Payne extolled the virtues of the library connected to the high school (ICY). He explained that "this library has been collected with great care, so as to exclude the poison and chaff of light literature while the pure wheat of useful knowledge is plenteously furnished without price to every parent and child." He also noted that three evenings a week the reading room was open to males, and one afternoon was set aside for females. Daniel A. Payne, *Bishop Payne's First Annual Address to the Philadelphia Conference of the AME Church* (Philadelphia: C. Sherman, Printer, 1853), n.p. The New York African Schools also reported their library holdings to the public. In 1830 they stated that the main campus had 450 volumes, while the female school had 200.

85. "To the Friends of Freedom and the Press," *North Star*, 26 April 1850. Elite women of color in Philadelphia also formed an organization, the Philadelphia North Star Association, to raise funds for Douglass's newspaper. "Visit to Philadelphia," *North Star*, 13 October 1848.

86. "Circular by the Provisional Committee of the Impartial Citizen," in *The Black Abolitionist Papers, Volume IV: The United States 1847–1858*, ed. C. Peter Ripley (Chapel Hill: University of North Carolina Press, 1991), 38–41.

87. Prince Saunders, "An Address before the Pennsylvania Augustine Society (1818)," in Newman, Rael, and Lapsansky, *Pamphlets of Protest*, 82.

88. David Gellman, *Emancipating New York: Politics of Slavery and Freedom, 1777–1827* (Baton Rouge: LSU Press, 2006), 6.

89. The links between Quakers, abolitionism, and free Black communities aided African Americans in their use of print culture. Philadelphia Quakers had long recognized the importance of print, creating a committee called Overseers of the Press in 1691. Anthony Benezet, a proponent of African American education, was appointed to this committee in 1757 and used the Quaker press to publish several antislavery tracts. While the Society of Friends' press was not widely utilized in the eighteenth century by African Americans, its power to support antislavery agendas provided a template for nascent Black print culture, which extensively published tracts, pamphlets, and speeches to promote equality throughout the nineteenth century. Jonathan D. Sassi, "With a Little Help from the Friends: The Quaker Tactical Contexts of Anthony Benezet's Abolitionist Publishing," *Pennsylvania Magazine of History and Biography* 135 (2011): 33–71.

90. Jacqueline Bacon, *Freedom's Journal: The First African-American Newspaper* (Lanham, Md.: Lexington Press, 2007), 51–53. Robert S. Levine argues that the list of agents that appeared in most issues of the paper served to demonstrate the relationship across locations and that as the list of agents grew it demonstrated "growing readership and the evolution of a black community" ("Circulating the Nation: David Walker, the Missouri Compromise, and the Rise of the Black Press," in *The Black Press*, ed. Todd Vogel [New Brunswick, N.J.: Rutgers University Press, 2001], 23).

91. Benjamin Fagan, *The Black Newspaper and the Chosen Nation* (Athens: University of Georgia Press, 2018), 27–29.

92. "Female Temper," *Freedom's Journal*, 20 April 1827.

93. *Freedom's Journal*, 16 March 1827.

94. In 1831 *The Liberator* published the prospectus for two new African American–edited newspapers. The *African Sentinel*, edited by John Stewart and published in Albany, New York, is believed to have had a limited run of approximately a year ("Proposals: The African Sentinel and Journal of Liberator," *The Liberator*, 12 March 1831). Junius Morel and John P. Thompson proposed *The American*; however, they were never able to get the paper off the ground ("Proposals: *The American*," *The Liberator*, 16 July 1831). Todd Vogel projects that over one hundred newspapers were published between 1827 and 1855 ("The New Face of Black Labor," in Vogel, *The Black Press*, 38). Given how few of these papers remain extant, this number is open to debate.

95. James Forten, "December 31st, 1830, Dear Sir," in *The Black Abolitionist Papers, Vol-*

ume III: The United States, 1830–1846, ed. C. Peter Ripley (Chapel Hill: University of North Carolina Press, 1991), 86.

96. James Forten, "May 6th 1832, Mr. William Lloyd Garrison, My Dear Sir," in Ripley, 87. Mr. Robert Purvis was Forten's son-in-law.

97. "For the National Enquirer, Invocation to Woman," *National Enquirer* (Philadelphia), 4 January 1838.

98. "Colonization Hints: To the Editor of the Liberator," *The Liberator*, 12 February 1831. Jane Dabel contends that there was a steady decline of African Americans in skilled labor through the nineteenth century. By 1860, 82 percent of African American wage earners were in service jobs, and by 1880 that number had surged to 93 percent. *A Respectable Woman* (New York: NYU Press, 2008), 66–67.

99. This is not to suggest that white women never took in boarders or ran boardinghouses; they were a necessity for the antebellum economy. However, many of these women who took in boarders were more likely to be on the fringes of the middle class and did not necessarily embrace middle-class standards of true womanhood.

100. "Agency in Behalf of Free People of Color," *Colored American*, 28 September 1839.

101. Theodore Hershberg, "Free Blacks in Antebellum Philadelphia," in *The Peoples of Philadelphia: A History of Ethnic Groups and Lower-Class Life, 1790–1940*, ed. Allen F. Davis and Mark H. Haller (Philadelphia: Temple University Press, 1973), 113.

102. Daniel Kilbride, *An American Aristocracy: Southern Planters in Antebellum Philadelphia* (Columbia: University of South Carolina Press, 2006), 91.

103. Carl Prince, "The Great 'Riot Year': Jacksonian Democracy and Patterns of Violence in 1834," *Journal of the Early Republic* 5 (1985): 14. New York City experienced significant rioting in 1834 and beyond. Much of this was a reaction to antislavery activism, as Carla Peterson explained: "White mob violence in northern cities rose in direct proportion to the spread of radical abolitionist activity" (*Black Gotham: A Family History of African Americans in Nineteenth-Century New York City* [New Haven, Conn.: Yale University Press, 2012], 99).

104. "Continued Riots in Philadelphia," *Maryland Gazette*, 21 August 1834.

105. *Fifth Annual Report*, 5.

106. *The Liberator*, 1 December 1837.

107. Harvey Kitchel, "In the Wolcott," 29 December 1839, Amy Kitchel Papers, Connecticut Historical Society, Hartford.

108. Pennsylvania Hall was built for $40,000 based on shares of $20 each. The building was built to provide a space for free speech and discussion, although it was not directly affiliated with any specific antislavery organization in the city. The motto that hung over the speaker's platform read, "Virtue, Liberty, and Independence." Women were significant subscribers to the builder. See *Report of a Delegate to the Anti-Slavery Convention of American Women: Addressed to the Fall River Female Anti-Slavery, and Published by Its Request* (Boston: I. Knapp, 1838), 4–5.

109. "The Terrible Riot in Philadelphia," *The Liberator*, 25 May 1838. This is a reprint of an article that appeared in the *Boston Centennial and Gazette* and does not reflect the views of *The Liberator*. Its extensive coverage of the riot included excerpts from other newspapers.

110. "Riot in Philadelphia and Conflagration of Pennsylvania Hall," *Maryland Gazette*, 24 May 1838.

111. "Abolition Riot at Philadelphia," *New York Morning Herald*, 19 May 1838.

112. Erica Armstrong Dunbar, *A Fragile Freedom: African American Women and Emancipation in the Antebellum City* (New Haven, Conn.: Yale University Press, 2008), 73–74.

113. *Report of a Delegate*, 16.

114. *Proceedings of the Third Anti-Slavery Convention of American Women, Held in Philadelphia, May 1st, 2d and 3d, 1839* (Philadelphia: Merrihew and Thompson, 1839), 5–6.

115. "Caustic Rebuke," *Pennsylvania Freeman*, 16 August 1838.

116. "Terrible Riot in Philadelphia," *New-England Weekly Review* (Hartford, Conn.), 6 August 1842. While the numbers vary, this report states that six individuals died from wounds received at the riot.

117. "The Riot in Philadelphia," *New York Spectator*, 3 August 1842.

118. Still, "An Appeal," 257.

119. James Oliver Horton, "Freedom's Yoke: Gender Conventions among Antebellum Free Blacks," *Feminist Studies* 12 (1986): 55.

120. Bella Gross, "*Freedom's Journal* and the *Rights of All*," *Journal of Negro History* 17 (1932): 259.

121. Frances Smith Foster, "A Narrative of the Origins and (Somewhat) Surprising Developments of African American Print Culture," *American Literary History* 17, no. 4 (Winter 2005): 720. Smith Foster qualifies this number by describing the difficulties of defining literacy at this time.

122. "The Female Literary Association," *The Liberator*, 3 December 1831. The language of the constitution of the African Female Benevolent Society of Troy is almost exactly the same. This suggests an awareness of the work of other groups across city and state lines and a commonality of purpose. In Newman, Rael, and Lapsansky, *Pamphlets of Protests*, 120–21.

123. Still, "An Appeal," 256–57.

124. "Domestic Habits," *Colored American*, 30 September 1837.

125. M. Carey, "Practical Rules for the Promotion of Domestic Happiness, Rules for Wives," *Colored American*, 3 November 1838.

126. Jacqueline Jones, *American Work: Four Centuries of Black and White Labor* (New York: W. W. Norton and Company, 1998), 284.

127. "The Intemperate Female," *Colored American*, 10 June 1837; and "Female Education," *Colored American*, 18 March 1837.

128. "Duties of Wives," *Freedom's Journal*, 21 February 1829.

129. "Female Education," *Freedom's Journal*, 9 January 1829.

130. "For the Colored American, Thoughts," *Colored American*, 12 June 1841.

131. "Religion in Woman," *Colored American*, 7 October 1837.

132. "From Henry H. Garnet to 'Dear Friend' (New York, May 13, 1837)," in *Love and Marriage in Early African America*, ed. Frances Smith Foster (Boston: Northeastern University Press, 2008), 71. In this letter, Garnet described Julia Williams, whom he eventually married.

133. Still, "An Appeal," 256.

134. Fagan, *Black Newspaper*, 50.

135. James Forten Jr., *Address to the Women of Pennsylvania* (Philadelphia: Marrihew and Gunn, 1836), 5, emphasis in the original.

CHAPTER 4. Creating an Empowered Private Sphere

1. While authorship opened doors for women, the process of becoming an author was not easy in the early nineteenth century. Typically, new authors had to underwrite much of the expense of their first books, and promotion of the work was largely left to the author. See Carolyn L. Karcher, *First Lady of the Republic* (Durham, N.C.: Duke University Press, 1994), 38–39. Child provided a breakdown of expenses with *Hobomok*, her first novel: "1000 copies were printed to be sold at 75 cts, which would have amounted to 750 dollars. Printing, paper, and binding 245$ commission & c., 250, making all expenses about 500$ A few more than half the edition are sold, which, allowing for the deduction of misprinted volumes, leave 98$ against me" (Lydia Maria Child to George Ticknor, 31 March 1825, Watertown, Massachusetts, in *Lydia Maria Child Selected Letters, 1817–1880*, ed. Milton Meltzer and Patricia G. Holland [Amherst: University of Massachusetts Press, 1982], 5).

2. Annie Fields, ed., *The Life and Letters of Harriet Beecher Stowe* (Boston: Houghton, Mifflin and Company, 1898), 104.

3. Mrs. (Sarah) Hale, *The Ladies' Wreath: A Selection from the Female Poetic Writers of England and America, with Notices and Notes, Prepared Especially for Young Ladies* (Boston: Marsh, Capen & Lyon, 1837), 388. By the time the *Ladies' Wreath* was published Hale was an established editor and could set her own terms. She wrote her publisher, "You wish to know my terms for the *Ladies Wreath*. I shall ask 10% on the first edition and I wish that edition to be not less than 2000. I do not choose to sell the copyright or I should value it higher than you would probably be willing to give" (19 November 1835, as quoted in Ruth E. Finley, *The Lady of Godey's* [Philadelphia: J. B. Lippencott Co., 1931], 92).

4. Mrs. Sarah Josepha Hale, *Northwood: or, Life North and South: Showing the True Character of Both*, 5th ed. (New York: H. Long and Brother, 1842), iii.

5. "Editors' Book Table: The Good Housekeeper," *Godey's Lady's Book*, June 1840, 282. The quote comes from the introductory paragraph of a review of Hale's new cookbook.

6. Hale, *Ladies' Wreath*, 384–85. Beecher, unlike Hale and Child, did not have older brothers and thus received more formal education outside the home than either Child or Hale did.

7. Hale, 386.

8. Nicole Tonkovich, *Domesticity with a Difference: The Nonfiction of Catharine Beecher, Sarah J. Hale, Fanny Fern, and Margaret Fuller* (Jackson: University Press of Mississippi, 1997), 53. The book opens with a poem of dedication to the "friends and patron" of the author. Sarah Hale, *The Genius of Oblivion and Other Original Poems* (Concord, Mass.: Jacob B. Moore, 1823), vi.

9. Sherbrooke Rogers, *Sarah Josepha Hale: A New England Pioneer* (Grantham, N.H.: Thompson and Rutter, 1985), 24–26.

10. Just prior to the U.S. Civil War, *Godey's* had 160,000 subscribers, making it the most widely read periodical in the country. Sarah C. O'Dowd, *A Rhode Island Original* (Lebanon, N.H.: University Press of New England, 2004), 16n2.

11. Tonkovich, *Domesticity with a Difference*, 60.

12. Laura Ingalls Wilder, *Little Town on the Prairie* (1941; repr., New York: Harper Collins, 2007), 109.

13. Finley, *Lady of Godey's*, 142.

14. Mrs. S. J. Hale, "Domestic Economy No. 1," *Godey's Lady's Book*, January 1840, 42.

15. Hale, 42.

16. S. G. Griffin, *A History of the Town of Keene* (Keene, N.H.: Sentinel Printing Company, 1904), 597.

17. Mrs. S. J. Hale, "Domestic Economy No. III," *Godey's Lady's Book*, April 1840, 154.

18. Mrs. Sarah J. Hale, *Traits of American Life* (Philadelphia: E. L. Carey & A. Hart, 1835), 265.

19. Hale, 265–66.

20. Hale, 121.

21. Hale, 126. This story was written before the founding of the Republican Party. Hale is likely speaking generically, or, given the time period in which the story is set, she is referring to the Democratic Republicans.

22. Hale, 127.

23. Elizabeth Oakes Smith, "Recollections of Sarah J. Hale," *Boston Daily Advertiser*, 8 July 1879.

24. Hale has few kind words for this character, Lydia Romalee. Her very choice of a southern husband called her character into question. While introducing Lydia, Hale more generally criticizes young women: "Those who have superintendence of female youth cannot too often nor too forcibly impress on their tender minds those lessons prudence, forbearance and humility, which the world is sure, sooner or later to force upon them. The art of self-government is indispensable to female felicity" (*Northwood: A Tale of New England* [Boston: Bowles & Dearborn, 1827], 12).

25. Hale, 27. In this short excerpt Hale unwittingly reveals the underlying sentiment of colonization.

26. Beverly Peterson, "Mrs. Hale on Mrs. Stowe and Slavery," *American Periodicals* 8 (1998): 36.

27. Sarah Josepha Hale, *Northwood*, 2nd ed. (New York: H. Long and Brother, 1852), iv.

28. Hale, 404.

29. Peterson, "Mrs. Hale on Mrs. Stowe," 32. While some argue that the politics of *Uncle Tom's Cabin* are difficult to categorize, the book is clearly antislavery, even if it isn't completely proabolition.

30. Tonkovich, *Domesticity with a Difference*, 5.

31. Fields, *Life and Letters*, 35.

32. Fields, 42.

33. Catharine Beecher to Edward Beecher, 3 March 1827, Hartford, Connecticut, Acquisitions, Harriet Beecher Stowe Center, Hartford, Connecticut.

34. Beecher to Beecher.

35. Elizabeth Elliot Foote to Harriet Foote, 28–28 January 1841, Foote Collection, Harriet Beecher Stowe Center.

36. Catharina Beecher, *Educational Reminiscences and Suggestions* (New York: J. F. Ford, 1874), 89.

37. Beecher, 86.

38. Catharine Beecher to Dear Sir, 9 November 1843, Acquisitions, Walnut Hills, Cincinnati, Ohio.

39. Tonkovich, *Domesticity with a Difference*, 52. This comes from a 24 April 1838 letter in the Hoadley Collection, Connecticut Historical Society, Hartford.

40. Kathryn Kish Sklar, *Catharine Beecher: A Study in American Domesticity* (New York: W. W. Norton and Company, 1976), 115–17.

41. Catharine Beecher, *Essay on Slavery and Abolitionism* (Philadelphia: Henry Perkins, 1837), 101–2.

42. Beecher, 5–6.

43. Beecher, 13–14.

44. Beecher, 102.

45. Beecher, 103–4. Beecher is referencing female slaves as the "oppressed females" and not speaking of white women seeking political rights.

46. Beecher, 104–5.

47. Beecher, *Educational Reminiscences*, 62–64. *To Benevolent Women of the United States* was written and distributed in secret, with the participants remaining silent. Perhaps this is one reason why Beecher was able to make her charge against Grimké without appearing to be a hypocrite. Harriet Beecher Stowe wrote her sister Catharine that "last night we teachers all sat up till eleven o'clock finishing our Cherokee letters. We sent some to the principal ladies of New Haven by Martha Sherman, to put in the Post-office there." Harriet stated that "the circular is making a great excitement in New York" (*Educational Reminiscences*, 69). Ronald and Mary Sarcino Zboray argue that this was "the earliest female national petition campaign" (*Voices without Votes: Women and Politics in Antebellum New England* [Durham: University of New Hampshire Press, 2010], 38).

48. Beecher, *Essay on Slavery and Abolitionism*, 107–8.

49. Beecher, 108.

50. Catharine Beecher to Georgina, 20 January 1849, Acquisitions, Boston.

51. The letter from Susan Warner to her sister as quoted in Mary Kelley, *Private Woman, Public Stage: Literary Domesticity in Nineteenth-Century America* (New York: Oxford University Press, 1984), 320. Warner further notes that the address was mostly read by Beecher's brother. Susan Warner (1819–85) published *The Wide, Wide World* in 1850, one of the most popular novels of the nineteenth century. Warner and her younger sister Anna turned to writing in the late 1840s to help supplement the family's income.

52. Beecher, *Educational Reminiscences*, 129.

53. Beecher, 123, emphasis in the original.

54. Catharine Beecher to Edward Beecher, 8 March 1826, Beecher Family Papers, 1822–1903, Mount Holyoke College Archives and Special Collections, South Hadley, Massachusetts.

55. Catharine Beecher to Edward Beecher, 25 April 1826, Beecher Family Papers.

56. Beecher, *Essay on Slavery and Abolitionism*, 30–31. Connecticut was never a bastion of antislavery sentiments and probably the most resistant to abolition of the New England states. William Lloyd Garrison famously described Connecticut as "the Georgia of New England."

57. Beecher, *Educational Reminiscences*, 7.

58. Patricia Holland, "Lydia Maria Child as a Nineteenth-Century Professional Author," *Studies in the American Renaissance*, 1981, 159. The *Juvenile Miscellany* was founded in 1826 and had an eight-year run. It followed the model of most early children's fiction, as it was a "primer, storybook, 'library of entertaining knowledge,' and purveyor of moral values" (Carolyn Karcher, *The First Woman in the Republic: A Cultural Biography of Lydia Maria Child* [Durham, N.C.: Duke University Press, 1998], 57). The $300 that Child added to her income through her work with the *Miscellany* was not insignificant. Calculating the value of $300 from 1828 to 2019 varies. The purchasing power of that amount of money is $8,350. Looking at the labor value for that amount of money (and comparing it to the 1828 wages of an unskilled laborer), the amount would be $100,000. I used the calculator at measuringworth.com to determine these values.

59. "The Works of Mrs. Child," *North American Review* 37 (1833): 138.

60. Holland, "Lydia Maria Child," 159.

61. In a letter directing how the proceeds could be used, Child allocated $260 to specific debts and then asked that the remainder be used to pay the interest on different notes. She suggested that these payments would take care of the entirety of her payment (Lydia Maria Child to Ellis Gray and Louisa Loring, 5 December 1838, Northampton, in Meltzer and Holland, *Selected Letters*, 95).

62. Lydia Maria Child, *The Mother's Book* (1831; repr., Bedford, Mass.: Applewood Books, 1992), dedication.

63. Lydia Maria Child to Lydia B. Child, 2 August 1831, Boston, in Meltzer and Holland, *Selected Letters*, 20.

64. Lydia Maria Child to Rev. Convers Francis, 30 October 1840, in Sewall, *Letters*, 39.

65. Lydia Maria Child to Dear John, "the change of tense," n.d., Sarah Hopper Palmer Family Papers, Friends Historical Library, Swarthmore, Pennsylvania, emphasis in the original.

66. Lydia Maria Child to Angelina Grimké Weld, 18 December 1838, in Barnes and Dumond, *Letters*, 725.

67. Lydia Maria Child to Angelina G. Weld, 26 December 1838, in Barnes and Dumond, 731.

68. Lydia Maria Child to Mrs. S. B. Shaw, Wayland, 1856, in Sewall, *Letters*, 79.

69. Lydia Maria Child to David Lee Child, 27 October 1856, Wayland, in Sewall, 83.

70. Lydia Maria Child to Lucy and Mary Osgood, 20 July 1856, Wayland, in Meltzer and Holland, *Selected Letters*, 289.

71. Lydia Maria Child to Mrs. S. B. Shaw, 27 October 1856, Wayland, in Sewall, *Letters*, 85.

72. Lydia Maria Child to Ellis Gray Loring, 3 July 1856, Wayland, in Meltzer and Holland, *Selected Letters*, 282.

73. Lydia Maria Child to Prof. Convers Francis, 6 December 1846, New York, in Sewall, *Letters*, 58.

74. Lydia Maria Child to E. Carpenter, 20 March 1838, in Sewall, 26. Angelina Grimké addressed a committee of the Massachusetts legislature on the subject of slavery on 21 February 1838 and on the two following days. She also gave a public lecture in Boston on 5 April 1838. In a letter to her mother-in-law, Child described Grimké's speech: "Last night I went to the Odeon to hear Angelina Grimké. It is a very large hall capable of holding more than three thousand people. It was crowded, gallery after gallery up to the very ceiling, and through a lecture of two hours there was perfectly hushed attention" (Lydia Maria Child to Lydia [Bigelow] Child, 6 April 1838, Boston, in Meltzer and Holland, *Selected Letters*, 73).

75. Lydia Maria Child to Miss Henrietta Sargent, 1838, in Sewall, *Letters*, 31.

76. "The Gray Mare," *Alexandria (Va.) Gazette*, 3 July 1841.

77. Lydia Maria Child to Ellis Gray Loring, 22 March 1842, New York, in Meltzer and Holland, *Selected Letters*, 167.

78. Lydia Maria Child to Louisa Loring, 17 November 1836, South Natick, in Meltzer and Holland, 58.

79. Lydia Maria Child to Lydia B. Child, 17 January 1837, South Natick, in Meltzer and Holland, 60.

80. Lydia Maria Child to Mrs. S. B. Shaw, 1852, West Newton, in Sewall, *Letters*, 69.

81. "Female Anti-Slavery Society," *The Liberator*, 14 July 1832.

82. Writing to the Boston group, Child explained: "My opinions concerning the formation of a distinct female society have remained unchanged since my first conversation with Mrs. Shipleigh; but I may be in the wrong and others in the right. . . . I am willing to pay my subscription, and to increase it by donations, as soon as we have fewer pecuniary difficulties to struggle with; but I had much rather not, in any way be connected with the government" (Lydia Maria Child to Charlotte Phelps, 2 January 1834, in Meltzer and Holland, *Selected Letters*, 28).

83. Lydia Maria Child to Lucretia Mott, 5 March 1839, Northampton, in Meltzer and Holland, 106.

84. *Fifth Annual Report of the Boston Female Anti-Slavery Society* (Boston: Isaac Knapp, 1838), 10.

85. "Mrs. Child's Appeal in Favor of the Africans," *Quarterly Christian Spectator*, 1 September 1834, 445.

86. "Appeal for the Africans," *Colonizationist and Journal of Freedom*, October 1833, 165.

87. "Literary Notices," *Ladies' Magazine and Literary Gazette*, September 1833.

88. Patricia Holland, "Lydia Maria Child as a Nineteenth-Century Professional Author," *Studies in the American Renaissance*, 1981, 157–67, 160, http://www.jstor.org/stable/30227480.

89. Lydia Maria Child to Louisa Loring, 30 April 1839, Northampton, in Meltzer and Holland, *Selected Letters*, 113.

90. Lydia Maria Child to Mrs. E. C. Pierce, 27 May 1841, New York, in Sewall, *Letters*, 42–43.

91. A decade later, women were using the power of their own editorships to engage in politics. Jane Swisshelm and Clarina Nichols were developing a national reputation and edited papers that were not just for women. See "Woman and Politics: The Next Presidency, &c.," *Frederick Douglass' Paper*, 25 February 1853.

92. Meltzer and Holland, *Selected Letters*.

93. Lydia Maria Child to Lucretia Mott, 5 March 1839, Northampton, in Meltzer and Holland, 107.

94. Lydia Maria Child to Ellis Gray Loring, 28 September 1841, New York, in Meltzer and Holland, 146–47.

95. Lydia Maria Child to Maria (Weston) Chapman, 19 May 1843, New York, in Meltzer and Holland, 197.

96. Lydia Maria Child to Louisa Loring, 22 June 1845, New York, in Meltzer and Holland, 223–24.

97. "To the Legislators of Massachusetts," *Boston Courier*, 29 April 1839.

98. "To the Legislators of Massachusetts." Child's "sisters in Lynn" refers to the location of the women who signed the petition.

99. "Additions to the Documentary History, Lydia Maria Child and Gov. Wise," *National Era*, 17 November 1859.

100. "Additions."

101. "Additions."

102. Kellie Carter Jackson examines the politics of violence among Black abolitionists as the movement splintered from its Garrisonian roots. She discusses Child's evolving rejection of nonviolence as the only response to slavery. *Force and Freedom: Black Abolitionists and the Politics of Violence* (Philadelphia: University of Pennsylvania Press, 2019), 94–96, 128.

103. L. Maria Child, *The Freedmen's Book* (Boston: Ticknor & Fields, 1865).

104. Lydia Maria Child to Miss Henrietta Sargent, 1838, in Sewall, *Letters*, 31–32.

CHAPTER 5. Rewriting Race and Respectability

The epigraph is from Monroe A. Majors, *Noted Negro Women: Their Triumphs and Activities* (Chicago: Donohue and Henneberry, 1983), viii.

1. Deborah Gray White describes the Jezebel character as emerging from the era of slavery: "In every way Jezebel was the counter image of the mid-nineteenth-century ideal of the Victorian lady. She did not lead men and children to God; piety was foreign to her. She saw no advantage in prudery, indeed domesticity paled in importance before matters of the flesh" (*Ar'n't I a Woman? Female Slaves in the Plantation South*, rev. ed. [New York: W. W. Norton & Company, 1999], 29). I believe that the Jezebel figure is not only a product of slavery and the domination of Black women by white men but also a by-product of true womanhood, an attempt to keep Black women from claiming the ethos of that status.

2. *The Register of Trades of the Colored People in the City of Philadelphia* (Philadelphia: Merrihew and Gunn, Printers, 1838), 5–6, lists over eighty women employed as dressmakers and tailoresses. The number greatly expanded in the 1856 census, with the number of

needlewomen listed as 486, suggesting the job had both broadened and lost status. The other occupations of Philadelphia women of color included washerwomen, 1,970; cook, 173; occupied at home, 290; day labor, 786; living in families, 156; trades, 213; raggers and boners, 103 (total 4,249). Benjamin Bacon, *Statistics of the Colored People of Philadelphia* (Philadelphia: T. Ellwood Chapman, Merrihew and Thompson, Printers, 1856), 18.

3. While the actual wealth of middle-class and upper-class families of color might be different, their social status remained the same; thus, I can classify the Fortens within the same social group as the more typically middle-class families such as the Robert Douglass family. Julie Winch notes that African American membership in the Philadelphia Female Anti-Slavery Society was drawn from the "city's elite families. Participation was confined for the most part to those not obligated to work to support their families. Only Sarah Dorsey, Sarah Douglass, and Margaretta Forten worked outside the home: all were teachers" (*Philadelphia's Black Elite* [Philadelphia: Temple University Press, 1988], 86).

4. Anti-Slavery Convention of American Women (Philadelphia), *Address to the Free Colored People of the United States* (Philadelphia: Merrihew and Gunn, 1838), 10. Mary S. Parker is typically credited with authorship of this document as the president of the convention. Parker was president of the Boston Female Anti-Slavery Society in the late 1830s and ultimately supported dissolving BFAS with the goal of creating a new anti-Garrisonian organization, which is reflected in the conservative tone of the address. For more information about women and antislavery activism in Boston, see Lee V. Chambers, *The Weston Sisters: An American Abolitionist Family* (Chapel Hill: University of North Carolina Press, 2014).

5. James Forten Jr., "An Address Delivered before the American Moral Reform Society by James Forten Jr., Philadelphia, August 17th, 1837," in *The Minutes and Proceedings of the First Annual Meeting of the American Moral Reform Society, Held at Philadelphia* (Philadelphia: Merrihew and Gunn, 1837; repr., Philadelphia: Rhistoric Publications, n.d.), 42–43.

6. Shirley Wilson Logan, *Liberating Language: Sites of Rhetorical Education in Nineteenth-Century Black America* (Carbondale: Southern Illinois University Press, 2008), 64.

7. Erica Armstrong Dunbar, "Writing for True Womanhood: African-American Women's Writings and the Antislavery Struggle," in *Women's Rights and Transatlantic Antislavery in the Era of Emancipation*, ed. Kathryn Kish Sklar and James Brewer Stewart (New Haven, Conn.: Yale University Press, 2007), 300.

8. "The Ladies' Department," *The Liberator*, 26 February 1833.

9. Sarah M. Douglass to William L. Garrison, 29 February 1832, 0149, reel 1, Black Abolitionist Papers, ProQuest.

10. James Forten to William L. Garrison, 28 July 1832, reel 1, 2007–8, Black Abolitionist Papers, ProQuest.

11. "Fair for the Benefit of the Female Vigilant Association," *Pennsylvania Freeman*, 27 December 1838.

12. "Miss Douglass, Boston 5 March 1832," Black Abolitionist Papers, ProQuest.

13. Todd S. Gernes, "Poetic Justice: Sarah Forten, Eliza Earle, and the Paradox of Intellectual Property," *New England Quarterly* 71 (1998): 232.

14. "Unnatural Distinction," *The Liberator*, 28 July 1832.
15. Gernes, "Poetic Justice," 232.
16. Forten, "An Address," 42–43.
17. "To Colored Americans," *Pennsylvania Freeman*, 10 October 1838.
18. "Woman's Rights," *Mirror of Liberty*, July 1838, 5.
19. Margaret Hope Bacon, *But One Race: The Life of Robert Purvis* (Albany: State University of New York Press, 2007), 41. Reading the letters of antislavery women, it is clear that networks were created that extended beyond city limits. For example, almost every letter Sarah Grimké sent Sarah Douglass included a long list of greetings to be passed along. An 1837 letter from Grimké includes near the end, "Love to the Fortens, Hetty Burr, the Smiths, S. A. Lewis, etc. Please ask James Forten if he knows what became of the slaves who served in the army in our revolutionary war; were they liberated according to promise, or were they as we suppose from circumstance turned from the battle to the cotton and rice field?" (Sarah M. Grimké, "Dear Sister Sarah, Holliston, 22 October 1837," Black Abolitionist Papers, ProQuest).
20. "Great Meeting of the People of Color," *National Enquirer*, 31 August 1835.
21. Dunbar, "Writing for True Womanhood," 303.
22. Anti-Slavery Convention of American Women (Philadelphia), *Address*, 10.
23. For a description of an early meeting to oppose colonization, see "James Forten Called to the Chair," *National Advocate*, 14 August 1817; for a retrospective of his anticolonization work, see James Forten, "Slavery," *The Liberator*, 1 August 1835. Forten was also president of the American Moral Reform Society, and his son James Jr. served as recording secretary.
24. A perusal of the antislavery press during the 1830s reveals a number of activists who wrote of visiting the Forten home and of meeting members of the Forten family. For example, Arnold Buffum wrote of visiting Philadelphia and taking tea at the home of Joseph Cassey, joined by the families of James Forten and Robert Purvis. See "Communications," *The Liberator*, 26 October 1833.
25. James Greenleaf Whittier, "For the Daughters of James Forten, Philadelphia," *The Liberator*, 3 September 1836.
26. James Forten, "To William Lloyd Garrison, 23 February 1831," in Ripley, *The Black Abolitionist Papers, Volume III*, 61.
27. *The Liberator*, 26 March 1831.
28. Julie Winch, "Sarah Forten's Anti-Slavery Networks," in Sklar and Stewart, *Women's Rights*, 147.
29. Sarah Forten to Elizabeth H. Whittier, 23 March 1835, Whittier Papers, Central Michigan University Special Collections, Mt. Pleasant, Black Abolitionist Papers, ProQuest. George Thompson (1804–78) was a British antislavery orator who made a successful lecture tour of the United States beginning in 1834.
30. Forten to Whittier.
31. The Forten family likely hired domestic labor, which allowed the women of the family to participate in a variety of organizations. The 1840 census lists seventeen free people of color as attached to the Forten home (and this would be after Harriet and Sarah and presumably at least one of the Forten sons had left home). Seven members are listed as

being employed in "trade or manufacture," suggesting that James Forten boarded some of his employees at the sail loft. See U.S. Federal Census, 1840, New Market Ward, Philadelphia, Pennsylvania, roll 484, p. 165, Ancestry.com.

32. Sarah Forten to Esteemed Friend, 15 April 1837, Philadelphia, Weld-Grimke Family Papers, William L. Clements Library, University of Michigan, Ann Arbor.

33. Forten to Esteemed Friend, emphasis in the original.

34. Harriet Forten Purvis married Robert Purvis on 13 September 1831. There has been some speculation as to why Sarah Forten eloped with Joseph Purvis to New Jersey to be married by a justice of the peace. Julie Winch speculates, based on when the eldest child was born, that Sarah was pregnant at the time of her marriage ("Sarah Forten's Anti-Slavery Networks," 153). Joseph Purvis was almost completely uninvolved in antislavery and reform movements and seems an odd choice for Sarah to risk her respectability with. Without any evidence, I wonder if because of his family connections, he was an easy solution for a more complicated problem.

35. See Bacon, *But One Race*, for a genealogy of Robert and Joseph Purvis. The estate that was divided between Robert and Joseph due to the early death of their brother was sizable.

36. Bacon, 49.

37. Harriet maintained a presence within the various organizations in Philadelphia during the years she was raising her young children. She was a member of various literary societies, continued leadership roles within PFAS, and was a member of the Colored Free Produce Association. Despite the high cost in money and time, as well as the often questionable quality of the goods, the Robert Purvis household shopped exclusively for free produce. The fact that Harriet was able to maintain this lifestyle when Sarah was not is likely due to several factors. Harriet spent the early years of her marriage in Philadelphia; she had a governess to help with the children and other domestic help and in her husband, Robert, a partner who believed in the equality of women. See Bacon, 96–97.

38. Winch, "Sarah Forten's Anti-Slavery Networks," 154. Sarah Forten Purvis's absences from various antislavery fairs are surprising. Both of her sisters continued to be listed as participants. Harriet Forten Purvis, who also lived outside the city by the middle of the 1840s, continued her work with the Philadelphia Female Anti-Slavery Society. See "Annual Fair," *Pennsylvania Freeman*, 18 November 1847; and "Pennsylvania A.S. Fair," *National Anti-Slavery Standard*, 20 December 1849. Even as late as 1849 Margaretta and Harriet were still active in the Pennsylvania Anti-Slavery Fair. In a letter to Gerrit Smith written from Byberry, Harriet mentioned the broadening scope of the fair and the desire for support outside Pennsylvania, and she included the printed call for the fair and list of volunteers. See Black Abolitionist Papers, ProQuest; Harriet D. Purvis to Gerrit Smith, 13 September 1859, Gerrit Smith Papers, Syracuse University, ProQuest.

39. Sarah Forten is listed as a manager of PFAS along with Lucretia Mott, Lydia White, Mary Needles, Grace Douglass, and Susan Haydock. See *Fourth Annual Report for the Philadelphia Female Anti-Slavery Society* (Philadelphia: Merrihew and Gunn, 1838), 19. Sarah Mapps Douglass is listed as corresponding secretary, and her sister Margaretta Forten is treasurer. Forten is not listed in the 1839 report, although Margaretta has moved from treasurer to the position of manager.

40. "Receipts, 16–23 January," *North Star*, 23 January 1851.

41. Jasmine Nichole Cobb, *Picture Freedom: Remaking Black Visuality in the Early Nineteenth Century* (New York: NYU Press, 2015), 106–7.

42. U.S. Federal Census, 1840, Bensalem, Bucks, Pennsylvania, roll 447, p. 211, Ancestry.com.

43. U.S. Federal Census, 1840, Cedar Ward, Philadelphia, roll 484, p. 251, Ancestry.com.

44. This is a substantial decrease in personal wealth from the time of his inheritance. Perhaps what is recorded here is inaccurate, or, as biographers of James Forten and Robert Purvis have noted, Joseph made bad financial investments in the late 1840s and throughout the 1850s.

45. Seventh Census of the U.S., 1850, Bensalem, Bucks, Pennsylvania, roll M432_798, 73B, image 154, National Archives microfilm publication M43, Record Group 29, Records of the Bureau of the Census, National Archives, Washington, D.C.

46. Bacon, *But One Race*, 129–30.

47. Although none of Sarah and Joseph's children are listed as part of the Charlotte Forten household in the 1860 census, given the relative proximity to the Bensalem farm, my guess is that the children were often long-term guests at the home. The superior opportunities for schooling further suggest that twelve-year-old Harriet might have lived there at that time.

48. U.S. Census, 1860, Population Schedule, Bensalem, Bucks, Pennsylvania, roll M653_1082, 47, image 52, National Archives microfilm publication M653, Record Group 29, Records of the Bureau of the Census, National Archives, Washington, D.C.

49. Tax records, 1782–1860, Bucks County, Pennsylvania, Ancestry.com.

50. Charlotte Forten, 6 July 1858, in *Journals of Charlotte Forten Grimké*, ed. Brenda Stevenson (New York: Oxford University Press, 1987), 322.

51. Sarah (Forten) Purvis to Dear Sir, 18 October 1869, Bridgewater, Bucks County, Weld-Grimké Papers, William L. Clements Library, University of Michigan, Ann Arbor.

52. Alfred Purvis died on 27 April 1865. James Purvis died on 18 February 1870. James had been declared a "lunatic" at least as early as 1858 after the death of his father (the findings of the orphan's court at the time Joseph Purvis Sr.'s estate was settled). Joseph Purvis Jr. enlisted in the military on 16 March 1864, became ill, and was discharged in July 1864. He reenlisted in March 1865 and continued to be plagued with ill health. See Bacon, *But One Race*, 150; Julie Winch, *A Gentleman of Color: The Life of James Forten* (New York: Oxford University Press, 2002), 365. Joseph's reenlistment card from 1865 lists him as a mulatto farmer born in Bucks County (twenty-five years old, five-foot-nine), this time with Twenty-Fourth Infantry Regiment, U.S. Colored Troops Military Service Records, 1861–65, Ancestry.com. At age nineteen it would seem that Alexander would also be at work on the farm. I would assume his listing as "at home" was in deference to class status. The two elder sons could be listed as "farmers," and as part owners of the farm, they were, in essence, gentlemen farmers. Alexander, who was under the age of twenty-one, would not want to appear as a farm "laborer."

53. Purvis to Dear Sir, 18 October 1869.

54. Winch, *A Gentleman of Color*, 365. By 1875 daughter Sarah Purvis had married and

was living in Kansas. Her brother was living with Sarah and her husband, William Bozeman, working on their farm. See U.S. Census, 1 March 1875, Kansas State Census Collection, Ancestry.com.

55. Forten to Esteemed Friend, 15 April 1837.

56. Monroe A. Majors, *Noted Negro Women, Their Triumphs and Activities* (Chicago: Donhue and Henneberry, 1893), 194.

57. Ada, "The Grave of the Slave," *The Liberator*, 22 January 1831. The poem was set to music by composer Francis Johnson (1792–1844).

58. "Dear Brother," *The Philanthropist*, 11 March 1836. This issue also included Forten's poem "A Prayer." *The Philanthropist* (Cincinnati, Ohio) was an antislavery paper edited by James G. Birney for the Ohio Anti-Slavery Society. Louisa was Sarah Forten's middle name.

59. Ada, "The Slave Girl's Address to Her Mother," *The Liberator*, 29 January 1831.

60. "Past Joys," *The Liberator*, 19 March 1831.

61. "The Prayer," *The Liberator*, 26 March 1831.

62. "The Farewell," *The Liberator*, 30 June 1832.

63. Sarah Forten to Esteemed Friend, 25 April 1837, Philadelphia, Weld-Grimke Family Papers.

64. "The Separation," *The Liberator*, 21 December 1833.

65. Sarah Forten, "An Appeal to Woman," *The Liberator*, 1 February 1834.

66. James Scott, "Reply to Ada," *The Liberator*, 22 February 1834.

67. "Reply to Ada," *The Liberator*, 1 March 1834.

68. Angelina Grimké, *An Appeal to the Women of the Nominally Free States, Issued by an Anti-Slavery Convention of American Women*, 2nd ed. (Boston: Isaac Knapp, 1838). Grimké begins the essay by including a quote from her sparring partner, Catharine Beecher, that implies that Beecher endorses women's antislavery activism: "The trembling earth, the low and murmuring thunders, already admonish as our danger and if females can exert any saving influence in this emergency, it is time for them to awake." While the context of this quote in its original publication calls for women to act quietly within their private world, I suspect Grimké took great glee in using Beecher's own words against her.

69. In an essay and letter of commendation for Angelina Grimké before she began her first lecture tour, Sarah Forten (as well as her mother, Charlotte Forten) is a signatory. Of the seventeen women whose names appear, Grace Douglass, mother of Sarah Mapps Douglass, is included, as well as the better-known officers of the Philadelphia Female Anti-Slavery Society (including Lucretia Mott, vice president; Sarah Pugh, recording secretary; and Mary Grew, corresponding secretary). "Female Philanthropy and Enterprise: An Important Mission," *National Enquirer* 13 (1836).

70. The timing of this claim is unusual, as it occurred five months before Nat Turner's Rebellion. Other famous slave rebellions, such as the Stono Rebellion (1739) and Denmark Vesey's plot, which never came to fruition (1822), seem too long before to be on Forten's mind. Presumably, she was familiar with David Walker's more recent *Appeal*, published in 1829, and was thinking in part of people of color acting on their own behalf.

71. Magawisca (Sarah Forten), "The Abuse of Liberty," *The Liberator*, 26 March 1831.

72. Findagrave.com lists her death as 29 October 1884, although there is no marker to confirm the date. Most sources list her death as occurring in 1883 but provide no specific date or source.

73. Pennsylvania, Philadelphia city death certificates, 1803–1915, index, Family Search, Salt Lake City, Utah, 2008, 2010, from originals housed in the death records at the Philadelphia city archives. The city record lists her date of death as 29 October 1884 (like Findagrave.com) and her burial as 2 November 1884. Ancestry.com provides no image of the document.

74. Julia Winch, *Philadelphia's Black Elite* (Philadelphia: Temple University Press, 1988), 50. Grace was the daughter of Cyrus Bustill, a baker who followed the Quaker faith and was a member of the Free African Society (founded in 1787). Anna Bustill Smith, "The Bustill Family," *Journal of Negro History* 10 (1925): 638–39.

75. Her father is listed as still practicing his trade as of 1838 and sometimes listed as a barber rather than a hairdresser. Her brothers Robert and William are listed as painters, although Robert could more accurately be described as an artist. See *Register of the Trades of the Colored People in the City of Philadelphia and Districts* (Philadelphia: Merrihew and Gunn, 1838), 6–7. William died in 1839 at the age of twenty-five. James is not listed in the 1838 trade register, although later in life he appears as a hairdresser.

76. "Robert Douglass, Jr.," *The Liberator*, 23 March 1833.

77. "Remittances," *The Liberator*, 17 November 1837. James Forten served as president and Robert Purvis as secretary to the college fund. The inclusion of Robert Douglass in a leadership position among elite men demonstrates the status of the Douglass family despite the fact that they were less wealthy. See "A Voice from Philadelphia," *The Liberator*, 13 April 1833. Robert Douglass also participated in the anticolonization meetings held in Philadelphia in 1817 that were chaired by James Forten Sr. and included Absalom Jones and Richard Allen on the committee.

78. "Our Friends in Hayti," *Colored American*, 3 March 1838; "Hayti, Extract of a Letter," *Colored American*, 3 March 1838.

79. Sarah Douglass to William Basset, December 1837, Black Abolitionist Papers, ProQuest, underlined in the original.

80. Why Douglass always served in this role is interesting to ponder. Was it her interest in corresponding with a wider world, was it the faith that society members placed in her due to her education, or was it because it was where Douglass felt she could wield the most influence? Unfortunately, in her surviving letters she doesn't reflect upon serving in this office; however, just a quick perusal of various women's organizations reveals that this was her preferred position within societies.

81. The *Weekly Anglo African*, published in New York, reported on a public examination held at the Institute of Colored Youth, where Douglass eventually taught. After praising the work of the students, the paper next turned to the teachers: "Of the three leading teachers, Mrs. Douglass, Miss Mapps, and Mr. Basett, no word of commendation is needed from us. The name of the first [Douglass] is identified with the cause of education in Philadelphia, and she still keeps on the student's harness" ("The Late Examination of the Institute for Colored Youth," *Weekly Anglo African*, 26 May 1860).

82. For some unknown reason, the name of the Forten/Douglass school never appears in historical narratives or official records. Perhaps the school was unnamed.

83. Margaret Hope Bacon, "New Light on Sarah Mapps Douglass and Her Reconciliation with Friends," *Quaker History* 90, no. 1 (2001): 29.

84. Letter to the Penn Abolition Society, 29 September 1836, correspondence, incoming, 1836–37, Pennsylvania Abolition Society, Historical Society of Pennsylvania, Philadelphia. This letter is designated as being from Lucretia Mott, Mary Needles, Sarah Pugh, Lydia White, and S. A. Lewis. While some historians state that her association with PFAS began in 1838, there was clearly some relationship between Douglass's school and PAS as early as 1836. In 1841 she separated herself from the abolitionist society but did apparently receive some additional financial support. In 1853 she moved her school to the facility owned by ICY and was eventually made part of the school in 1854, with Sarah serving as head of the primary school, a position she held until her retirement in 1877 (Bacon, "New Light," 29).

85. Angelina Grimké to Dear Sarah, 3 April 1837, New York, Weld-Grimké Family Papers.

86. "Editorial Correspondence," *Colored American*, 2 December 1837.

87. *A Statistical Inquiry into the Condition of the People of Color of the City and Districts of Philadelphia* (Philadelphia: Kite & Alton, 1849), 22. Her science cabinet must have been truly special. The 2 December 1837 "Editorial Correspondence" article in the *Colored American* also makes note of this: "Miss Douglass has a well-selected and valuable cabinet of shells and minerals well-arranged and labeled. She has, also, a mind richly furnished with a knowledge of these sciences, and she does not fail, through them, to lend up the minds of her pupils through Nature, to Nature's God." Forty years later, ICY purchased it for enough money that it served to replace some of her postretirement wages.

88. For a detailed discussion of nineteenth-century pedagogy, see Sarah Anne Carter, *Object Lessons: How Nineteenth-Century Americans Learned to Make Sense of the Material World* (New York: Oxford University Press, 2018).

89. Benjamin C. Bacon, *Statistics of the Colored People of Philadelphia* (Philadelphia: T. Elwood Chapman, 1856), 8.

90. Sarah Mapps Douglass to Rebecca White, 30 May 1855, Quaker and Special Collections, Magill College, Haverford College, Haverford, Pennsylvania.

91. Sarah Mapps Douglass to Rebecca White, 19 December 1858, Quaker and Special Collections.

92. According to Measuringthewealth.com, the historic standard of living of $1,000 in 2019 would be $33,800; however, when calculated to determine income value for that sum, it would be $588,000, suggesting a degree of wealth for the three siblings.

93. Seventh Census of the U.S., 1850, High Street Ward, Philadelphia, Pennsylvania, roll M432_816, 176A, image 356, National Archives microfilm publication M43.

94. The marriage announcement was brief: "In Philadelphia, July 23rd, by Rev. Peter Van Pelt, Rev. Wm. Douglass, Rector of St Thomas's Episcopal Church, to Sarah M. Douglass, all of that city" ("Married," *Provincial Freeman*, 22 August 1855).

95. "At the Concert of Prayer," *Colored American*, 2 December 1837.

96. Julie Winch, *Philadelphia's Black Elite* (Philadelphia: Temple University Press, 1988), 158.

97. Sarah Mapps Douglass to Rebecca White, 30 May 1855, Quaker and Special Collections.

98. Sarah Moore Grimké to Sarah Douglass, 1855, Miscellaneous Manuscripts Collection, University of Chicago Special Collections, Chicago, Illinois.

99. Sarah Moore Grimké to Sarah Douglass, 19 June 1855, Newark, Miscellaneous Manuscripts Collection.

100. Brande Guisbert posted a family tree on Ancestry.com where William Douglass's mother is listed as Ruth Bustill, sister of Grace Bustill Douglass, the mother of Sarah. While I have not independently verified this information, a personal e-mail with Guisbert confirms her belief in this relationship. While I am neither convinced or not of this relationship, it does provide some rationale for Douglass's surprising decision to marry. The will of Cyrus Bustill lists both Ruth and Grace Bustill as children. See Philadelphia County, Pennsylvania will index, 1682–1819, Ancestry.com.

101. According to Measuringtheworth.com, $300 in 2019 based on the historic standard of living would be merely $9,520; however, when calculated to reflect the income value of $300, the sum would be $141,000, a total that more accurately reflects the status of the household.

102. Born in 1806, Sarah would have been older than the forty-five years indicated on the census. William Douglass was born on 6 September 1805. U.S. Census, 1860, Ward 5, Southern Division, Philadelphia, Pennsylvania, roll M653_1155, 563, image 569, National Archives microfilm publication M43. While the 1860 census lists all of the Douglass children as being born in Philadelphia, the oldest children were born in Maryland. Several Douglass children have disappeared from the household. Martha Ann, who would have come of age in the 1850s, is not included. William P. Douglass, who was ten in 1850, and Georgianna were also absent.

103. Sarah Mapps Douglass to Rebecca White, 30 July 1855, Josiah White Papers, Quaker and Special Collections.

104. Sarah Mapps Douglass to Rebecca White, 29 October 1860, Philadelphia, White Papers.

105. "Obituary," *Christian Recorder*, 31 May 1862.

106. U.S. Census, 1870, Ward 5, District 14 (2nd enumeration), Philadelphia, Pennsylvania, roll M593_1419, 90B, image 184, National Archives microfilm publication M43.

107. Grace and Sarah M. Douglass to *The Liberator*, 21 June 1839.

108. "Female Literary Association," *The Liberator*, 30 June 1832.

109. "To a Friend," *The Liberator*, 30 June 1832.

110. "To a Friend."

111. Sarah Douglass, "Mental Feasts," *The Liberator*, 21 July 1832. There is something somewhat uncomfortable about a white man issuing a call to free women of color in particular to sympathize "over the fate of the unhappy slaves" rather than issuing a call for all people to ponder their plight.

112. Sarah Douglass, "Mental Feasts," *The Liberator*, 21 July 1832.

113. Douglass.
114. Zillah (Sarah Mapps Douglass), "A Mother's Love," *The Liberator*, 28 July 1832.
115. Zillah.
116. "Our Philadelphia Letter," *Weekly Anglo-African*, 14 April 1860.
117. Angelina Grimké to Dear Sarah, 3 April 1837, New York, Weld-Grimké Family Papers.
118. Sarah Douglass to My Dear Abby, 18 May 1838, Philadelphia, Black Abolitionist Papers, ProQuest. Abby Kelley Foster (1811–87) was a lecturer and organizer for the American Anti-Slavery Society. She not only advocated immediate abolition but also supported full equality for African Americans and was a proponent for women's rights.
119. "For the Pennsylvania Freeman," *Pennsylvania Freeman*, 21 June 1838.
120. "To the Abolitionist of Eastern Pennsylvania," *National Anti-Slavery Standard*, 25 April 1844.
121. Sarah Mapps Douglass to Rebecca White, 28 November, Josiah White Papers. For information about her college training, see Bacon, "New Light," n32.
122. "Mrs. Douglass' Lectures," *Weekly Anglo-African*, 23 July 1859.
123. "Mrs. Douglass' Lectures," *Weekly Anglo-African*, 24 November 1860.
124. "Banneker Institute," *Christian Recorder*, 28 April 1866.
125. Robert Douglass to Esteemed Friend, 9 September 1882, Philadelphia, as quoted in Bacon, "New Light," 45.
126. Bustill Smith, "The Bustill Family," 644.

CONCLUSION. Reconstructing Womanhood

1. Ellen Carol Dubois, *Suffrage: Women's Long Battle for the Vote* (New York: Simon and Schuster, 2020), 72–73.
2. Minor v. Happersett, 88 U.S. 162 (1875). Apparently, this decision was used by those who claimed that former President Barack Obama is not a natural-born citizen and thus was not eligible to be president of the United States. The section of the court decision used by "birthers" does not provide a definitive definition of what constitutes a "natural-born citizen" and thus did not constitute a successful challenge to the legitimacy of Obama's presidency.
3. *Minor*, 88 U.S. 162 (1875).
4. Catharine Beecher and Harriet Beecher Stowe, *The American Woman's Home* (Hartford, Conn.: Harriet Beecher Stowe Center, 1975), 13.

INDEX

abolition. *See* antislavery activism; emancipation
Adams, Abigail, 17, 19, 22
African American men, 2, 79, 99, 135, 145; civic status, 16, 41–42, 96, 136, 165–66; elite status, 71–72; libraries for, 87; military enlistment, 22; natural rights claims, 17, 27–28, 165; patriarchy, 4, 18, 91, 96, 136–37; societies for, 138, 139, 161; stereotypes, 94; voting rights, 32–33, 167–68
African American middle-class women, 15–16, 66, 111, 160; civic identity or civic status of, 44, 136–37; emergence of, 70–73; performance of domesticity, 12–13, 135; self-help and antislavery societies, 137–42, 161–62; in teaching positions, 83–84, 154–55, 191nn66–67, 208n84; true womanhood and respectability of, 25, 63, 69–71, 95–99, 134–36
African Episcopal Church of St. Thomas (Philadelphia), 30, 74–75, 78, 143, 188n16; William Douglass of, 155–56, 157, 158
African Methodist Episcopal (AME) Church, 5, 76, 83, 88–89, 158, 192n84
African Society (Boston), 28, 175n47
Alcott, William, 48, 62, 181n13, 186n84
Aldrich, Hannah Thompson, 40
Allen, Richard, 5, 75–77, 189n30, 207n77
American Anti-Slavery Society, 115, 141, 210n118
American Cookery (Simmons), 26, 55–57, 65
American Frugal Housewife (L. M. Child), 57–58, 61, 97, 122–23; Hale's critique of, 58–59, 185n68; reprinting of, 62, 185n82
American Ladies' Magazine, 30, 46, 58

American Revolution, 1, 17, 18, 22, 117, 141
American Woman's Home, The (Beecher and Stowe), 48, 53, 59, 113, 168
Anderson, Benedict, 9; imagined communities, 44, 55, 89, 180n3
Anglo-African, The, 30
anonymity, 102, 105, 128, 137, 140; use of pseudonyms, 142, 150–52, 159
antislavery activism, 50, 52; African American women's organizations for, 139–40; Beecher's position on, 115–18, 120; bigotry and, 77, 161–62; Child's participation in, 125–32; Hale's views on, 109–10; moral elevation and, 68, 72–73, 141; in New England, 120, 199n56; petitions, 14, 27, 117, 126, 141; racial integration and, 141–42, 150; Sarah and Grace Douglass's, 153–54, 158–62; Sarah Forten and family's, 142–45, 148–52, 204nn37–38; for schools and education, 79–86; suffrage and, 33–34; violence and, 92–94, 131, 194n103, 201n102; women's rights and, 35, 38–39, 125. *See also* antislavery press; *Dred Scott* decision
Anti-Slavery Convention of American Women: in New York (1837), 151, 161; in Philadelphia (1838), 79, 93–94, 100, 137, 148; in Philadelphia (1839), 94, 127–28
antislavery press, 13, 36, 89–90, 117, 155, 203n24; African American women's presence, 136, 138–40, 142, 158, 162, 164. See also *Liberator, The*
Appeal in Favor of That Class of Americans Called Africans (L. M. Child), 125, 127–28

211

Appeal to the Women of the Nominally Free States, An (A. Grimké), 152, 206n68
"Appeal to Women, An" (S. Forten), 151–52
Armstrong, James, 179n104
Articles of Confederation, 6
authorship, 23, 55, 102, 174n28, 196n1. *See also* anonymity

Barrett, Zeloda, 54
Baumgartner, Kabria, 70
Beecher, Catharine Esther, 16, 49, 67, 81, 101–4, 135, 166; *The American Woman's Home*, 48, 53, 59, 113, 168; antislavery politics, 115–17; colonization beliefs, 119–20; *Educational Reminiscences and Suggestions*, 117–18, 198n47; *An Essay on Slavery and Abolitionism*, 116, 120; family and educational activities, 111–15, 118–19, 196n6; on female household management, 120–21; *Miss Beecher's Domestic Receipt Book*, 52; *A Treatise on Domestic Economy*, 44, 50, 58, 59–62, 113, 119, 168
Beecher, Edward (brother), 113, 119
Beecher, Lyman (father), 59, 113, 114, 115, 176n51
Beecher, Mary (sister), 112
Beecher Stowe, Harriet (sister). *See* Stowe, Harriet Beecher
benevolent societies, 14, 30, 73, 116–17; African American female, 74, 81, 86–87, 97, 188n16, 195n122; Beecher's circular to, 18, 198n47; schools sponsored by, 79–81
Benezet, Anthony, 193n89
Berthoff, Rowland, 29
Bethel Church (Philadelphia), 75, 87
birthright citizenship, 5, 6, 41, 165, 167, 210n2
Black press: cookbooks, 65–66; domestic advice manuals, 63–64, 67, 186n90; financial support for, 87, 193n85; growth of, 28–29, 34, 175n49; institutions and, 73–74; masculine mediation of, 95–96; middle-class standards and, 72; newspapers, 79, 87, 88–90, 95–96, 141; promotion of womanhood in, 12, 95–99, 171n31; Quakers and, 193n89; women's participation in, 138–41. *See also* antislavery press
Blackstone, William, 19
boarders, 91, 158, 194n99
book trade, 54–55, 183n55
Boris, Eileen, 171n35
Boston, 23, 76, 77, 129, 130; domestic labor in, 51, 52; literacy rate, 97; schools, 85–86

Boston Female Anti-Slavery Society, 26, 93, 127–28, 190n50, 200n82
Boydston, Jeanne, 24, 50, 58, 181n24, 185n67
bread baking, 107
Brotherly Union Society of Philadelphia, 28
Brown, Elsa Barkley, 13
Brown, John, 131–32
Brown, Kathleen, 174n38
Brown, Pamela, 54
Buffum, Arnold, 203n24
Burchard, Ely, 55
Bustill, Cyrus, 209n100
Bustill, Grace. *See* Douglass, Grace Bustill

Campbell, Tunis, G., 64, 186n93
Carey, Matthew, 80, 98, 190n43
celebrity chefs, 57
Chateauvert, Melinda, 9
Child, David Lee (husband), 1, 123–24, 126, 129
Child, Lydia Maria, 1, 16, 63, 101–4, 109, 169n1, 184n65; *American Frugal Housewife*, 57–58, 61, 62, 97, 122–23, 185n68, 185n82; antislavery activism, 124–32; *Appeal in Favor of That Class of Americans Called Africans*, 125, 127–28; domestic labor and farm life, 123–24, 133; early writings, 121–22; editorship of *National Anti-Slavery Standard*, 125, 126–27, 129–30, 131, 138; *The Freedmen's Book*, 132; *Hobomok, a Tale of Early Times*, 122, 196n1; *Juvenile Miscellany*, 122, 129, 199n58; marriage, 105; *The Mother's Book*, 122–23; support for women's suffrage, 124–25
childhood, African American, 135
child-rearing. *See* motherhood, republican
children's magazines, 122, 199n58
Christianity, 60, 150, 151–52, 160
Christian Recorder, 88–89, 158
churches: African American, 13, 71, 73, 74–77, 128, 188n16; publications, 88–89; segregated, 77, 99, 135, 140; social status and, 155–56
Cincinnati, 114–15, 120
citizenship, meanings and definitions, 5, 6–8, 10, 165
citizenship rights, 7, 8–9, 15; African American, 22, 27–29, 31, 40–41, 73, 165–66; domesticity and, 12–13; of free Blacks, 70, 81, 91, 136; state legislatures and, 18, 172n4. *See also* natural rights claims; voting rights
civic status, 3–4, 5, 7, 15, 103, 172n35; African American, 12–13, 16, 27–29, 41–42, 68–69,

96, 165–66; for Black female authors, 136–37, 164; coverture and, 19–20; emancipation and, 30–31; gender and race and, 8–10, 45; military service and, 18–19, 41; property ownership and, 29–30; white males and, 18; women's political participation and, 35, 39–40, 115–17
Clark-Pujara, Christy, 22
Clarkson Institute of Pennsylvania, 80
cleanliness, 48, 61, 65, 171n31
Cobb, Jasmine Nichole, 145
colonization, 5, 94, 142, 207n77; Child's critique of, 128–29; Hale and Beecher's support for, 81, 103–4, 109–11, 115, 119–20, 133, 197n25
Colonizationist and Journal of Freedom, 128–29
Colored American, 33, 49, 97–99, 155, 208n87
Colored Reading Society for Mental Improvement, 87
Compleat Housewife, 55, 184n57
Connecticut, 27, 81–82, 120, 177n74, 199n56; Hartford Female Seminary, 102, 112–13
consumerism, 123, 133
Continental Congress, 1, 17
cookbooks, 26, 43, 45, 55–58, 184n62; by African American women, 65–66; fund-raising, 50; by men, 62, 186n84
Cott, Nancy, 49
counterpublics, 15–16, 74, 88, 104, 136, 166; definition, 38, 45, 179n104
coverture, 19–20, 29, 34–35, 136, 137
Coxe, Mrs. Daniel, 51, 54, 182n32
Crandall, Prudence, 81–83, 120, 190n53
Crenshaw, Kimberlé, 13
Crummell, Alexander, 163
cultural citizenship, 4–6, 9, 26, 31, 44–45, 59, 73
cultural norms, 8, 23, 51, 107, 132; femininity and, 3, 4, 52, 166

Dabel, Jane, 194n98
daughters-mothers relations, 46, 47, 107
Declaration of Independence, 22, 27, 165
democracy, 49, 60; Jacksonian, 23, 32
diaries, 54
Dill, Bonnie Thornton, 63
Domestic Cookbook by Mrs. Malinda Russell, A (Russell), 65–66, 187n97
domesticity: African American women and, 12–13, 64, 69–70, 100; Beecher's vision of, 59–62, 67, 112–14, 115, 119, 120–21, 135, 168; citizenship or civic standing and, 9–10, 16, 25, 43–45, 104; femininity and, 52, 101; middle-class, 45–46;

62–63; nation building and, 14, 26, 53; politics and, 24; promoted in press, 72, 98–99; true womanhood and, 3, 4, 50–51, 68–69, 132–33, 168
domestic labor, 9–10, 12, 43, 67, 133, 182n35; Child's performance of, 123–24; Douglass household, 155; foreign-born, 52; Forten household, 203n31; indentured servants, 119–20; managing, 46, 47, 52, 107; market economy and, 49–50; Purvis household, 145–46, 204n37; shortage, 51
domestic literature, 3, 14, 103; advice manuals, 9–10, 26, 45–46, 48, 57–65, 67, 122–23; journals, 49–50; novels, 47–48, 182n25; overview of, 17–18, 43–44; race and, 72, 96–99. *See also* cookbooks
Douglass, Frederick (no relation), 37, 85, 155; *Frederick Douglass' Paper*, 38, 84, 191n59, 191n70; *North Star*, 87, 89, 145
Douglass, Grace Bustill (mother), 153, 159, 206n69, 207n74, 209n100
Douglass, Robert, Jr. (son), 153, 155, 158, 163, 207n75
Douglass, Robert, Sr. (father), 153, 157, 202n3, 207n75, 207n77
Douglass, Sarah Mapps (daughter), 16, 37, 100, 135, 137, 177n71, 189n32; antislavery and racial elevation work, 139, 140, 153–54, 158–63, 204n39; birth and death, 163–64, 209n102; family and faith, 153, 158, 207n75; marriage, 155–58, 164; teaching career and public lectures, 154–55, 162–64, 207n81, 208n84, 208n87
Douglass, William (husband of Sarah), 155–58, 209n100, 209n102
Dred Scott decision, 31, 40–41, 166, 179n112, 190n56
Du Bois, W. E. B., 72
Dunbar, Erica Armstrong, 94, 138

economy. *See* market economy
Edgeworth Society, 140
education: of African American children, 70, 78–86, 135, 189n35, 190n41; Beecher's promotion of, 112–15, 119–20, 121; Hale's interest in, 104–5, 106–7, 108, 109; household, 62; literary societies and, 87–88, 97, 140; promoted in Black press, 89; Sarah Douglass's pursuits, 154–55, 162–64, 207n81, 208n84, 208n87; teaching positions, 83–84, 191nn66–67, 191n70

Educational Reminiscences and Suggestions (C. E. Beecher), 117–18, 198n47
emancipation, 22, 24, 90, 136, 160, 164; Child's view on, 128, 132; citizenship rights and, 30–31; equality and, 162; freedom of movement and, 36–37; Hale and Beecher's views on, 104, 109, 116, 119; independence and, 27–28; response in North, 33, 128; Thirteenth Amendment and, 132, 166. *See also* free African Americans
Emlen, Ellen, 184n62
employment opportunities, 12, 72, 83–84, 91, 136, 201n2. *See also* domestic labor
equal adulthood, 170n22
equality: citizenship and, 9, 17; education and, 21, 79; emancipation and, 162; gender, 60, 204n37; institutions and, 70, 77–78; movements for, 167; political, 1, 49; racial, 25, 27, 31, 100, 104, 140–41, 166. *See also* integration
Essay on Slavery and Abolitionism, An (C. E. Beecher), 116, 120

fairs: antislavery, 127, 128, 139, 144, 162, 204n38; ladies', 107–8
"Farewell, The" (S. Forten), 150, 151, 159
farms: Child family, 123–24, 133; Purvis family, 144–46, 148, 205n47, 205n52
fashion, 96, 105–6
federal censuses: of 1790, 6; of 1840, 145, 203n31; of 1850, 145, 146, 155, 171n24; of 1860, 146, 157, 205n47, 209n102; of 1870, 147, 148, 158
Female Literary Association (FLA; Philadelphia), 87, 97, 139, 140, 159, 161
femininity: Beecher's vision of, 112; cultural constructions of, 3, 4, 5, 8, 26, 52, 166; *Godey's* magazine and, 105, 106; middle-class, 71, 165
Field, Corrine T., 170n22
financial independence, 51, 113, 115, 133, 136; Child's struggle for, 122–24, 199n58, 199n61; Hale's achievement of, 102–3, 105, 196n3; Sarah Forten's struggle for, 146–48
Finkelman, Paul, 177n74
Fisher, Abby, 65
Flower, Ann, 78, 189n35
Fluke, Sandra, 9
Forten, Harriet (daughter), 100, 144, 145, 162, 204n34, 204nn37–38
Forten, James, Jr. (son), 137–38, 203n23
Forten, James, Sr. (father), 137, 139, 140, 154, 203n19, 203n23; employees, 203n31; wealth and social standing, 90, 142, 147, 176n55, 202n3, 203n24
Forten, Margaretta (daughter), 141, 146, 147, 162, 204nn38–39
Forten, Sarah (daughter), 16, 135, 137, 162, 206n69; "An Appeal to Women," 151–52; children and financial struggles, 145–48, 205n52, 205n54; death, 152–53, 207nn72–73; "The Farewell," 150, 151, 159; "Grave of the Slave," 149; marriage and end to antislavery work, 144–45, 164, 204n34, 204nn37–39; "Past Joys," 149–50; poetry and pen names, 148–52, 159; "The Separation," 150–51; "The Slave Girl's Address to Her Mother," 149; upbringing and interest in writing, 142–43
Foster, Abby Kelley, 162, 210n118
Fraser, Nancy, 45, 179n104
free African Americans, 29, 31, 41, 66, 73, 104, 203n31; discrimination and violence, 91–95; importance of churches, 74–77; literacy rates, 87, 97, 192n81; middle-class status, 71–72; mobility rights, 36–37; newspapers for, 89–90, 128, 193n94; organizations, 86–88; Quakers and, 193n89; schools and teachers, 78–86, 120; suffrage, 32, 33. *See also* racial elevation
Free African Society, 75, 207n74
Freedmen's Book, The (L. M. Child), 132
Freedom's Journal, 5, 79, 89, 96, 128, 138, 193n90
Frémont, Jesse Benton, 111, 124
Frémont, John Charles (husband), 40, 124–25

Garnet, Henry Highland, 86, 99, 195n132
Garrison, William Lloyd, 127, 130, 134, 137, 142, 199n56; as publisher of *The Liberator*, 90, 128, 139–40, 148–52, 159–60
gender: Black press and, 95–96; citizenship and, 6–7, 8–9, 19–20, 165, 172n9; education and, 78, 189n35; household manuals and, 57–58, 64, 184n65, 186n84; ideologies, 3; libraries and readers, 87, 192n84; norms, 7, 46, 69, 70, 104; racial difference and, 3, 25, 120, 175n38; and racial identity, 72
Genius of Oblivion and Other Original Poems, The (S. J. Hale), 105
Gilman, Caroline Howard, 47–48
Gilman, Charlotte Perkins, 185n79
Ginzberg, Lori, 18
Godey, Louis Antoine, 106
Godey's Lady's Book, 49, 58, 96, 103, 104, 105–8; total subscribers, 197n10

INDEX

Good Housekeeper (S. J. Hale), 58–59
"good wife" construct, 3, 35, 49, 53, 181n22
Graham, Sylvester, 48, 181n13
"Grave of the Slave" (S. Forten), 149
Green, Frances Harriet, 59
Grimké, Angelina (sister), 143, 154, 161–62, 177n71, 206n69; *An Appeal to the Women of the Nominally Free States*, 152, 206n68; Beecher's critique of, 115–16, 198n47; friendship with Child, 124, 126, 200n74; Pennsylvania Hall riot and, 93–94; public speaking, 26, 127
Grimké, Forten Charlotte (niece), 83, 146–47
Grimké, Sarah Moore (sister), 26, 115; friendship with Sarah Douglass, 36–37, 156, 189n32, 203n19
Guisbert, Brande, 209n100

Habermas, Jürgen, 88, 169n5
Hale, David (husband), 105
Hale, Sarah Josepha, 16, 35, 81, 166, 196n3; critique of Child's writings, 129, 185n68; editorship of *Godey's Lady's Book*, 49, 58, 96, 103, 105–8; education and marriage, 104–5, 196n6; *The Genius of Oblivion and Other Original Poems*, 105; *Good Housekeeper*, 58–59; ideology of true womanhood and, 101–4, 106–9, 132–33; *Northwood*, 103, 105–6, 109–10, 197n24; *Traits of American Life*, 107–8, 197n21
Hambleton, Henry, 37
Harris, Leslie M., 12
Harris, Sarah, 81–82
Harris-Perry, Melissa, 7
Hassler, Jane, 57
health reformers, 48, 59, 108, 164, 181n13
Hermes, Joke, 44
Hobomok, a Tale of Early Times (L. M. Child), 122, 196n1
Hoff, Joan, 23
Holcomb, Martha, 84
home, 10, 24, 26, 50; Black women and creation of, 12–13, 180n11; cultural function of, 50, 58; motherhood and, 49, 53; sanctity of, 35, 49, 51, 54; slavery and, 149–50; white middle-class, 62, 69, 121, 126
Horton, James, 96
Hotel Keepers, Head Waiters, and Housekeepers' Guide (Campbell), 64, 186n93
household labor. *See* domestic labor

household management, 4, 26, 46, 47–48, 98; Beecher's views of, 61–62, 112, 120–21
household manuals, 17–18, 26, 45–48; Beecher's, 59–62, 67, 113–14; Child's, 57–59, 122–23, 129; overview of popular, 55–59; race and, 62–66, 95
House Servant's Directory, The (Roberts), 64
husbands-wives relations, 19–20, 49, 60, 71–72, 137

identity: African American civic, 12, 28, 69, 85, 99–100; citizenship and, 4, 5, 6–7, 13; concealing, 27, 142, 149; feminine civic, 7, 10, 18, 27, 35, 44–45, 54, 71; national, 2, 18, 22; political, 5, 7, 43, 137; racial, 72, 88, 140, 142; republican, 19, 21; shared, 2, 3, 9, 13, 180n3; true womanhood and, 16, 168. *See also* anonymity
imagined communities, 44, 55, 89, 180n3
immigrants, 167; European, 38, 52; naturalization and, 6, 170n16
indentured servitude, 22, 31, 119–20
Institute of Colored Youth (ICY; Philadelphia), 84–85, 191n69; library, 87, 192n84; Sarah Douglass's teaching position at, 155, 156, 157, 208n84, 208n87
institutions, 70, 73–74, 86–87, 128, 166. *See also* churches; schools
integration, 70, 77, 78, 128, 141–42, 148; schools and, 80, 84, 85–86
interracial marriage, 125, 126, 128, 130–31

Jackson, Kellie Carter, 201n102
Jacobson, Matthew Frye, 6
Jefferson, Thomas, 23, 174n28
Jeffries, Julie Roy, 170n19
Jennings, Elizabeth, 38
Jocelyn, Simeon, 159–60, 190n53, 209n111
Jones, Absalom, 28, 75, 77, 207n77
Jones, Jacqueline, 98
Juvenile Miscellany (L. M. Child), 122, 129, 199n58

Kerber, Linda, 19, 21, 36, 172n9
Keyssar, Alexander, 178n77
Kitchel, Harvey, 93

Ladies' Magazine and Literary Gazette, 106, 129. See also *Godey's Lady's Book*
Ladies' Wreath, 49, 181n22, 196n3
Lane Theological Seminary, 114–15, 120

215

Lapsansky, Emma, 71
Lee, Jarena, 76
legal status, 1, 5, 7, 20, 40–41, 139
Leslie, Eliza, 62
Levine, Robert S., 193n90
Liberator, The, 11, 28, 77, 90, 128, 193n94; anonymous publications, 140; anti-abolitionist violence and, 93; Child's abolitionist vision and, 129–30; employment discrimination and, 91; Female Literary Association and, 159; integrated schools and, 85–86; promotion of African American women's groups, 138–39; Robert Douglass's paintings and, 153; Sarah Douglass's essays, 160; Sarah Forten's poetry and absence from, 137, 142, 144–45, 148–52
libraries, 54–55, 87, 129
Lindsley, Adaline, 39–40, 55, 183n53
literacy rates, 46, 67, 87, 97, 171n24, 180n7
literary societies, 90, 92, 116, 204n37; racial elevation and, 87–88, 97, 138, 140; Sarah Douglass's role in, 139, 159–60, 161. *See also* Female Literary Association
Litwack, Leon, 176n64
Locofocos, 39, 179n106
Loring, Ellis Gray, 1, 125
Loring, Louisa, 127
Lovejoy, Elijah, 92–93, 94

Majors, Monroe A., 134, 148
market economy, 12, 15, 58, 61, 133, 181n24; changing labor practices and, 4, 23–25, 165; true womanhood and, 49–50
Martin, Trayvon, 9
Martineau, Harriet, 62
masculinity, 5, 69, 95–96, 99
Massachusetts Abolition Society, 91–92
middle class. *See* African American middle-class women; white middle-class women
migration, 36, 65, 159
military service, 18–19, 22, 41, 205n52
Miner, Myrtilla, 83
Minerva Literary Society, 87, 140
Minor v. Happersett, 41, 167, 210n2
Mirror of Liberty, 141
Miss Beecher's Domestic Receipt Book (C. Beecher), 52
mixed economy, 58
mobs, 92, 94, 100, 194n103
moral reform societies, 14, 26, 69, 137–38, 203n23

motherhood, republican, 24, 26, 53, 60, 72, 114, 122; activism and, 50; ideology of, 21–22, 49
Mother's Book, The (L. M. Child), 122–23
Mott, Lucretia, 94, 100, 141, 204n39, 208n84
movement, freedom of, 36–38, 131, 159
mulatto designation, 146, 148, 155, 157, 205n52
Murray, Judith Sargent, 2, 21

National Anti-Slavery Standard, 125, 126–27, 129–30, 131, 138
National Enquirer, 90, 141
nation building, 1–2, 24, 32, 107, 115; cookbooks and, 56, 57; cultural citizenship and, 26, 44, 101; domesticity and, 4, 59, 119, 135, 168; women's roles in, 6, 11, 14, 59, 101, 120
naturalization, 6, 166, 170n16
natural rights claims, 13, 22, 150; African American men's, 17, 27–28, 165; publication of, 28–29; voting and, 34–35, 167–68
needlework, 106, 107, 108, 127, 202n2
Nell, William Cooper, 85
Nelson, Mary Ann, 53–54, 183n46
Newell, Eliza, 83–84
newspapers, 9, 30, 98, 143, 175n49; for African American women, 95–96, 138–39, 141; Black-edited, 72, 88–90, 99, 138, 139, 141, 193n94; financial assistance for, 87, 193n85; white-edited, 28–29, 38. See also *Liberator, The*; *National Anti-Slavery Standard*
New York, 12, 130, 163, 194n103; African American societies and organizations, 86, 87, 190n41; African free schools, 79, 81, 192n84; voting rights, 32, 177n74; women's rights, 29–30
New York Manumission Society (NYMS), 190n41
Nichols, Clarina, 201n91
Northwood (S. J. Hale), 103, 105–6, 109–10, 197n24
Norton, Mary Beth, 24

Obama, Barack, 210n2
obligations of citizenship, 4–6, 12, 13, 16, 17, 18–19, 165; Black males and, 32; domesticity and, 10, 104, 111; white middle-class women and, 44, 133
Ocasio-Cortez, Alexandria, 41

parades, 20–21, 22, 92, 95
Park, Louisa Adams, 39
Parker, Mary S., 202n4

Parks, William, 55
passports, 36–37
"Past Joys" (S. Forten), 149–50
Paterson, N.J., 30
patriarchy, 24, 26, 69, 164; Black male, 4, 18, 91, 96, 136–37
Payne, Daniel, 192n84
Pennsylvania, 28, 31, 79, 136; Bensalem (Purvis farm), 144–46, 205n47; constitution, 32–33, 177n66. *See also* Philadelphia
Pennsylvania Freeman, 27, 28, 38, 139
Pennsylvania Hall Riot (1838), 93–94, 100, 162, 194nn108–9
Pennsylvania Society for Promoting the Abolition of Slavery (PAS), 80–81, 83, 154, 208n84
performance of citizenship, 4–6, 12, 41, 70, 73, 168
Peterson, Carla, 194n103
petitions, 4, 128; antislavery, 14, 27, 126, 141; Beecher's reaction to, 117–18, 198n47; for emancipation, 27–28; for interracial marriage, 125, 126, 130–31; for voting rights, 33, 34
Philadelphia, 28, 100, 129, 146; antislavery convention (1833), 150–51; churches, 74–76; elite families, 137, 144, 155–56, 157, 202n3, 207n77; employment opportunities, 136, 202n2; free Black community, 73, 79, 86–87, 92, 192n81; libraries and literary societies, 87, 140, 161, 192n84; riots, 92–95, 194n108, 195n116; schools, 78–80, 84–85, 154–55, 190n43, 191n70
Philadelphia Female Anti-Slavery Society (PFAS), 139, 202n3; prominent members, 141, 153, 204nn37–39, 206n69, 207n80; Sarah Douglass's position with, 153, 154, 162, 208n84; Sarah Forten's resignation from, 144, 151, 204n39
Philanthropist, The, 149
poetry, 15, 88, 140, 141; Sarah Forten's, 142, 148–52, 159; Wheatley's, 22–23
political participation, 20–21, 101, 128, 173n19; of Black men, 22; Child's, 126–27, 128; Hale's view on, 107–9; movements for equality, 167; through private writings, 39–40. *See also* antislavery activism; public speaking
Post, Mary Robbins, 68, 187n2
power, 38, 50, 71, 101, 127; of Black men, 135, 137; citizenship and, 23, 41; hierarchies, 8, 20, 96; household, 34–35; political, 115, 116, 118, 164; of print word, 132, 140, 143. *See also* patriarchy

print culture, 2, 11, 15–16, 23, 45, 180n3; African American, 38, 88–90, 136, 138–39, 164, 193n89; civic status and, 4, 5, 9, 18, 166; domesticity and, 3, 9–10, 13, 26; ideology of true womanhood and, 3, 54, 95–99, 101–4. *See also* antislavery press; Black press; domestic literature
property ownership, 29–30, 34, 92, 176n55, 188n7
Pryor, Elizabeth Stordeur, 37
public speaking, 26, 35, 38–39, 87, 109; Angelina Grimké's speech, 126, 200n74; church platforms for, 76; Sarah's Douglass's lecture series, 162–64
public sphere: African American women and, 16, 99, 136, 139, 143, 164; Black press and, 88–90; exclusion from, 11, 16, 18, 45, 73, 166; female print culture and, 2, 4, 15–16, 18, 101–4; Habermas's description of, 169n5; political participation in, 20–21, 22, 35–36, 173n19; private sphere divide from, 10–12, 49–50, 60
publishing expenses, 122, 196n1
purity and piety, 69, 99, 115; of Black women, 135, 160, 201n1; true womanhood and, 11, 25, 133
Purvis, Harriet Forten (wife of Robert). *See* Forten, Harriet
Purvis, Joseph (brother), 144–48, 204nn34–35, 205n44
Purvis, Robert (brother), 33, 144, 153, 176n55, 204n34, 207n77; household, 86, 145, 204n37; success in obtaining passport, 36–37; wealth, 71
Purvis, Sarah Forten (wife of Joseph). *See* Forten, Sarah

Quakers, 77, 79, 115, 135, 159, 189n32; Douglass family and, 153, 207n74; press, 193n89
Quarterly Christian Spectator, 128

race: Beecher's views on, 119–20; citizenship and, 11, 12–14, 16, 18, 30–31, 40–41; civic identity and, 44–45; colonization and, 103–4, 109; household manuals and, 62–65; labor and, 12, 24, 91, 97, 194n98; riots, 11, 92–95, 162, 194n103, 195n116; schools and, 81–86; true womanhood and, 95–99, 133, 164; voting rights and, 31–34
racial elevation, 14, 29, 90, 93, 133; Beecher's opposition to, 120; civic standing and, 68, 73, 166; education and literacy and, 78–79, 87–88, 97, 139, 159; purity and piety and, 77, 99; Sarah

racial elevation (*continued*)
  Douglass's reputation for, 153–54, 158–64; true womanhood and domesticity and, 63, 69–70, 98; women's societies for, 137–42
racism, 77, 99, 140, 143–44, 153, 167; antislavery movement and, 132, 161–62; in Cincinnati, 120; employment discrimination, 91–92; stereotypes, 94; U.S. history of, 41. *See also* segregation
Rael, Patrick, 63
Reeve, Tapping, 29, 176n51
reproductive labor. *See* domesticity
respectability, 4, 15, 64, 89, 104, 204n34; Black middle-class, 12, 25, 94, 100, 135–36, 165, 166, 171n31; challenges to notions of, 38–39; European immigrants and, 38; property ownership and, 30; racial elevation and, 68, 70, 79, 86, 133, 140, 141; of students and teachers, 154–55; white middle-class, 16, 63, 99
Reynolds, Elizabeth, 84, 191n67
Roberts, Robert, 65, 66; *The House Servant's Directory*, 64
Romeo, Sharon, 5
Russell, Malinda, 65–66, 187nn97–98
Ryan, Mary, 21, 24, 173n19, 184n65

Sanderson, Jeremiah, 68
Schloesser, Pauline, 172n9
schools, 107, 146, 153, 157, 164; for African American children, 70, 74, 78–86, 120, 154–55, 190n41, 191n59; Beecher family and, 112–13, 114–15, 119, 120; cooking, 62. *See also* teachers
Scott, Joan, 8
seamstresses, 136, 157, 201n2
Sedgwick, Catharine Maria, 47, 48, 54, 106–7, 152, 180n9
segregation, 11, 91, 135, 138; in churches, 75, 77, 78, 99, 135, 140; in schools, 81–82, 85–86
"Separation, The" (S. Forten), 150–51
sexual difference, 8, 19
Shaw, Adaline, 51
Sigourney, Lydia Huntley, 43, 48, 53, 81, 114, 183n44
Simmons, Amelia, 26, 55–57, 65
single women, 34, 74, 112, 113, 115, 136, 137
Sinkler, Emily Wharton, 54, 57
Sklar, Kathryn Kish, 3
"Slave Girl's Address to Her Mother, The" (S. Forten), 149

slavery, 22–23, 31, 50, 90; Beecher's position on, 116–17, 120; Child's stance on, 125–32; Hale's novel on, 109–10; Jezebel figure and, 201n1; rebellions, 206n70; Sarah Douglass's essay on, 160; Sarah Forten's writings on, 149–51, 152. *See also* antislavery activism; emancipation
Smith, Eric Ledell, 176n64
Smith School (Boston), 85–86
social status, 8, 37, 66, 70, 100, 103; church attendance and, 155–56; of Douglass and Forten families, 135, 142–43, 148, 202n3. *See also* wealth
Spires, Derrick R., 5
Stanton, Elizabeth Cady, 14, 31, 111, 166, 167
state constitutions, 165, 172n4, 176n64; Connecticut, 82; Massachusetts, 34; Missouri, 167; New Jersey, 34; New York, 32, 176n63; Pennsylvania, 32–33, 36–37, 177n66, 177n71; Vermont, 31. *See also* U.S. Constitution
state legislatures, 5, 18, 22, 37, 172n4; Black migration and, 36, 159; Massachusetts, 126, 130, 200n74; petitions and, 27; voting rights and, 32, 35, 176n64
stereotypes, 7, 25, 94, 135
Stewart, Maria, 5, 27, 35, 72, 76, 170n9
St. George's Methodist Church (Philadelphia), 75–76, 77, 189n30
Still, Mary, 76, 95, 99
Stokley, Jane, 84
Stowe, Harriet Beecher, 52, 83, 111, 114, 182n35, 198n47; *The American Woman's Home*, 48, 53, 59, 113, 168; *Uncle Tom's Cabin*, 105, 110, 127, 197n29
submissiveness, 25, 50, 89, 99, 135
suffrage. *See* voting rights
Swisshelm, Jane, 201n91

taxes, 17, 32, 86, 125, 146, 174n38
teachers, 80, 83–85, 122, 191nn66–67, 202n3; ad for, 191n70; Beecher's career, 111–15, 118–19; Sarah Douglass's career, 154–55, 207n81, 208n84, 208n87
temperance, 26, 95, 137, 153. *See also* moral reform societies
textbooks, 102, 103, 113–14
Theophano, Janet, 56
Thomas, Susan, 75
Thompson, George, 143, 203n29
Tocqueville, Alexis de, 60, 168, 185n75

Tonkovich, Nicole, 106
Traits of American Life (S. J. Hale), 107–8, 197n21
travel, 36–38, 186n93
Treatise on Domestic Economy, A (C. E. Beecher), 44, 50, 58, 59–62, 119, 168; reissued as *The American Woman's Home* (with Stowe), 48, 53, 59, 113, 168
true womanhood: of African American women, 66, 134–37, 143, 148, 149, 163, 164, 201n1; civic status and, 7, 18, 44–45, 132–33, 165; concept and cultural importance of, 2–4, 25; education and, 114; middle-class status and, 46, 62–63, 72, 91, 194n99; new economy and, 49–54, 181n24; politics of respectability and, 38, 68; of prominent antebellum writers, 101–4, 106–9, 124, 128, 132, 133, 168; property rights and, 30; public speaking and, 38–39; purposeful, 70, 91, 100; racial difference and, 16, 25, 62–64, 69–71, 95–99; tenets of, 11, 135
Twitty, Michael W., 186n94

Ulrich, Laurel Thatcher, 51
Uncle Tom's Cabin (Stowe), 105, 110, 127, 197n29
unpaid labor, 52, 58, 185n67
U.S. Civil War, 5, 19, 41, 43, 83, 166. *See also* military service
U.S. Constitution, 6, 18, 31, 82, 110; Thirteenth Amendment, 132, 166; Fourteenth Amendment, 5, 9, 40, 41, 165, 166–68; Fifteenth Amendment, 167, 168
U.S. Supreme Court, 40–41, 165, 167, 190n56

vigilance societies, 139
violence, 131, 167, 201n102; riots, 11, 92–95, 162, 194n103, 195n116
voting rights, 1, 13, 19; African American, 30, 31–34, 167–68, 176n64, 177n66, 177n74; women's, 14, 31, 34–35, 41, 124–25, 166–67, 178n77

wage labor, 24, 49, 52, 66, 91, 136
Walker, David, 5, 128, 170n9, 206n70
Warner, Clarissa, 66

Warner, Susan, 118–19, 198n51
Washington, D.C., 76, 83, 117, 126, 191n59
Watkins, William J. (uncle), 77–78, 85, 189n33
Watkins Harper, Frances Ellen, 83, 189n33
wealth, 55, 71, 73, 136; Douglass family, 155, 157, 208n92, 209n101; Forten family, 142, 143, 176n55, 202n3; Purvis family, 144, 145–48, 205n44
Weekly Anglo-African, 161, 162, 207n81
Weld, Angelina Grimké. *See* Grimké, Angelina
Weld, Theodore (husband), 115, 147
Welter, Barbara, 3, 25, 50, 60, 95
Wheatley, Phillis, 2, 17, 22–23, 174nn27–28
White, Deborah Gray, 201n1
White, Rebecca, 156, 157, 162, 163
white middle-class women, 3, 63, 69, 104, 194n99; civic identity and citizenship obligations, 10, 13, 44, 121, 133, 165; household advice manuals for, 61–62, 67, 95; racial difference and, 25–26, 41, 72, 95–99; skills, 107
whiteness, 9, 12, 67, 144; true womanhood and, 14, 16, 18, 45, 99
Whittier, Elizabeth (sister), 143
Whittier, John Greenleaf, 142
Wilder, Laura Ingalls, 106, 111
Willson, Joseph, 71
Wilson, Harriet E., 47–48, 180n11
Winarnita, Monika Swatsi, 44
Winch, Julie, 144, 147, 202n3, 204n34
Wise, Henry, 125, 131
womanhood. *See* true womanhood
women's rights, 14, 15, 118, 141, 170n22, 210n118; property ownership and, 29–30, 34; to public speaking, 38–39, 76; suffrage, 31, 34–35, 41, 124–25, 166–67, 178n77; to travel, 37, 186n93
Wright, Nazera Sadiq, 72

Yee, Shirley, 25

Zafar, Rafia, 66
Zuck, Rochelle Raineri, 5

www.ingramcontent.com/pod-product-compliance
Lightning Source LLC
Chambersburg PA
CBHW030647230426
43665CB00011B/988